ARTHUR
O'CONNOR

ARTHUR O'CONNOR

The Most Important Irish Revolutionary You May Never Have Heard Of

Clifford D. Conner

iUniverse, Inc.
New York   Bloomington

Arthur O'Connor

The Most Important Irish Revolutionary You May Never Have Heard Of

iUniverse books may be ordered through booksellers or by contacting:

iUniverse
1663 Liberty Drive
Bloomington, IN 47403
www.iuniverse.com
1-800-Authors (1-800-288-4677)

ISBN: 978-1-4401-0516-6 (sc)
ISBN: 978-1-4401-1734-3 (dj)
ISBN: 978-1-4401-0517-3 (ebook)

Printed in the United States of America

iUniverse rev. date: 01/21/2009

Other books by Clifford D. Conner

Jean Paul Marat: Scientist and Revolutionary
Colonel Despard: The Life and Times of an Anglo-Irish Rebel
A People's History of Science

Arthur O'Connor

by J. D. Herbert

Engraved by W. Ward the Elder, 1798
Source: National Gallery of Ireland

Contents

ABBREVIATIONS

used in the footnotes

AAE	Archives des Affaires Étrangères, Paris
BIF	Bibliothèque de l'Institut de France
CBF	Château du Bignon, France
NAF	National Archives of France, Paris
NAI	National Archives of Ireland, Dublin
NLI	National Library of Ireland, Dublin
PRO	Public Record Office, Kew, England
SHAT	Service Historique de l'Armée de la Terre, Château de Vincennes, Paris
TCD	Trinity College Library, Dublin

Cover: Hugh Douglas Hamilton's *Portrait*

of Arthur O'Connor, c. 1796–97

Acknowledgments

Thanks are due above all to Anne, Countess de la Tour du Pin, for her kind permission to allow me to consult Arthur O'Connor's personal papers at her home, the château du Bignon, which is about seventy miles southeast of Paris in the *départment* of Loiret. The château, which was General O'Connor's home from 1807 to the end of his life, has remained continuously in the possession of his descendants, and its magnificent library—dominated by a heroic portrait of *le Général* himself—contains a great deal of his correspondence as well as his unpublished memoirs. Scholars and researchers frequently visit the château du Bignon, not so much on O'Connor's account but more often to see the papers of the Countess's late husband, the prominent French poet Patrice de la Tour du Pin, who was Arthur O'Connor's great-great-grandson, or those of O'Connor's celebrated father-in-law, the Marquis de Condorcet. I also owe thanks to the Countess's daughter, Marie-Liesse d'Aboville, a great-great-great-granddaughter of Arthur O'Connor, who had previously arranged and catalogued his papers, greatly simplifying my task. In addition to allowing me access to O'Connor's papers, the Countess extended the warmest hospitality imaginable to my wife and myself, and we are very grateful to her for that. We were happily surprised to find that the château, despite its old-world elegance, was equipped with that most useful of modern conveniences for researchers: a photocopying machine.

Professor Marianne Elliott is routinely thanked by authors who write about the United Irishmen because of her irreplaceable, groundbreaking scholarship on the subject, and I am indeed in her debt for that, but in the case of this book her contribution was even more fundamental and direct: It was she who originally called my attention to the need for a biography of Arthur O'Connor. My deepest thanks also to Dr. Fintan Lane for his help and encouragement, including a number of specific research suggestions that proved very valuable. I have likewise benefited very much from the collaboration of Dr. Maria Luddy of the University of Warwick.

I am particularly indebted to Richard Aylmer for his unique insights into the period of the 1798 Rebellion. Although not all of the bold hypotheses generated by his fertile mind proved viable, they invariably challenged me to deepen my research and profitably rethink some of my interpretations. The record of our collaboration extends, I would estimate, to hundreds of pages of e-mail between Dublin and New York; I hope it has been at least partially as fruitful for him as it has been for me.

Several research institutions were essential to the writing of this biography, and I want to express my appreciation to them and their staffs. First of all, the research division of the New York City Public Library kindly allowed me the use of its Wertheim Room—a haven of calm where authors can study and work—for an extended period of time. The Columbia University Law Library provided me with transcripts of some of the trials in which O'Connor was a central figure.

In France, the Service Historique de l'Armée de la Terre (SHAT) at the Château de Vincennes gave me access to General O'Connor's military dossier. At the Archives des Affairs Etrangères at the Quai d'Orsay I was able to read the diplomatic correspondence regarding O'Connor's important negotiations with General Hoche in 1796. At the Bibliothèque Nationale I found the entire run of O'Connor's short-lived *Journal de la Liberté Religieuse*. Thanks to the kind support of Professor Pierre Aigrait of the Académie des Sciences, I gained entry to the library of the Institut de France, where I examined the papers regarding O'Connor's efforts in compiling and editing the complete works of Condorcet. And finally, the Archives Nationales also provided me with numerous documents pertinent to O'Connor's many years in France.

At the manuscripts division of the National Library of Ireland I was able to consult its newly augmented collection of Fitzgerald family correspondence. Pertinent documents at the National Archives of Ireland included the police-informer reports of the turncoat Leonard McNally and of the "Sham Squire," Francis Higgins. The manuscripts division of Trinity College Library allowed me to peruse the papers of R. R. Madden, including his correspondence with O'Connor. In England, the Public Record Office at Kew provided prison correspondence and more police spy reports; I thank Tim Hughes for his help with my research there.

I am grateful to my friends Gerry Foley and the late Paul Siegel for reading the manuscript and offering valuable advice and suggestions drawn from their fields of expertise (Irish political history and literature of revolution, respectively), and to military historian J. B. M. Frederick for providing answers to my queries. Special thanks also to Anne-Françoise Bender for making the arrangements for our visit to Le Bignon.

Most of all, I thank my spouse, Marush Conner, whose inspiration and influence on everything I do are beyond measure.

PART I

The Making of a Revolutionary
1763–1795

1

Who Was Arthur O'Connor?

✦

"MANY WILL SNEER," ARTHUR O'CONNOR wrote to his son late in life, "to hear your father speaking of taking the place of Washington." Nonetheless, he believed that his place in Irish history only narrowly missed being the equal of George Washington's in American history. "In the judgment and the justice of men," he continued,

> *Washington is a great man, a great patriot or hero, and deservedly [so], and I am in the eyes of the same world a traitor and a rebel worthy to pass six years of his life in eight different prisons, of being disinherited by his parents, his future ruined and in exile for his life from home, friends and country.*[1]

Only an accident of weather, he believed, had prevented him from becoming the George Washington of Ireland. Had a storm not prevented a French army led by General Lazare Hoche from landing at Bantry Bay in December 1796, Ireland would have been liberated and he would have been the general at the head of the liberation army.[2]

Arthur O'Connor was indisputably one of the most important leaders of the United Irishmen in the era of the Rebellion of 1798—arguably the most important—and he played a significant role in the origins of Irish republicanism and Irish nationalism. Today, however, his name and reputation are not nearly as well remembered as are those of Wolfe Tone, Lord Edward Fitzgerald, Robert Emmet, and several others of his United Irish colleagues. Statues of these men and streets named in their honor abound in Ireland, but it is not uncommon to meet Irish people of good education to whom the name of Arthur O'Connor is unknown.

The other United Irish leaders have been the subjects of numerous biographies, but no life of Arthur O'Connor existed when I began work on this one. I was not the only person who noticed the glaring omission; just as this biography was nearing completion another one appeared under the authorship of Jane Hayter Hames, who refers to O'Connor as "my kinsman."[3] Her book is a welcome and worthwhile addition to the literature of the 1798 Rebellion, but in honoring her ancestor she has tended to uncritically report his own view of his life. In doing so, she has left room for other biographers, myself included, to offer a more objective assessment of O'Connor's activities and ideas.

One reason for the historians' and biographers' previous neglect of O'Connor, most likely, is that although Irish nationalists have traditionally done a splendid job of keeping the names of martyrs to their cause alive, O'Connor—unlike Tone, Fitzgerald, and Emmet—did not die a martyr's death. He survived the Rebellion and lived for more than a half century after 1798. After being released from prison in 1802, he spent the rest of his long life in comfortable exile in France (notwithstanding his lamentation of having had "his future ruined").

But although O'Connor's part in the revolutionary events of 1798 has remained in relative obscurity, that does not mean that it deserves to be forgotten. To the contrary, it could be argued that his contributions to the effort to free Ireland from English rule were more substantive than those of more colorful characters such as the adventurous Lord Edward Fitzgerald and Robert Emmet.

Although he has not become the subject of romantic legend, O'Connor's revolutionary career was not lacking in color, drama, and controversy. He was a skilled conspirator and a charismatic orator who was capable of charming the likes of Charles James Fox, Richard Brinsley Sheridan, and Napoleon Bonaparte. Many of his allies expected—and his rivals feared—that O'Connor would have become Bonaparte's anointed king of Ireland had the French succeeded in driving the British out.

PERSONAL IMPRESSIONS

Theobald Wolfe Tone, who knew O'Connor only by reputation, obviously held him in high esteem. He wrote in his diary in February 1797:

"I would give a great deal for an hour's conversation with O'Connor. I see he has thrown himself, body and soul, into the revolution of his country. Well, if we succeed, he will obtain, and deserves, one of the first stations in government. He is a noble fellow, that is the truth of it."[4]

Among the United Irishmen who knew O'Connor personally was John Binns, who later became "one of the leading journalists in America."[5] In his memoirs, published in 1854, Binns recalled his impressions of O'Connor in 1798:

> *At that time Arthur O'Connor must have been thirty-five years of age, about five feet nine inches high, stout built, dark eyes and eyebrows, black hair and whiskers. His features were handsome, expressive, and manly; his manners fascinating, and his information, especially upon Irish affairs, extensive. His conversational powers were of the first order. . . . He was an eloquent public speaker, and his society courted by the most talented public men of the Democratic and Whig parties in Ireland and Great Britain.*

It was Binns's opinion that if O'Connor had "been as willing to barter the independence of his country, as was my Lord Castlereagh, he was quite as likely to have become Prime Minister of the United Kingdom."[6]

Appraisals of O'Connor were also recorded by another United Irish veteran, William Drennan, and his sister, Martha McTier. Drennan was a prominent figure in the earliest years of the movement, but dropped out of membership in 1794 after the government tried, but failed, to prosecute him on treason charges. (Drennan wrote to another United Irishman in 1794: "the good truth [is] that my political quiver is spent and I am tired of the hobby."[7]) Nonetheless, he maintained close contact with many who remained active in the movement and the voluminous correspondence between him (in Dublin) and his sister (in Belfast) provides invaluable eyewitness accounts of the activities of the United Irish Society in the years surrounding the events of 1798.[8]

Although Drennan acknowledged that "with O'Connor I am but little, very little acquainted,"[9] he and his sister discussed him frequently in their letters. In November 1796 Drennan provided this physical description:

> *O'Connor . . . wears a black silk handkerchief tied on his head so as to resemble a black crop, having lost his hair in a fever and disdaining a wig. He is an odd figure, tall, dark and penetrating with that native vulgarity of face you observe in the Irish—his manner is plain—he is silent and no way attractive.*[10]

This latter assertion, however, was contradicted in another letter a few months later: "He is certainly a singular looking man as Grattan also is, but the ladies might, and I believe many do think O'Connor singularly handsome."[11]

Prior to the Rebellion, Martha McTier thought very highly of O'Connor and considered him "a man evidently born for great events."[12] On the first day of 1798 she wrote:

> The Press *has not been delivered here for the three last usual days. Arthur O'Connor I am told stands forth as the publisher. If so the demand will be trebled and its cowardly opposers baffled. He is a clever spirited fellow, and perfectly fitted for his present post—in everything good he ought to be supported.*[13]

Five days later she added: "I am an avowed admirer of the brave and spirited A. O'Connor."[14]

The harsh events and outcome of the Rebellion, however, greatly distressed her, causing a dramatic shift in her political outlook, and her appreciation of O'Connor was transformed accordingly. "If in his power," she fretted in 1802, O'Connor

> *will conduct the French to Ireland, make them believe he is heir to a king, head the Irish Catholics, and by his art and eloquence madden more than ever Castlereagh will soften them. I never liked him, but on paper—powerful indeed he was there. He has a bad, very bad countenance, and will never rest till he is somehow exalted. I like him not and hope he never may come to Ireland—tis not for such as him, we should forfeit peace. He would try to be an Irish Buonaparte.*[15]

This charge reflected the hostility that marked O'Connor's post-Rebellion relationships with some of the other United Irish leaders—most notably Thomas Addis Emmet—which no doubt arose in part from O'Connor's patrician deportment. His personality was not at all what would be expected of a revolutionary; he was certainly not a "man of the people." In early 1797, before she had turned against him, McTier commented on O'Connor's aloofness: "O'Connor keeps to a *set*" when he is in Belfast.[16] Drennan replied, "What you say of O'C[onnor] keeping to a set is a fault that I find with many here, of thinking none to be communicated with but such as are exactly on a masonic level with themselves."[17] R. R. Madden, the first authoritative historian of the United Irishmen, remarked that O'Connor's "manners, external appearance, bearing in public, and demeanor in society, his notions of all things in general, with one exception, were aristocratic." The one exception was that "Arthur O'Connor was a democrat" and remained so to the end of his life.[18]

NEGOTIATING FOR A FRENCH INVASION

A strong case can be made that O'Connor's comparison of himself with George Washington was not at all far-fetched. The attempted French invasion of Ireland led by General Hoche was the pivotal event leading up to the Rebellion of 1798. "The failure of the French to land," one historian recently wrote, "does not . . . detract from its historical significance."[19]

Although most credit for negotiating that expedition has traditionally gone to Wolfe Tone,[20] O'Connor argues persuasively in his unpublished memoirs that in fact Tone was not taken seriously by the French government, the Directory, and that the invasion plans only became a reality when he and Lord Edward Fitzgerald joined the negotiations. This is corroborated by military historian Édouard Desbrière: "The missions of Wolfe Tone . . . from the beginning of 1796 were, in fact, no more than semiofficial"; with O'Connor and Fitzgerald, however, "it would become a matter of formal negotiations with duly accredited agents."[21] O'Connor admired Tone and described him as "a man whose talents, integrity and unflinching principles I set at the head of those who served their country, with the sole exception of my beloved Lord Edward."[22] Nonetheless, he demonstrated from Tone's own memoirs that the Directory had simply been humoring Tone for several months.

In May 1796 O'Connor and Fitzgerald set out on a voyage to the continent to meet with French negotiators. Fitzgerald, however, was mistrusted by the French due to his wife's family connections to the *ci-devant* aristocracy, and was refused entry into France. O'Connor therefore went on alone to conduct negotiations with General Hoche, who was to command the invasion. Whatever influence their mission had could therefore more correctly be attributed to O'Connor.

What O'Connor and Fitzgerald brought to the negotiating table was credibility. Although Tone is today a household name in Ireland and O'Connor has been all but forgotten, their reputations were quite the opposite in 1796. The French military planners knew little about Tone and were not at all inclined to stake a military invasion on the authority of an unknown Irish patriot. But O'Connor had gained international renown for a courageous, electrifying speech he had made in the Irish Parliament in 1795 calling for Catholic emancipation, and Fitzgerald, son of the Duke of Leinster, was known as a scion of Ireland's premier aristocratic family. Once reassured of Lord Edward's trustworthiness, General Hoche and the Directors were willing to seriously consider their proposal to invade Ireland—a proposal that differed hardly at all from the one Tone had been urging to no effect for the previous several months.

O'Connor made bold claims in his memoirs, writing of "the treaty I made personally and individually with the Directory," and contending that "if I had succeeded in separating Ireland from England," the history not only of Ireland, but of all Europe, would have been considerably altered.[23] "There cannot be a shadow of doubt," he added, "that if the expedition of Hoche, which was my wish, had succeeded, I would have been the author of the separation."[24] These assertions, however, must be weighed against evidence that the French invasion plans had already been solidly formulated even before O'Connor's meeting with Hoche.[25]

Nonetheless—and although his analysis of Tone's relations with the French government is greatly oversimplified[26]—his conclusions are not altogether unjustified. It can be fairly said that Tone initiated United Irish diplomacy with the Directory, but O'Connor and Fitzgerald—with O'Connor in the lead—transformed it and gave it substance.

O'CONNOR AND THE UNITED IRISHMEN

An analogous point can be made about the respective roles of the three men in the creation of the United Irishmen. In 1791 Tone was a guiding spirit behind the founding of the United Irish Society in Belfast; he wrote its founding documents and supplied the organizational talent and energy necessary to bring it into being.

The original United Irish Society of 1791 was not, however, the United Irish Society that was to provide the organizational framework of the Rebellion of 1798. "The organizational history of the early United Irishmen is hardly impressive," writes Nancy Curtin, but after 1794 it underwent a complete transformation.[27] From a small propaganda group devoted to the goal of reforming the Irish parliament by peaceful and legal means, the United Irishmen became a mass underground army dedicated to overthrowing the Irish government and breaking the connection with England by military force.[28] While this transformation was the product of historical forces and circumstances beyond the control of any individual leaders, it coincided with, and was greatly enhanced by, the adherence of O'Connor and Fitzgerald to the United Irishmen in 1795.[29] As a leading historian of the United Irishmen explains, "the stature of the two men and their recognized position as social leaders raised the nascent and still very fragmented Irish revolutionary movement on to a new plane."[30]

Again, what O'Connor and Fitzgerald brought to the movement was credibility. Gaining these two highly influential figures as leaders greatly enhanced the prestige of the United Irish and gave it an appearance of authenticity and social breadth that it had previously lacked. O'Connor's reputation as a champion of Catholic rights, for example, was instrumental in winning the ranks of the Defenders, a nationwide Catholic secret society, to the United Irish banner.

O'Connor did not claim priority over Fitzgerald in historical importance; to the contrary, he consistently described his political relationship with "my beloved Edward" as one of perfect collaboration. As for Lord Edward's view of O'Connor, he declared that his friend's soul was "twin to his own."[31] Their comradeship, however, was not one of perfect symmetry. Fitzgerald had a personal charisma of legendary magnitude, but O'Connor was considerably more gifted in the essential qualities of political leadership such as oratorical, theoretical, and organizational ability. Lord Edward was attracted to O'Connor as someone who could articulate his own political feelings better than anyone else. It would not be at all unreasonable, therefore, to conclude that at the crucial moment of the United Irishmen's transformation into a mass revolutionary organization Arthur O'Connor was playing the primary leadership role.

At the time of the outbreak of the Rebellion of 1798, however, Arthur O'Connor, like most of the other top leaders of the United Irishmen, had been removed from the scene of action by a successful campaign of governmental repression facilitated by the treachery of disloyal members acting as police informers. Most had been arrested in Dublin at a meeting of the United Irish executive committee held at the house of Oliver Bond on 12 March 1798. At that time O'Connor was already in prison in England awaiting trial on a charge of high treason. Although acquitted in a spectacular show trial that backfired on his prosecutors, he was immediately rearrested on yet another charge of high treason. This time the government—unwilling to risk a second embarrassing acquittal—declined to put him on trial, but simply held him in prison for five years before sending him into permanent exile. O'Connor was thereby denied the opportunity of being put to the ultimate test of revolutionary leadership.

After the collapse of the Rebellion, O'Connor and the other surviving United Irish leaders were in imminent danger of being hanged. That O'Connor was eventually exiled rather than executed was the result of an agreement he and other imprisoned leaders—especially Thomas Addis Emmet and William MacNeven—made with the British government. Although this "Kilmainham pact" required substantial political concessions on their part, they maintained that it required no betrayal of principle. Readers can judge that claim for themselves by perusing the documents in the first two appendices, which contain the official "position papers" of O'Connor and the other two principal United Irishmen with regard to their organization and the Rebellion.

Once in exile O'Connor did not abandon the quest to liberate Ireland from English rule. In France he quickly rose to the rank of general and for more than a decade continued preparations to lead a French invasion of Ireland under the auspices of Napoleon Bonaparte. Although Bonaparte was undoubtedly serious about wanting to attempt such an expedition, none of his plans ever reached fruition, and General O'Connor was thus left perpetually on the sidelines, never to smell powder in real military action.

The highlights of O'Connor's career as an Irish rebel—the famous speech on Catholic emancipation, the negotiations with Hoche, the treason trial at Maidstone, and the Kilmainham pact, among others—are recounted in more detail in chapters 3 through 7 below, as are some related issues of historiographical interpretation that have attached to O'Connor's reputation. Revolutionary leaders cannot avoid being the focus of dispute—it is an essential element of their calling—and O'Connor generated his full quota of controversy. Was he an opportunistic demagogue or a principled revolutionary leader (or a combination of both)? Can it be argued that his imprisonment in 1798, which effectively removed him from the field of action, materially affected the outcome of the Rebellion? Was the Kilmainham pact an act of cowardice and betrayal on his part or a defensible, intelligent act of compromise? Did subsequent events tend to vindicate his radical stance in the internal disputes of the United Irishmen, or did they lend retrospective weight to his factional opponents' arguments? These and other issues will be confronted as they arise in the course of examining the events of O'Connor's life.

EXILE IN FRANCE

Although the central significance of his life was defined by his activities surrounding the revolutionary events of 1798, the half-century O'Connor spent in French exile amounted to considerably more than half of his lifetime and therefore an account of those years is an indispensable part of his biography. His marriage to the daughter of the renowned *philosophe* Condorcet gave him entrée into leading French social and intellectual circles. As hopes of a French expedition to Ireland faded, he turned to more private pursuits, especially with regard to defending his own financial interests both in Ireland and in France. He considered himself a pioneer of rational agriculture in France, and involved himself in bitter disputes and lawsuits with family members in Ireland over his Irish properties. He also devoted a great deal of literary effort to defending the legacy of the United Irishmen as he understood it, which often brought him into conflict with radicals of the younger generation—most notably his own nephew, the Chartist leader Feargus O'Connor—and with reformers such as Daniel O'Connell. All of this will be the subject of chapters 8 and 9.

Among the literary efforts to which he dedicated the most time and attention was the writing of his personal memoirs, which in the end remained unpublished. An earlier account of O'Connor's life—Frank MacDermot's 1966 article—drew on those memoirs, but only partially. MacDermot must not have seen the most significant entries because he stated that they end in 1793 when in fact they continue through 1798.[32]

Because O'Connor's own view of the events he lived through and participated in obviously constitutes a fundamental biographical resource, his memoirs have been frequently quoted in this book. His claims, of course, cannot simply be taken at face value but must be carefully evaluated and weighed against pertinent evidence, which I have attempted to provide. I have also introduced those of his assertions that deserve most caution with phrases such as "O'Connor claims" or "according to O'Connor," but even those that appear without such qualification deserve the reader's critical attention.

One of O'Connor's acquaintances who did not fully share his political outlook judged that his memoirs would be trustworthy because "he was a man of truth, and incapable of misrepresentation, though, of course, liable to misconception, in his recital of events."[33] Although his account of his life seems to be essentially honest and for the most part factually accurate,[34] O'Connor acknowledged that he was often unable to check his memory of events against documentation due to "the numerous seizures Government has made of my papers in Ireland and in England."[35] Furthermore, his memoirs are characterized by subjectivity and unconscious biases not untypical of the genre. While generally avoiding overt braggadocio or falsehood, his narratives tend toward heroic melodrama and idealization. In every situation O'Connor portrays himself in the best possible light.

Most significantly, O'Connor wrote his memoirs relatively late in life when his social attitudes had become somewhat more inflexible than they had been in his younger years—especially with regard to Catholics and Catholicism. As a revolutionary-minded young man O'Connor was able to devote himself wholeheartedly to the struggle against the oppression of Ireland's Roman Catholics, but in his old age he became increasingly preoccupied with what he perceived as the perfidy of "papists." He did not, however, traverse the familiar path of ex-revolutionaries (of every place and every era) who become rabid conservatives. His increasing aversion to priests and the Pope was expressed as militant anticlericalism, and he never ceased to sympathize with the Catholic poor and to execrate their oppressors. That is not to suggest that the complexities and contradictions of O'Connor's anti-Catholicism can simply be reduced to anticlericalism or attributed to dotage; more will be said on this subject in the following chapters.

O'Connor's position as the proprietor of a large landed estate also no doubt colored his social outlook, and his long forced separation from his native land affected his views of contemporary Irish politics. In spite of their deficiencies, however, there is no substitute for O'Connor's memoirs as a window to the way he saw his world and his life.

Arthur O'Connor's remarkable persona was to some degree based on accident of birth. He was favored in his genetic inheritance: He was gifted with keen intelligence and great personal charm, and by all accounts—corroborated by his portraits—he was a handsome man. The strength of his personality attracted many important people to him, and repelled others. Yet nature alone cannot account for the vagaries of his revolutionary career, and so it will be necessary, first of all, to consider the environmental elements that shaped his early life.

2

The Conners and O'Connors of Connorville

✦

ARTHUR'S LAST NAME AT birth was not O'Connor but Conner, the surname of his father and of all previous generations of his family. He would only become Arthur O'Connor later, by conscious choice, when as university students he and his brother Roger decided to emphasize their Irishness and claim descent from Rory O'Connor, the last high king of Ireland.[1] The name change was by no means a frivolous matter; it represented a political division in the family that came close to being drawn by a line of blood.

Arthur and Roger's three older brothers, who chose to retain "Conner" as their name, "were Orange in their politics" (conservative supporters of the Protestant ascendancy and Ireland's connection with England) while Arthur and Roger both became outspoken radicals and United Irish militants.[2] One of the loyalist brothers, Robert Conner, a local magistrate and captain of a corps of yeomanry, so vehemently loathed his younger brothers' republicanism that he made a determined effort to have Roger arrested and hanged for subversion. In a letter to the English authorities on 1 August 1797, Robert expressed the fear that he, his wife, and their two children "would be butchered in cold blood, and this by the desire of Mr. Roger O'Connor, and this I have on oath that he said so." Robert urged the government not to "leave him at liberty to be the firebrand and assassin to set the nation on fire and to massacre all loyal subjects," but to prosecute him on charges of high treason.[3] Robert's wish that Roger be executed was not fulfilled, and they were reportedly reconciled in later years,[4] but the depth of bitterness between the brothers on the eve of the 1798 Rebellion was evident.

The Conners were a wealthy Protestant landowning family that had lived in Cork for several generations. A chronicler of the family described them as "remarkable . . . for eccentricity and talent."[5] Arthur was born on 4 July 1763 at Mitchelstown in County Cork. One of eight children, he was the fifth and youngest son; the other boys, from oldest to youngest, were Daniel, William, Robert, and Roger. The three sisters died young and "without issue." One of them drowned—accidentally, according to the Conner family version[6] but other reports say she took her own life when refused permission by her parents to marry a Catholic man.[7]

The original patriarch of the clan was one Cornelius Conner, a successful London merchant who had settled in Cork in the seventeenth century. His son Daniel greatly expanded the family's landholdings, allegedly taking advantage of the expropriation of Catholics in the wake of William of Orange's triumph of 1690. Daniel Conner's second son, William Conner,

> *settled at Connorville, then called Ballyprevane, in 1727. He built Connorville House, and planted the domain. The mansion was large and commodious. The offices nearly surrounded two courts, and were on a scale of such magnitude as to resemble rather a village than the establishment of a country gentleman.*[8]

William Conner's son Roger Conner, who was Arthur's father, inherited Connorville, which was thus home to Arthur in his boyhood years.

The social status of Arthur's family was greatly augmented by the eminence of his maternal lineage. His mother was Anne Longfield, the only sister of Richard Longfield, who became Baron Longueville in 1795 and Viscount Longueville in 1800.[9] Arthur's aristocratic uncle was a very wealthy and influential man; the income from his County Cork estates was estimated at £20,000 per annum in 1811.[10] Having no sons of his own, Lord Longueville named Arthur his heir and actively promoted his nephew's political career—until he became alienated by the young man's radicalism. Arthur, the chronicler recounts,

> *forfeited, by espousing the popular cause, all that selfish men hold most dear—wealth, patronage, and title. He was Lord Longueville's favorite nephew, and his destined heir; and his Lordship had sufficient*

influence to have obtained for him a peerage, had Arthur been a pliant
disciple of the school of Pitt and Castlereagh.[11]

In his memoirs O'Connor describes the relationship as one of great mutual affection: "I was cherished, adored by my beloved uncle."[12] By his own account, Lord Longueville "gave him a seat in parliament in 1791 for the borough of Philipstown,"[13] facilitated his election as high sheriff of Cork, and even arranged for British Prime Minister Pitt to offer him a high political position in England, which he declined. Intent on establishing that he was not simply his uncle's political hireling, he recounts an occasion on which Longueville recommended him to another man by saying that "to his knowledge from my infancy he never knew me to swerve an iota from Republican principles or ever acknowledge any rightful government but that which was in the interest of all."[14] But in 1795, when Arthur went beyond espousal of abstract republicanism to make his powerful speech on Catholic emancipation, and stormily resigned from parliament, the relationship came to an end. "Here lies the greatest sacrifice I have ever made," says O'Connor; the break with his uncle was the price he paid when he undertook to "give my life to free my country from the oppression and misery that made it the wretchedest in all the world."[15]

THE NOTORIOUS ROGER O'CONNOR

None of the family combined eccentricity and talent more fully than Arthur's brother Roger, who was a little more than a year older than Arthur. Roger's personal charm was not inferior to Arthur's; both brothers moved equally easily in the highest social circles of Ireland and England. A leading political and cultural figure of the era, Richard Brinsley Sheridan, described Roger in 1798 as "one of the finest Fellows I ever saw."[16]

Roger, like Arthur, was educated at Trinity College and originally intended to practice law. In 1783 he was called to the bar, but "never attended, being cursed, as he has often said, with too good an estate to make diligence at a profession necessary."[17]

Roger's devotion to the cause of Irish separatism ran as deep as Arthur's. As the French ships carrying General Hoche's army were approaching Bantry Bay in December 1796, Roger feigned loyalty to the government by entertaining its soldiers at Connorville while meanwhile organizing his tenants to join Hoche's forces.

In their youth and through the era of the Rebellion, Arthur and Roger were inseparable in spirit. They were both arrested on a number of occasions and were in prison together from 1798 through 1800. The bonds of fraternal love and political comradeship uniting them were evidently strong. In early 1799 Arthur called Roger "the twin brother of my soul."[18]

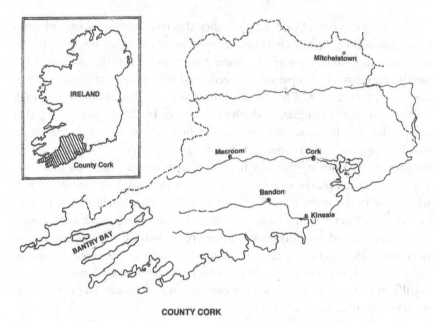

COUNTY CORK

In later years, however, Roger apparently became somewhat unhinged. When Arthur was forced into exile, he left his financial affairs in Ireland in Roger's hands, but Roger proved to be thoroughly irresponsible and untrustworthy. In the heat of the dispute Arthur condemned him as a "wretch who has violated every principle of honor and justice, by plundering an exiled brother."[19]

Widespread notoriety attached to the name of Roger O'Connor as a result of his involvement in a series of bizarre incidents, including marital scandals, a mail coach robbery, and the suspicious burning of a house he had heavily insured.[20] The controversy he created extended to historical scholarship as well. In 1822 he published a lengthy work purporting to give the "hidden history" of the Irish race, *The Chronicles of Eri*,[21] which has been interpreted variously as a pure literary fraud or as a clever satire in the spirit of Montesquieu's *Persian Letters*.[22]

Roger died insane in 1834 and Arthur later gave this very judicious appreciation of his troubled brother:

> *Roger, who was called after his father, had the talents of our mother and was the cleverest of the family. It would be difficult to find a man with so prodigious a memory. Had his application equaled his genius,*

he would have risen high in science, but his disorderly imagination
spoiled all the precious gifts of nature.[23]

A ROYAL HERITAGE?

When the rascally protagonist of William Makepeace Thackeray's novel *Barry Lyndon* claims the eleventh-century Irish king Brian Boru as a direct ancestor, a Prussian officer comments wryly that he had never yet met an Irishman who "was not descended from the kings of Ireland." The O'Connor brothers were no exception; Roger's *Chronicles of Eri* was partially designed to bolster the family legend of royal lineage.

Both Roger and Arthur changed their surname to O'Connor when their father told them of their ancestry in the royal Kerry line of the O'Connor clan, but Arthur seems not to have taken the story quite so seriously.[24] Although his factional opponents in the United Irish movement frequently charged him with harboring royalist ambitions, they were attempting to visit the sins of his brother upon him. Arthur remained in fact dedicated to republicanism and opposed to monarchy. There is evidence that he believed the family's claim to a royal pedigree—his descendants in France continue to this day to display the family crest of the ancient Gaelic kings—but he did not actively promote it or seek like Roger to use it for political ends.[25]

Some imaginative tales were utilized to explain away the undeniable fact that the first of their ancestors in Cork was Cornelius *Conner* rather than *O'Connor*. In one, Cromwell's soldiers allegedly killed one of their O'Connor forebears in Tralee, County Kerry, in 1652. His widow escaped to Bandon in County Cork with the infant Cornelius and in defense against further persecution changed the name to Conner and converted to Protestantism.[26] In a variant account, Cornelius was acknowledged to be a Protestant immigrant from England, but was nonetheless said to be directly descended from "the line of O'Connor Kerry, whose chiefs were kings of Kerry for centuries previous to the Anglo-Norman invasion in the twelfth century."[27]

The legend was put to political use in the mid-nineteenth century by Roger's son Feargus O'Connor, who became one of the most important leaders of the radical English working-class movement known as Chartism. According to his biographers, Feargus "was constantly to repeat to humble Chartist audiences, that his family was descended from Roderick O'Connor, high king of Ireland in the eleventh century."[28]

ARTHUR'S EDUCATION

In 1842, in response to a request for information from Dr. Madden, O'Connor summarized his education:

> Arthur O'Connor, at an early age, was placed at a public school at Lismore, and subsequently at one in Castle Lyons. He had a great taste for poetry when very young, but his parents and preceptors discouraged it. He entered Dublin College, as fellow-commoner, in 1779, under Mr. Day. . . . He was educated in the Protestant religion—in rigid Protestantism. . . . He was devoted, from the period of his college life, to serious studies, but political economy was the favourite study of his life. His literary tastes were formed on the classical education he received.[29]

The "Dublin College" he entered in June 1779 at age fifteen was Trinity College,[30] which many of the leading United Irishmen attended; he graduated with a BA degree in 1782. He also studied law in London and was called to the Irish bar in 1788 but, like Roger, never practiced law.

In his memoirs, he credits his mother with being the primary intellectual influence in his young life; his father receives no mention in this regard:

> It was my good fortune to have a mother who was not only capable to instruct me but that had for me all the affection which could induce her to undertake the task. To this adored mother I am indebted that the foundation of my education was laid on the most liberal principles. She began by instructing me in history and geography and in the writings of the great moralists of the 17th and 18th centuries.[31]

As for his formal education, after beginning at a public school in Lismore and then attending one at Castlelyons for several years, he spent a year at a school in Bandon, nine miles from Connorville. He then returned to the school at Castlelyons, where, it seems, he engaged in political controversy for the first time:

> Here I found some sixty or seventy scholars [students]. The war against American independence had begun and divided us in Americans and English. I need not tell you I was American and Republican. We were in minority, but having more energy we kept the upper hand. On quitting this school to go to Dublin College I received the public thanks of the master for my conduct.[32]

O'Connor attributes the initiation of his military education to Major Apollos Morris, a very close family friend.[33] Major Morris, O'Connor tells us, "was esteemed one of the best officers in the British army." However, "not relishing a war against American liberty he quitted the British service and went to America." Morris fought under Washington with distinction, but because he did not want to forfeit his property in Ireland he did so under a "feigned name," and therefore "the services he rendered has been lost to his fame, but not to the glorious cause of American liberty." When he returned to Ireland, he "fixed his abode in our family," and asked and obtained permission from Arthur's father to undertake the young man's military education. "If I was his son," O'Connor says, "he could not have taken more pains and pleasure with my education." But the young man did not begin his military training completely unprepared:

> *I had been bred from my infancy to all the manly exercises which could fit me for a military profession and nature gave me a constitution of steel. I became an adept in swimming, riding, shooting, fox hunting and all kinds of exercises at an age when others generally begin to learn them. It was with this stock Apollos Morice [sic] undertook my education.*[34]

The instruction began with Morris having Arthur estimate "the space a thousand men would occupy in line three deep." After each guess they would measure the space with a chain, and before long "I conquered the greatest accuracy," and "could give a pretty accurate calculation of the space any number would occupy." Soon "there was not a military position for miles around Connorville I had not made an object for my instruction."[35]

In 1782 Morris organized a group of the Conners' tenants into a corps of Volunteers, the extragovernmental military movement inspired by the American revolution that exerted armed pressure on the Irish government to make political concessions. This, Arthur reports, "gave me an occasion of perfecting myself in the practical parts of military evolutions. Nothing could exceed the rapidity and exactness of our movements, thanks to our instructor."[36] From that time until he became a French officer, whenever O'Connor wished to present himself in public as a military man he wore the uniform of the Volunteers.

As for his academic studies, he says he supplemented his formal schooling by memorizing the speeches of Demosthenes and Cicero, which he read "in the originals and in the best translations." He also copied out the Junius letters as well as "all the principal parts of Milton, Shakespeare and all the best English tragedies," and he "took delight in Homer and Virgil, in the wit of Horace and Lucian's dialogues."[37]

Arthur tried his hand at mathematics, but found that "though they gave great accuracy to the mind they did not extend it, and they were easily forgotten without constant application to them." The science that he says most pleased him was astronomy, to which he attributes the origins of his enlightened religious views:

> *The grandeur of the subject and the vast expansion it gave my ideas took me from the state of a groveling, creeping selfish insect on the earth by making me acquainted with the transcendent majesty of the heavens. It was there I acquired my convictions of a God and of the attributes he must have to create, move, direct, and govern a world it was easier to suppose infinite than to set bounds to.*[38]

But of all subjects, the one that made the deepest impression and to which he put the most ideological use was economics:

> *A year before I entered college I had gotten the* Wealth of Nations *of that great and good man Adam Smith, the father of the economical science. I read and reread it with the greatest desire to make it all my own, and such was the conviction and satisfaction it brought to my reason that it engrossed my thoughts more than all my college courses and on it I have formed all my political principles.*[39]

EARLY TRAVELS

The final major element of Arthur's education was foreign travel. After completing his studies at Trinity College he spent two years in England, and then in 1784 he visited France, accompanied by two young aristocratic friends, Standish O'Grady (later Lord Guillamore, "Chief Justice of the Exchequer," and the prosecutor of Robert Emmet) and John Waller ("the great proprietor of the domains of Castle Waller")[40]. After a brief stay in Paris he and his two traveling companions "set off for Dijon to pass the year in perfectioning ourselves in French, fencing and dancing."[41] While his accomplishments as a dancer and swordsman are not known, his attempt to perfect his French apparently fell somewhat short. An account of his activities in France in 1830, after nearly three decades in exile in that country, says he was even then speaking "un assez mauvais français."[42]

Most importantly, his travels served to provide him with invaluable lessons in comparative politics. "The national government in France," he observed, "gave her an immense advantage over Ireland, whose government was the corrupted agent to another nation." On the other hand, what he saw in prerevolutionary France seemed to him "far inferior to England," because the French people were simply "the instruments of a court, the nobles and the clergy." He "was forcibly struck with the contrast between the independence of Englishmen and the degradation" of Frenchmen.[43]

As a landowner himself, it was to be expected that O'Connor would take an interest in the cultivation of the soil. He expressed surprise at the inferiority of the state of agriculture in France as compared with England:

> *It approached nearer the disorder and slovenliness of Ireland. The few cows I saw were held by the roadside, none feeding in the fields. My astonishment was how the flocks of sheep I saw could find nourishment. Artificial grasses, turnips, beet root, etc. seem total strangers to French culture, and all means of manure.*[44]

After a few months of study in Dijon, he and Waller left O'Grady behind and made an excursion to another country, an experience that strongly reinforced O'Connor's nascent republicanism:

> *On entering Switzerland I found another and a stronger contrast with other countries I had seen. It was the antipode to French despotism and is opposite to English aristocracy . . . . In Switzerland I found the manners of a republic which seemed to rest in the air, and in the soil, and in the hearts and nature of the people. . . . Here for the first time I saw the fruits of equality—a society where no man was exalted at the debasement of his fellow citizens. Every citizen from the highest to the lowest, from the richest to the poorest possessed the consciousness he was a free and independent man.*[45]

After returning to France, O'Connor rejoined O'Grady and they went back to London, "leaving Waller to continue his travels on the continent."[46] Arthur visited France again in 1787. In his memoirs he notes "the rapid progress the public mind had made" in the intervening period, and says "it was obvious" to him in 1787 that "the diseases which centuries of feudal and priestly despotism had accumulated in the body politic could not be dissipated but by a revolution."[47] This prescient observation, however, undoubtedly owed a great deal to hindsight.

CONNORVILLE AND THE FAMILY FORTUNE

O'Connor had become a landowner in his own right two years before his first trip to France, but it was precipitated by an event he called the "greatest misfortune that could befall me": the unexpected death of his mother at the relatively young age of 48.[48] He received news of her illness in Dublin just as he was leaving for London in 1782 to study law. Instead he set off in the opposite direction, to Kinsale, arriving just before she died.

His mother's death led to "the breaking up of the paternal house." In exchange for an annuity, his father

> divided his fortune amongst his children, which put me in possession
> of a considerable fortune before I was of age. As I had always shown
> a strong predilection for agriculture, vast flocks of sheep and horned
> cattle with immense provisions came to me, besides an extensive wood
> of the finest timber.[49]

It is interesting to note that although opposition to what he called "the monopoly feudal law of primogeniture" was a lifelong pillar of his political ideology, and although Arthur himself was a younger son, he and his brothers were not greatly inconvenienced by it. The oldest son, Daniel, gained possession of Connorville during his father's lifetime, but an adulterous affair with a Mrs. Gibbons led to a court case in which heavy damages were assessed against him, obliging Daniel to leave Ireland and to sell Connorville to his brother Roger for £5,000.[50] Daniel's oldest son, also named Daniel, later returned to Ireland and reclaimed part of the property.

The second brother, William, was named after his grandfather, "who left him a large fortune independent of his father," thus (Arthur notes dryly) obviating the need for William to acquire a profession.[51] William, however, later descended "into abject poverty, and died about 1822 or 1823 in misery in Dublin, and, it is said, in confinement for debt."[52]

Robert, the third brother, broke his thigh in a fall from a horse just before he was scheduled to embark on a military career in the East Indies. "This accident," Arthur says, "kept him at home where he became a country squire and a fox hunter."[53] Robert built a large mansion that he named Fortrobert atop a hill adjacent to the Connorville demesne.

Connorville remained in Roger's possession through the year of the Rebellion, when he and Arthur were imprisoned together at Fort George in Scotland. Roger was released in late 1800 and although permitted to return to Ireland in 1803, he was not allowed to reside in County Cork, so he divested himself of Connorville and purchased a large estate named Dangan in County Meath for £40,000—a sum far beyond his means. Thus ended the Conners' and O'Connors' connection with Connorville forever.

The property that Arthur O'Connor inherited—his fundamental means of support—produced an income estimated at £1,500 a year. (A standard rule of thumb for comparing monetary sums of the eighteenth and twentieth centuries is to multiply the earlier figure by sixty. By that formula, O'Connor's inherited income was roughly equivalent to £90,000 a year in "today's money.") In order to avoid having it confiscated by the government in reprisal for his revolutionary activities, he transferred legal title to his property in Ireland to one of his closest political allies in England, Sir Francis Burdett. When Arthur was permanently banished from Ireland, however, he entrusted it to Roger's stewardship, but Roger, struggling to maintain a lifestyle at Dangan that he could not afford, embezzled Arthur's property, leaving the latter seriously financially embarrassed in France and almost helpless to do anything about it. After many years of acrimonious lawsuits Arthur eventually recovered at least part of his inheritance.

O'CONNOR'S SOCIAL AWAKENING

Following his mother's death O'Connor left for England as previously planned. His subsequent years in England and France "greatly added to the little store of knowledge" he had earlier acquired, but he felt that what he had learned was not well ordered in his mind, and therefore he needed to take some time to "give it an arrangement to enable me to call it out as I might want it." Consequently, he "sought retreat," but first had to take care of his pecuniary affairs, "which had suffered some confusion in my absence."

> I began by purchasing a large estate in the neighborhood of Kinsale, which had been mortgaged to my grandfather for more than it was worth, but by the indolence of my father he suffered it to be entangled with conditions which rendered the recovery of the mortgage a most difficult affair. My brothers and I had shares in it and to render the payment practicable I purchased all the shares and in a short time I became sole possessor of the whole estate. Here I sat down to cultivate my property and my mind. I built a handsome house with numerous out offices together with several farm houses and undertook as practical farmer the culture of a considerable domain.[54]

He named his handsome house "Fort Arthur." Although the activities he lists must have kept him exceptionally busy, O'Connor describes himself as being in a "retired state" at this time, "forgetting the world and by the world forgot." For two years he immersed himself in studies, focusing particularly on the history of Ireland. But suddenly "a circumstance awoke me from my passive life to enter on the duties of an active citizen."[55]

He had joined a sailing club at Kinsale that met under a cliff near the entrance to Kinsale harbor. One evening the group was surprised by the approach of a ferocious storm. Arthur immediately made for the shore and began running toward his house, two miles away.

> I had not gone a half a mile when the most violent tempest assailed me. On a barren heath in the midst of which I was running along, I passed a wretched cabin from which I saw a woman issuing who, with scanty clothing and long disheveled hair blown by the winds, set violently to tear the thatch from her house. I followed her in and never did I witness so great a scene of wretchedness; two fine boys, two and three years old, naked as they were born, on a moist cold clay floor without an atom of furniture but an iron pot full of raw potatoes. I asked her what induced her to uncover her cabin in such weather. She showed me her little ones and told me she had no other fuel to boil the potatoes for their supper and her own.[56]

O'Connor claimed that he was struck by the contrast between the ugliness of the poverty he saw and the beauty of the young woman, who "was of those celestial forms that might have been the ornament of the highest station."[57] He was moved to offer her assistance: a few pounds were enough to repair her cabin, prepare a few acres around it for farming, and buy her some clothing and utensils, "which raised her state from the lowest depths of misery to be on a level with the ordinary wretchedness which has been so long the lot of the mass of the Irish."[58]

Readers in the post-Freudian era might suspect that O'Connor had other than altruistic motives for providing financial support to the vulnerable young beauty he first encountered in scanty clothing. Nonetheless, he describes this experience as a sort of social epiphany; it "made such an effect on my feelings that it made me form the resolution to devote my life, fortune and efforts to change this state of Ireland."[59] By his own account, this was the beginning of his political career, which eventually led him to the forefront of the revolutionary movement in Ireland.

3

Political Beginnings

ARTHUR O'CONNOR'S FIRST PUBLISHED political writing was an anonymous open letter that he subsequently never mentioned to anyone, not even to his brothers. Although his account in his memoirs of the letter's reception sounds somewhat exaggerated, the story in general is not entirely implausible.[1]

The occasion was a session of the assizes of Cork. He neglects to tell us the year in which it occurred, but says it came after "the development which two years at college had given to my mind," so the events he describes must have taken place in about 1781, when he was nineteen. His initial motive for attending was that it was a time and place "where hundreds of the handsomest women in the world filled the ballrooms with their charms." But his uncle, Lord Longueville, and the other country gentlemen were assembled there for political purposes, and it was expected that young Arthur would take an interest in their affairs. However, his first reaction was indignation at seeing so many men "of independent fortunes" acting as "the obsequious slaves of the great Borough monger Lord Shannon."[2]

Lord Shannon had monopolized the nominations to a number of boroughs, and he had access to considerable government patronage.[3] O'Connor found it especially galling "to see my uncle, who had double Lord Shannon's fortune, among his humble servants." And even Lord Kingsborough, "who had a still larger fortune," was "in the same vile servitude."[4]

His dismay at this state of affairs moved him to draft an anonymous open letter to his uncle and Lord Kingsborough, appealing to them to "come forward in defense of the liberty of their country by placing themselves at the head of the Liberal men of the county."[5] He surreptitiously slipped his letter into the mailbox of a local newspaper at midnight. Some days later he went to a coffeehouse in the morning and came upon a great deal of agitated discussion about his letter, which had just been published. From there he went to breakfast with his uncle, who immediately asked him if he had read the latest newspaper and whether he knew who was the author of the offending polemic. "The room was filled with his friends who came to learn what he thought of the address," O'Connor says, "and all equally at a loss to discover a person to whom they could attribute it." O'Connor was worried that his uncle would guess that he was the culprit, "for I had given an opinion on this subject some days before at his table." Fortunately, however, "no one suspected it to be the work of a young collegian."[6]

Although the letter created a sensation, it had no immediate political consequences. However, over the next several years—in O'Connor's immodest opinion—"the opposition it recommended and that it gave rise to [was] brooding in men's minds," and at the end of 1788 it "produced its fruits." At that time, opined O'Connor, "a revolution" in Irish politics occurred as a result of King George III's lapse into insanity: "Upon this occasion most of the old mercenaries deserted the King to place their faith in the rising son," the Prince of Wales. But when the King recovered, he punished Shannon and his cronies by transferring his favor from them to their opponents. This immediately transformed Lord Shannon into a reluctant member of the opposition party. Conversely, Arthur's uncle and Lord Kingsborough suddenly found themselves thrust into the unfamiliar role of government allies.

A general election for the county was called and a public meeting was held where the two parties—one headed by O'Connor's uncle and Lord Kingsborough and the other by Lord Shannon—were to present themselves and appeal to the electorate for its votes. Arthur claims that this was the occasion of his first political speech. The Shannonites' strategy was to portray themselves as principled oppositionists and their opponents as obsequious government toadies. Arthur took to the hustings against these "new-made Patriots," allegedly exposed their mercenary motives, and played a significant role in undermining their electoral ambitions.[7]

He had prepared for the meeting by researching the measures the Shannonites had previously supported, prior to their recent metamorphosis. After reciting the details of the Shannonites' political past, he says, "I asked the electors what confidence they could have that such profligate men would not return to their old and confirmed habits."

> *I defied any elector to come forward and deny the conclusive facts I advanced. I found for an answer not a soul dared speak. I took the engagement that if anyone attempted I would answer him by giving the enumeration of all the measures he had supported for twenty years by which he sold the rights, the industry, the commerce and every thing that could contribute to Ireland's prosperity. The triumph was complete. I had put these pretended Patriots to silence. My uncle pressed me to his head before the whole assembly and I received the warmest of solicitations [from] all the independent electors.*[8]

The electoral victory of his uncle's faction gave impetus to O'Connor's political career and opened up sources of patronage to him. Although Arthur had studied law and had been admitted to the Irish bar, he "had never followed the profession."[9] Nonetheless, Lord Kingsborough hired him as one of his lawyers to represent his interests during the 1790 elections in County Cork. O'Connor sat on a panel of lawyers made up of representatives of opposing candidates; its function was to rule on allegations of voter fraud. The election process lasted three months and the panel sat for eight hours every day. Its primary activity was trying to determine whether individual voters were really eligible to vote, as they claimed, or whether they were perjuring themselves.

O'Connor was but one of eight lawyers representing the Kingsborough faction (which he calls "the independent side"), but he tells us that he was able to make a unique contribution to their work:

> *The profound study I had made of the doctrine of evidence was here of the greatest use to me and though my seven collaborators were infinitely my superiors in matters of law I took the lead in the subjects of evidence. The application of its principles enabled me to detect a great number of those votes supported by fraud and perjury.*[10]

THE HIGH SHERIFF OF CORK

O'Connor thus once again demonstrated his usefulness to his uncle's political friends and as a result more of the fruits of patronage soon came in his direction. During the elections, the high sheriff of Cork proved to be too indecisive and hesitant to perform the job effectively, so it was generally agreed that he should be replaced before the next elections. "By the change of politics the choice of the High Sheriff devolved on my uncle and Lord Kingsborough," Arthur says; "They resolved in nominating me." Hence, within a short time of entering political life O'Connor had succeeded in obtaining one of the most prestigious posts in the county. He claims that during the subsequent elections he fulfilled his duties so successfully that he received the "hearty thanks" of the assembled electors.[11]

In his memoirs O'Connor reports an incident that occurred during 1791, his year as high sheriff, that helped to put him in good stead with the Catholic population, not only in Cork but throughout Ireland. He had requested a leave of absence to go to England on his private affairs, but before he left he heard that the Shannonites intended to stir up political mischief by encouraging agrarian discontent. Learning that they were holding a private conclave to plan their skullduggery, he went to the meeting himself.

> On entering I could perceive my appearance was as unwelcome as unexpected. It caused a dead silence. I remained a silent spectator until at length one man bolder than the others asked me if I was of the assembly. To this I answered by a severe rebuke to the whole by informing that they were an illegal meeting, that to be legal they should have advertised me of their meeting and the neglecting this necessary form must give me to understand there was an underhand plot in being.[12]

O'Connor asserts that the Shannonites had hoped to discredit him by secretly fomenting an agrarian insurrection of the poor Catholics in the Macroom area. Then they would help to put the insurrection down, thus boosting their own stock in the eyes of the government. The Catholic peasants were to be the unwitting victims of the Shannonites' machinations.

It is difficult to know what to make of this claim by O'Connor and, while it may be based on real events, it is highly improbable that the Shannonites actually aimed at stirring up a Catholic rebellion. Nonetheless, O'Connor's intervention served to calm fears among local Protestants. He wrote a public notice and had it published in a local newspaper in which he denounced those who spread rumors of an insurrection and promised to soon "drag the true delinquents before the public."[13] Meanwhile, he enlisted the help of his steward, who he described as "a good Irish peasant that knew all the arts and wiliness of their race," and sent the man to Macroom to infiltrate nocturnal meetings of the would-be insurrectionaries and "find out the leaders."[14] O'Connor says it was not his intention to make arrests, but that he instructed his agent to convince the agitators *that they were the dupes of their bitterest enemies who had incited them to those barbarous risings to furnish themselves with arguments against granting the indulgences to the Catholics that were held out for the meeting of the Parliament; that I was their real friend and would vote for them.*[15]

Some days later O'Connor set out from Cork with a few soldiers, but when he arrived his steward assured him that no force would be necessary to quell the agitation. O'Connor himself met with the agrarian leaders, who he says told him that a Shannonite magistrate had urged them to revolt as a means of instilling fear in the local gentry, to frighten the latter into lowering the tithe and the rents.

The following Sunday morning O'Connor held an open-air meeting a few miles from Macroom. "The crowds were immense," he reports. "Every rising ground was covered with men anxious to know what I should say."[16] In order to reassure the local peasantry, he had no soldiers accompanying him. His speech—in which he blasted "the intrigues of a Protestant faction to inveigle the lowest class into nocturnal meetings," and declared that he "stood guarantee for the good conduct of my Catholic countrymen"—was warmly received, and afterwards the crowd dispersed peacefully.[17]

With the threat of insurrection dissipated, O'Connor returned to Cork, where he says he "reestablished commercial credit, which had been shaken by this attempt of the Shannonites to disturb the country." Before long he learned that his speech at Macroom "was received throughout all of Ireland as the most welcome news. From every town and village I received addresses of the most warm thanks. They filled a large trunk."[18] O'Connor reproduces several of these expressions of appreciation in his memoirs. One representative example, dated 15 December 1791, reads in part:

> The Catholic Committee of Dublin return you their thanks for the liberal manner in which you declared yourself relative to the Catholics of the county of Cork . . . . We hope the Roman Catholics of Ireland will ever merit the approbation of such officers of executive power who, like you, unwarped by prejudice and independent in station, do justice to injured truth. Signed by order of the society, Thomas McKenna.[19]

O'Connor says he had not expected a response of this magnitude: "What I had done was but an ordinary act of justice towards men foully calumniated by their oppressors."[20] This outpouring of Catholic gratitude, he opined, was an indication of the depth of "the cruel state of oppression of the Irish papists."[21]

Although O'Connor portrays himself in this narrative as an enlightened public officeholder who was able to use reason rather than repression to prevent an uprising, he does not explicitly mention that the fundamental social problem—the oppressively high tithe and rents—remained unsolved. That omission indicates the limitations of his empathy with the plight of the poor Catholic peasants, both at the time the events occurred and at the time he was writing about them.[22]

O'CONNOR IN PARLIAMENT

In the narration above, when O'Connor told the Catholics at Macroom "I will vote for you," he was alluding to his position as a member of the Irish parliament. Before he had become high sheriff of Cork, his uncle had offered him a seat in the Irish parliament, which he had accepted.[23] In his memoirs he goes to great lengths to insist that he did not sell his soul to advance his career. His uncle, he says,

> knew me too well to offer [the parliamentary seat] on any other condition but that of the most perfect independence. His words were: "You know the love I bear you. I am proud of your talents, and the greatest satisfaction I can feel is the being instrumental in enabling you to bring them to the service of your country. I have observed you from your infancy. I have attentively observed the principles which invariably guided you. Were I to propose to you the smallest deviation from them I am convinced you would reject them. In offering you a seat in Parliament I leave to you your entire independence."[24]

Does O'Connor protest too much? While his account of his earliest political experiences may be factually accurate, he has certainly interpreted them to make it appear that his political outlook remained perfectly consistent from 1790 through 1798 and up to the 1830s when he began writing his memoirs. There are problems with this scenario. The evidence suggests that he had not developed solid political principles by the time he took his seat in parliament. As time went by, he seems to have evolved first into a liberal reformer of the Grattan or Fox variety, and then, by 1795, into a radical revolutionary who would not shrink from the use of "physical force" to topple an unjust government. In his memoirs, however, he sought to portray himself as a life-long consistent moderate revolutionary of the type of Lafayette or Condorcet. An examination of his public actions undermine this depiction.

O'Connor was admitted to the Irish parliament in 1790, representing the borough of Philipstown in King's County. Describing that moment in retrospect, he says:

> *In the state of the Assembly I was entering, a man of my principles could do little to serve Ireland. . . . I may safely assert there never did exist in any country a more profoundly corrupt body than this Irish representation, which represented nothing but its own individual selfish interest, where the votes of the most vital interests of the Nation were bought and sold as the vilest offal.*[25]

At first, O'Connor had expected that his uncle's faction, which he continued to call "independents," would be less corrupt than the Shannonites it had replaced. However, he quickly became disillusioned:

> *I soon discovered that our independents had resolved to follow the example of the men they had just dispossessed and support government for the distribution of the patronage they had obtained. This discovery made me regret I had opened my life in a House where nearly all was so corrupted.*[26]

O'Connor did find one kindred soul in parliament, however; a friend from college named Sir Laurence Parsons, who he calls "the honestest member in the House."[27] He and Parsons discussed what men in their position could do in parliament to serve Ireland and concluded that because they were impotent to effect change, "the post of honor was a private station." Therefore, O'Connor says, "I remained a whole year a silent looker-on."[28]

THE "INDIA TRADE FOR IRELAND" QUESTION

In the parliamentary session of 1792 an issue arose that prompted him to break his silence: the question of the India trade for Ireland. His uncle's political allies, now members of the government party, were obliged to vote for a measure that would severely restrict Ireland's ability to engage in trade with India. They were, however, in a quandary because they believed they were being forced to cast a vote against the interests of Ireland. The government's position was dictated by English commercial interests that sought to discourage competition by all means possible.

The day before this issue was scheduled to be debated in parliament, Lord Longueville invited twenty-five of the government members to his house for dinner to discuss what they would do. They unanimously agreed that the measure would cause Ireland "the most ruinous injury" and lamented having to vote for it.[29] O'Connor then rose and declared that to the contrary, it would be damaging for Ireland to attempt to break into the India trade. His remarks were met with laughter and he was accused of intentionally putting forward a paradox merely for sport.

Longueville, however, encouraged him to speak on the question in parliament the next day, sensing that perhaps his nephew might provide them with a way out of their dilemma. Arthur agreed to do so, although he said he did not like appearing to support a government he "knew to be essentially inimical to the dearest interests" of Ireland, even in this most unusual instance when that government happened to be proposing a measure he thought should be supported.[30]

The following day, before going to the House of Commons, he rode to the Wicklow mountains and spent the morning there thinking about what he would say. When the debate began, George Ponsonby and many others spoke, O'Connor says, but "not one of them in conformity to the economical principles by which the question should be decided."[31] When he rose to speak he noticed smiles on the faces of the men who had been at his uncle's house the previous night: "They all imagined I had gotten into an inextricable difficulty."[32]

He began by stating that "it was not a question of right but of utility." If it was to Ireland's advantage to trade with India, he declared, "no power on earth should prevent her." But to carry on that trade, Ireland

> *must find capital and this she could not do but by taking it from some of the trades she now carried on. Was it from agriculture she could take it? They all knew she had not the twentieth part for supporting this first of all industries. Was it from her manufactures she was to take it? At the time I was speaking there were thousands of manufacturers that filled the streets with their cries for bread from want of capital to employ them. I asked the advocates for embarking Ireland in the India trade if they thought in the cruel dearth Ireland felt of capital, her diminutive portion would serve her industry better by sending it to India and awaiting a return in two or three years than by employing it in the home trade or in the foreign trades where the return was monthly or (if farther) half yearly.[33]*

He paused, waiting for an answer but was met with silence. He repeated the question and paused again. The silence continued. In his memoirs he remarks that his "triumph was complete" at this stage.[34] His uncle was pleased because O'Connor had "set to sleep one of the questions that had embarrassed the government most."[35] Aside from winning his uncle's approval he had also displayed considerable skill as a public debater.

It is evident that O'Connor's outlook was changing and that he was beginning to develop principles that were clearly incompatible with his those of his uncle. He was forced to recognize that "the party of the independents who had driven the old sinners out of their places and had got possession of the patronage of government had fallen also into their unconditional support of every ruinous measure."[36]

Meanwhile Lord Longueville tried to rationalize every twist and turn, but finally turned to his nephew for advice on how to extricate himself from the political morass. O'Connor says that he urged his patron to quit being a tool of the government and to "place himself at the head of the independent men of Ireland." Longueville wistfully replied that in his youth he might have been able to lead a crusade, but he no longer had the energy to buck the "vile and corrupt" system. Realizing that his uncle would not challenge the Irish government, O'Connor advised him to ignore it and direct his attention instead to the real source of political power: the English ministers. "My uncle made me no answer, but a few days after, he told me he had reflected on the advice I gave him and asked me if I would accompany him to London, to which I willingly consented."[37]

O'CONNOR AND PITT

At this time O'Connor was beginning to develop a serious interest in the revolutionary events transpiring in France. It seems that he accepted his uncle's invitation to go to England partly because he hoped to be able to go on from there to the continent. Meanwhile, Longueville had arranged to see Prime Minister William Pitt. Pitt, O'Connor says, "was well pleased to have a man of my uncle's political importance in his immediate direct dependence."[38]

Longueville told Pitt "of the service his nephew was capable of rendering to government,"[39] and described O'Connor's triumph on the India-Ireland trade question. "Pitt acknowledged I had shown a knowledge of the economical science," O'Connor reports, and agreed that it "certainly entitled me to fill a most important station." But when Longueville asked the prime minister to appoint O'Connor to the position of chancellor of the exchequer, Pitt objected that he was too young. O'Connor claims that the prime minister did consent to make him commissioner of the revenue, however, and promised to promote him to chancellor of the exchequer at a future time.[40]

According to O'Connor's narrative, he had little interest in Pitt's offer but was deeply distressed at the prospect of hurting his uncle's feelings by refusing it.

> *When my uncle told me what had passed between him and Mr. Pitt, I don't know that in all my life I felt more sensibly than on that occasion the sense of affection for the evident intentions with which my uncle had acted toward me, and the disappointment my refusal must cost him entered into my head like a dagger.*[41]

Nonetheless, he told his uncle that he could not "receive any place under the gift of the Crown on conditions of supporting the Irish government."[42] Longueville took the rejection better than he had expected, and their good relationship remained temporarily intact.

There is no independent evidence that Pitt made such offers of positions, and it is difficult to believe that O'Connor's claims are not considerably overstated. It should also be noted that they are contradicted by O'Connor's later insistence, during a 1797 election campaign, that he had not allowed his uncle to make such a solicitation on his behalf.[43] But however exaggerated, any such discussion that Longueville had with Pitt is remarkable, and certainly highlights the seriousness with which O'Connor was viewed by contemporaries. He was clearly a man of significant abilities.

VIEWING THE FRENCH REVOLUTION

With the unpleasantness of disappointing his uncle out of the way, O'Connor was free to leave for France. John Hely-Hutchinson (later Lord Donoughmore), whose father was Provost of Trinity College, offered to join him and to share the expenses; O'Connor gladly accepted. At that time, he says, Hely-Hutchinson "was a red hot Democrat, in love with the French Revolution to excess."[44]

O'Connor procured "two capital riding horses and a good traveling carriage."[45] They traveled as military men; Hely-Hutchinson wore the uniform of a colonel in the English army and O'Connor the uniform of a colonel in the Irish Volunteers. Their equivalence of rank, however, was in name only. The English army was a state institution under centralized command and Hely-Hutchinson had risen to the rank of colonel in competition with other officers. The Volunteers, by contrast, consisted of decentralized units headed by self-appointed officers who purchased their own uniforms. Nonetheless,

O'Connor's credentials were sufficiently legitimate to gain him entry to military circles during his travels.

O'Connor and Hely-Hutchinson were able to acquire letters of introduction to the French generals stationed on the German frontiers as well as to some important men in Paris. Their first stop was at Lille, where Arthur visited the local Jacobin club in full session.

> *The hall where they met was vast yet it was full to excess. Never before did I see such an uproar. It seemed to me I was the only hearer. All the rest were bawling as loud as their lungs could go. Hundreds seeing me a silent spectator addressed themselves to me and all the same time. After passing an hour in this Hell on Earth I could not imagine it was not a madhouse I had been in.*[46]

The following day he went to the town square to witness the execution of a man who he identifies as "the assassin of an Officer Dillon" (a French commander killed by his own troops on 29 April 1792)[47]. The fact that O'Connor describes the condemned man as a "traitor" places him on the moderate end of the spectrum of French revolutionary opinion, because more radical revolutionaries (Jean Paul Marat, for example) considered Dillon the traitor and those who killed him heroes.

O'CONNOR AND LAFAYETTE

From Lille, O'Connor and his traveling companion went on to visit the frontier encampments at Maubeuge, Valenciennes, Sedan, and elsewhere. He was particularly impressed with meeting General Lafayette:

> *On arriving at the camp of Sedan where Lafayette commanded, nothing could be more kind than the reception I met with from the general. The time he served in America had taught him to distinguish between the Irish and the English. He was as much at home with the former as he was a stranger with the other. [Hely-Hutchinson] was extremely nearsighted, which gave him the appearance of the extreme reserve of the English. This led Lafayette to take him for an Englishman. The Irish of my character led him to give me all his confidence from the first.*[48]

O'Connor and Hely-Hutchinson had been invited by Lafayette to accompany him on his army's forthcoming campaign, but one of the great *journées* of the Revolution, 10 August 1792, intervened as a massive insurrection in Paris brought the first French Republic into being. When O'Connor heard the news of this momentous event from a man who had just arrived from Paris, he hastened to see Lafayette "and found him less well informed than I was on several particulars."[49]

Lafayette had already been on a collision course with the revolutionary government in Paris. O'Connor says that "some days before, when he arrested the *Commissaires* sent by Government to his army, I did all I could to dissuade him from it. His ideas and mine were totally different on the march the Revolution must take." Lafayette, O'Connor says, "fondly imagined his army was more attached to him personally than to the public opinion which was against him. I told him that before a week he would find himself deserted." The prophesy came to pass; his French host acknowledged that O'Connor "had judged his army more justly" than he himself had, and said that he intended to leave France that very night.[50]

During their sojourn, Hely-Hutchinson's near-sightedness almost cost both him and O'Connor their lives. Upon hearing that Lafayette had struck camp, O'Connor asked his friend to go to ascertain whether the report was true. Hely-Hutchinson went to the site of the camp, which indeed had been abandoned, and looked around with a hand-held lens that he depended upon to see anything more than a few yards away. A woman who saw this foreigner repeatedly raising what appeared to be a spyglass to his eye assumed he was a German spy and alerted an army patrol. Just as Hely-Hutchinson was about to be arrested O'Connor joined him; both were taken into custody and conducted to a nearby army post where they were surrounded by a crowd that threatened to lynch them on the spot. The officer in charge decided to take them to the city hall in Sedan where the two "German spies" would at least be allowed an informal trial.

O'Connor was confident that the mayor of Sedan, who was Lafayette's uncle, would vouch for them and arrange their safe release. Unfortunately, when they arrived at city hall they discovered that all of the officials had gone to dinner, and the informal trial proceeded. Hely-Hutchinson compounded their difficulties by becoming belligerent and insisting on his prerogatives as a nobleman. "Now of all men living," O'Connor comments, "the slovenly appearance of Hely-Hutchinson at this moment gave him the least pretension to any thing aristocratic."[51] Not surprisingly, the townspeople sitting in judgment of them greeted his haughty airs with derision and contempt. O'Connor took a more pragmatic approach:

> On being asked what and who I was, I answered I was a member of the democratic chamber of the Irish parliament . . . that I came to regale myself with the sight of the French nation in the enjoyment of

her infant liberty and hoped they would not give so bad an example of it as hanging us and judging us after; that if there was a single man in all Sedan who spoke English he could convince them we were English and not German; that if they would give us a few moments time I could produce the testimony of the Mayor that we were the friends of General Lafayette and had frequently dined with him at the General's table.[52]

Fortunately for O'Connor and Hely-Hutchinson an aide-de-camp of Lafayette's arrived and corroborated everything he had said. They were freed and "everywhere we went we received the expressions of everyone of the universal regret for the mistake that was made in arresting us."[53] O'Connor says that he was perfectly satisfied with the outcome of the affair, but Hely-Hutchinson's pride was so wounded by the way he had been treated that he underwent a 180-degree political conversion. From previously having been "in love with the French Revolution to excess" he turned into its sworn enemy. Hely-Hutchinson wanted to leave immediately for Belgium, which was under Austrian control, but O'Connor was able to convince him that such a precipitous departure would appear very suspicious, so he prevailed upon him to wait a few days and then they left together.

WITH THE AUSTRIANS IN BELGIUM

In Brussels they met an Austrian general of Irish extraction named O'Grady, who introduced them at the Austrian viceroy's court and invited them, together with a group of British army officers who happened to be mostly Irishmen, to review the troops encamped at Jemappes. At breakfast, before setting out, a discussion arose over whether those who had seen the French fortifications and outworks were free to tell the Austrians "what they had seen on the faith of a neutral nation." Of all the British officers only Hely-Hutchinson maintained that it was acceptable to disclose what they had seen in France. O'Connor felt that this "would be acting the part of a spy," and expressed strong disagreement with his friend's views.[54]

After dinner that evening a General Harney approached O'Connor and put a sheet of paper on the table in front of him. It showed a sketch of the defenses of Maubeuge, and Harney asked O'Connor if he thought it appeared accurate. O'Connor indignantly pushed the paper away and told Harney that he knew nothing about it. A short while later O'Connor was told by General O'Grady that he and the other generals were appalled by Harney's improper request and had demanded that he offer an apology to O'Connor, which he did, and which O'Connor accepted. This little drama may have been staged as a test of O'Connor's trustworthiness, because he and the British officers were then invited to see the Austrians' advance posts—a confidence, O'Connor says, never before bestowed upon foreigners.

INFLUENTIAL FRIENDS IN ENGLAND

O'Connor's visit to France and Belgium ended in December 1792, and he returned to England. He already knew a few influential people in that country, but from that time through 1795 he made the acquaintance of many more very important men and women and became a familiar face at Devonshire House, a primary gathering place for the cream of English society. His friends old and new—Charles James Fox, Richard Brinsley Sheridan, Charles Grey, Samuel Whitbread, Thomas Erskine, George Tierney, Edmund Burke, Sir Francis Burdett, Georgiana, Duchess of Devonshire, the Duke of Norfolk, and the Earls of Suffolk, Oxford, Lauderdale, Thanet, and Moira, among others—readily accepted the talented young Irishman into their rarified social and political circles. Although a reader of O'Connor's memoirs may be excused for judging him to be somewhat humorless and egocentric, when he was a young man his personality seems to have been characterized by a gentle, self-effacing sense of humor.

Except for Burke, his friends in England formed the backbone of the parliamentary opposition to the King's ministers in the era of the French Revolution. O'Connor was enchanted by "these highly honorable, independent men."[55] He planned to parlay his relationship with Fox and his friends into a parliamentary career for himself in England. Although it did not come to pass, Fox negotiated with a Mr. Lambert to purchase O'Connor a seat in the House of Commons for IR£3,000.[56] Disgusted with the abject servility of the Irish parliament, O'Connor saw the English parliament as a place where he could be among "men discussing their country's interests without their opinions being perverted by the corruption which sold them to another nation."[57]

It might be expected that O'Connor, as an Irish patriot, would not have wanted to serve in the legislature of his country's colonial masters, but he was convinced that oppressing Ireland was ruinous to England. The American experience proved it, he argued: "Who does not know that free trade with twenty millions of an independent nation is more profitable than a trade of stunted monopoly with three millions that existed before the American Revolution?"[58] O'Connor therefore believed that by joining the parliamentary opposition in England he could fight for the best interests of both Ireland and England simultaneously.

Although his plans to enter the English parliament were ultimately superseded by his revolutionary activities, his English friends undoubtedly saved his life in 1798 when many appeared as character witnesses at the Maidstone trial, where he was acquitted on charges of high treason. In his memoirs, after many years of complete separation from them, he recalled his association with most (Lord Moira was an exception) in the warmest possible terms.

O'Connor's introduction into the upper strata of English society was due partly to Lord Suffolk, whose acquaintance he made in Ireland in 1787, and partly to his uncle. Among the first of the influential men he met was Lord Shelburne, Marquis of Lansdowne,[59] who had held high political office in the Rockingham administration, and briefly served as prime minister following Rockingham's death. The Marquis and Arthur's uncle had been educated at the same school. To the Marquis, Arthur says, "I owe many days of happy and instructive society."[60]

SIR FRANCIS BURDETT

It was at the Marquis of Lansdowne's house that Arthur met Sir Francis Burdett, who was to become the foremost radical politician in England since John Wilkes. They forged a bond that O'Connor described as "one of the most intimate friendships that ever bound man and man together."[61] Their first encounter was at a dinner party at the Marquis's, but O'Connor—distracted by the presence of an attractive French duchess—hardly noticed Burdett. The Marquis posed some questions to O'Connor about "the economical science," which he at first declined to answer on the grounds that "it was too serious a subject for the entertainment of a young and beautiful woman like the duchess." The Marquis, however, persisted: "You are mistaken—she occupies herself with the sciences." O'Connor then relented and held forth at length on "the science as founded by Turgot, Condorcet, and Adam Smith."[62]

The next day O'Connor was walking down St. James Street when a young man jumped from a horse and ran up to him. It was Burdett, who said he had two requests to make of O'Connor: first, his friendship, and second, to be instructed in economics. O'Connor says that he was so impressed with Burdett's frankness that "I readily granted all he asked, and for years after we were inseparable. We studied together and such was the unity of our hearts that neither had a secret [from] the other."[63] That would imply that O'Connor kept Burdett fully informed of his revolutionary activities during the period leading up to the Rebellion of 1798.

O'Connor says that Burdett even urged him to marry his sister-in-law, Susan Coutts (later Lady Guilford), and promised half of his fortune as her dowry. O'Connor declined, telling Burdett: "The vow I made to devote my life to the relieving Ireland had forbid me to involve any woman in a union with a man whose life was already disposed of, rendering marriage impossible."[64] His pledge to remain unmarried remained in effect until after 1802, when he was permanently banished from Ireland and felt his life was no longer entirely defined by revolutionary duty.

Burdett was a protégé of one of the seminal figures of English radicalism, John Horne Tooke. O'Connor, however, tested the limits of Tooke's radicalism on at least two occasions. Tooke was critical of British policy toward Ireland, but he was not in favor of Irish independence. According to O'Connor:

> Horne Tooke himself told me one day [when] I was maintaining the necessity to which England had driven Ireland to separate, that he would do all he could to dissuade me, but if words would not do, he would hold me by the sleeve of my coat, and if this should tear, he would seize the collar.[65]

On another occasion a favorable comment by O'Connor on the abolition of primogeniture in French law provoked Tooke to violent disagreement:

> In my youth I passed a day with Horne Tooke at his house at Wimbledon. The French law of succession was the subject of discussion; in the midst of it, Tooke drew a long poniard-knife from his pocket, opened the blade, and presenting it towards me with a furious look: "This," said he, "is the argument I employ with men who take the side of this question that you do." I took an early moment to quit the room, and was followed by sir Francis Burdett, who was so shocked with this action of Tooke's, that he expressed his sorrow and astonishment so superior a man should, in his own house, break off a discussion in so brutal a manner.[66]

THE PARLIAMENTARY SESSION OF 1793

O'Connor had ended his travels on the continent in December 1792 in order to return to Ireland for the parliamentary session of 1793, but he passed through England on his way home. England, he says, was "in a most violent state. Never was a country so intrigued, so wrought upon by every species of terror and imposture." A "war of political opinion" was raging, sparked by "the arts of an ambitious minister," Pitt. England was "inundated with publications" of all descriptions "paid for by the Treasury at an enormous expense," all aimed at creating enmity toward the French Revolution rather than embracing it as a giant step toward the liberation of humankind.[67]

When O'Connor arrived in Dublin and went to the House of Commons he found himself the only member of the Irish parliament who was not dressed all in black. Pitt had required the English parliament to observe deep mourning for Louis XVI, who had been guillotined in Paris on 21 January 1793, and the Irish legislators had decided to follow suit. "On entering the House," O'Connor reports,

> *a crowd surrounded me to demand why I was not in black. I answered them that I was perhaps the only man amongst them who had a right to condemn the killing of the French king from my having constantly maintained that society had no right to take the life of any of its members.*[68]

But he refused to join them in their political act of mourning because he "denied the right of any nation to interfere in the internal regulation of any other."[69] This defiance, it seems, was O'Connor's first overt act of radicalism, and it earned him a certain amount of notoriety.

During the session of 1793 O'Connor discovered that the French Revolution was being condemned not only by the corrupt majority, but by "Grattan, Forbes, and most of the honestest men in opposition" as well. In a conversation with Grattan he "found his mind had been perverted" by O'Connor's erstwhile traveling companion, Hely-Hutchinson, who "was esteemed as a very honorable man and was in the highest confidence with Grattan." O'Connor attempted, but with uncertain effect, to undo the damage of Hely-Hutchinson's misrepresentations by dining with Grattan and Forbes and telling them "the unvarnished facts as they had happened" to himself and Hely-Hutchinson in France.[70]

In any event, O'Connor soon became "so disgusted with the vile spirit" he found in Ireland that he decided to leave and spend the summer of 1793 with a friend, John Knox, at Ryde on the Isle of Wight.[71] Ironically, within a few years Knox and O'Connor would find themselves on opposite sides of the barricades, figuratively speaking, as Brigadier-General Knox would then be actively promoting "the most drastic measures of repression" against the United Irishmen in Ulster.[72]

While vacationing with Knox on the Isle of Wight, O'Connor gave vent to his frustration by writing a political pamphlet that he sent off to a printer/bookseller named Eaton in London, "telling him to print it if he thought it would pay the publication."[73] It bore the rather unwieldy title *The Measures of Ministry to Prevent a Revolution Are the Certain Means of Bringing It On* and was published anonymously under the pseudonym "A Stoic." The 71-page pamphlet was essentially a polemic against the "ruinous war" the Pitt ministry was waging against revolutionary France; "the abuses of power," it warned, "which led to a Revolution in France would lead to another in England."[74] O'Connor later claimed that after he sent the manuscript to the printer he never gave it another thought until he encountered it quite unexpectedly three years later, in 1796. However, its publication was undoubtedly an important milestone in his shift toward radical republicanism.

LAUDERDALE AND GREY

By 1796 he had already become fast friends with Fox and his colleagues. One evening a dozen of them agreed to meet for dinner "at the famous beefsteak chophouse Dolly's, in the City."[75] As he and the Earl of Lauderdale were walking toward the restaurant, Lauderdale, O'Connor later recalled, "quitted my arm suddenly and ran into a bookseller's shop," which happened to be none other than "the famous Eaton's." He followed his friend into the shop and witnessed him buying a stack of pamphlets. Lauderdale, he says, told him, "I have found here a pamphlet which when it came out puzzled Fox and all of us to divine who could be the author. It is a most extraordinary work."[76] Lauderdale handed a copy to O'Connor who recognized it as the antiwar tract he had written earlier on the Isle of Wight and he told Lauderdale that he was the author.

When they arrived at Dolly's, they found Fox, Sheridan, Grey, and Tierney sitting around a table, waiting for the others. Lauderdale tossed one of the pamphlets to Grey, who read the title and said he had heard of it; that it was reputed to be "a most wicked pamphlet." Lauderdale then gleefully announced, to Grey's chagrin, that O'Connor had written it.[77] Grey apologized to O'Connor and blasted Lauderdale for his insensitivity. He told O'Connor that he had in fact never read the pamphlet. O'Connor responded by asking him to read it and "if he found anything reprehensible or that he thought unfounded to communicate it to me."[78]

Some days later O'Connor chanced to meet Lady Grey, who told him that Lord Grey would very much like to see him, and invited him to dinner that evening. The first thing Grey said to him, according to O'Connor's account, was, "Well, I have read your little work with the greatest attention and I declare that I subscribe to every letter of it."[79]

This indicated to O'Connor that "Grey's mind was expanding out of the old routine," because the pamphlet had at least implicitly espoused radical republicanism.[80] A short while later, at a dinner party hosted by the Duchess of Devonshire, Grey was present and the Duchess observed publicly that since he had become friends with O'Connor he had become a republican. The future prime minister replied, according to O'Connor, that "he had the strongest conviction that to serve his country he should be a Jacobin but he acknowledged to his shame he had not the resolution to do what he ought."[81]

BURKE AND SHERIDAN

Although it may seem peculiar that O'Connor would have been drawn to the most prominent ideological opponent of the French Revolution, he claimed to be gratified that "Edmund Burke had favored me with his friendship." The two Irishmen, he said, shared an important conviction: "The interest we both took in freeing our countrymen from their religious persecution was the bond of this friendship." Although O'Connor abhorred Burke's *Reflections on the French Revolution*, he says that when they were at Bath together in the winter of 1793 they "were scarce an instant from each other's society." Because of their deep differences over the French Revolution, "I took special care never to utter a syllable" on that subject, "leaving our Irish bond entire."[82] O'Connor's description of his relationship with Burke gives the impression that they had been close friends for a long time, but Burke later wrote, after O'Connor's radicalism became widely known, that their encounter at Bath was the one and only time they had met. "I saw," Burke said of O'Connor, "he had a mind of great energy, and was capable of much good or of much Evil."[83]

Burke, O'Connor says, "passed his evening tete-a-tete at my lodgings where, stretched full length on my sopha, he enjoyed his ease."[84] In spite of Burke's age (O'Connor estimated it at 73 when it was in fact 63), "yet his legs were as fine and neat as a young man's of twenty, which he attributed to his taking an horizontal position as often as he could take that liberty." Their "intimate conversations turned on the parties, the intrigues and politics" of the day. "From him I learned of the subjects what is not to be found in books."[85]

In the crucial field of political economy, however, O'Connor deemed his older friend to be deficient. "In all my most intimate conversations with Edmund Burke I perceived his disdain of this indispensable science. It was always 'your economical science,' with a sneer." But O'Connor found it "quite natural" that a man of Burke's brilliant imagination could not "bear the shackles of positive, unflinching principles of science."[86] Moreover, O'Connor believed Burke harbored "prejudices which obscured his reasoning faculties" that stemmed from his "having been a converted Protestant from Popery."[87]

On one occasion O'Connor asked Burke to rate the great orators of the day. He realized immediately that the request seemed to trouble Burke. "You put me a question which is most disagreeable," he told O'Connor, "but I can refuse you nothing." The difficulty was that honesty required Burke to concede that the greatest of them all was his hated rival, Richard Brinsley Sheridan. "You know that since my disagreement with Charles Fox I never rise to speak in the House that Sheridan does not plunge a dagger in my side," Burke said, "but truth obliges me to say that Chatham, Fox, Townsend, Barré, Pitt—they do me the honor to class me in this list—we are all but children [compared] to Sheridan."[88] Burke continued (according to O'Connor):

> I think I know the speeches of the greatest orators of antiquity. I have heard those of modern times; all these are nothing to Sheridan's. You have heard him as well as me and have seen what a succession of flashes of lightning and peals of thunder they were, how they command the attention of his audience.[89]

O'Connor had indeed heard Sheridan speak; he had been present when Sheridan gave some of the greatest oratorical performances of all times. In 1787 Sheridan presented the indictment when Warren Hastings was charged (in O'Connor's words) with committing "the cruelest extortions and plunder" against "the mild and patient millions in India" while governor-general of that colony.[90] Later, at Hastings' trial in the House of Commons, Sheridan was again the primary speaker for the prosecution. "Though his first speech lasted six hours," O'Connor recalled, "such was the fascinating powers of this first of orators" that "no one thought it was more than half an hour."[91] The sequel was even more brilliant: "When I heard his first speech I thought it was the greatest effort of eloquence the mind of man could achieve; what was my astonishment at hearing four months after the same man surpass himself by a speech that lasted four days?"[92] Sheridan's oratory "fell so heavily on Hastings that he appeared crushed by a thunderbolt," and succeeded in turning even his most ardent supporters against him.[93] Against all prior expectation, the House of Commons found Hastings guilty. (It was a foregone conclusion, however, that the verdict would eventually be overturned by the House of Lords.)

O'Connor did not know Sheridan at the time of the Hastings trial but, he says, "his matchless speeches on this occasion gave me the greatest desire to converse with the man that could make them."[94] When O'Connor arrived in London in 1795 he set out to make Sheridan's acquaintance. He could have asked a mutual friend to arrange an introduction, but instead he wrote directly to Sheridan "to know when I could find him at home."[95] In response,

O'Connor says, "he received me with the warmest expression of his desire to cultivate my friendship and from that moment never did a warmer nor a more sincere friendship unite two hearts together."[96]

But Sheridan was a flawed genius: "It was the failing of this great-minded man to impair his reason by excess of wine."[97] O'Connor relates an incident that occurred around the dinner table one evening, when Burdett and Robert Fergusson attacked Sheridan for failing to maintain his old zeal in defense of the French Revolution. Sheridan attempted to defend himself, but "as the discussion continued, Sheridan was losing ground from the confusion of his ideas." O'Connor then jumped into the fray and argued that the fault lay not with Sheridan, but with the turn of the French Revolution toward "sanguinary demagogy." Sheridan was the same, he maintained; "it was the principles of the French Revolution which had changed."[98] After receiving Sheridan's thanks for defending him, it fell to O'Connor to help his inebriated friend into bed.

Such incidents led a distraught Mrs. Sheridan to reproach O'Connor for "being the cause of her husband's excesses." O'Connor responded that he would give anything to prevent Sheridan from drinking, "but that being impossible, what would be gained by my standing off? Would she find then anyone who would take more care of him than I did?" If O'Connor, who never drank at all, were not his companion, he would surely seek others who might make matters much worse by joining him in his excessive drinking. "The poor woman threw herself into my arms, and sobbing, entreated me to forgive her and impute no injustice to her sorrow."[99]

Sheridan, according to his most recent biographer, "clearly admired" O'Connor.[100] He testified at the Maidstone trial that he had known O'Connor "very intimately" for about three years and declared, "I was particularly anxious for his society on account of his character, and the recommendations I received respecting him from Ireland."[101] When asked "Have you ever conversed with him confidentially upon political subjects?" he replied:

> I think most confidentially, because I treated him, and I think he treated me, with a confidence and unreservedness that might have been expected to have arisen alone from a much longer acquaintance; but from my opinion of his principles and character, and such communication that we had, and we did communicate without the smallest reserve whatever, upon all political topics relating to England or Ireland.[102]

FOX AND FITZGERALD

O'Connor also made the acquaintance of the great parliamentary leader Charles James Fox early in 1795, and, he says, their intimacy "augmented every day until it arrived on the most entire mutual confidence."[103] Half a century later O'Connor would fondly recall their "delicious conversations" at Fox's villa where "till midnight we walked amidst the warbling of his nightingales he so delighted to hear."[104] It was "in those confidential colloquies I perceived the noble sentiments of this great and good man's heart."[105]

O'Connor describes Fox as "incapable of deceit," but makes allowances for his position as "the chief of an hereditary party."[106] Although Fox "embraced the French principles," a major split in the Whig party in 1794 (in which a large majority abandoned Fox to join a coalition government with Pitt) had "made Fox cautious to shock the opinions of those who remained faithful to him by a too great predilection for democratical politics."[107]

Fox's testimony at the Maidstone trial indicates that he held O'Connor in high regard. When asked whether he thought O'Connor was capable of dissimulation he replied, "Perfectly the contrary—I should describe him as a man of the openest carriage." O'Connor, he added, was "very ardent and affectionate in his friendships, and totally without any reserve, I should think as much as any man I have the honour to be acquainted with."[108]

After the Kilmainham pact of 1798 some members of Fox's social circle looked upon O'Connor as a man who had betrayed them. One of them, Harriet Duncannon, claimed that Fox in fact "never liked [O'Connor] and always thought him a fool and disagreeable."[109] It is likely, however, that she was projecting her own retrospective disdain for O'Connor onto Fox. In the late summer of 1802 when Fox visited France it was apparent that he and O'Connor were still on good terms. They met in Calais, where they went to dinner and attended the theater together, and they later met again in Paris.

Exactly how O'Connor first came to know Fox in 1795 is a matter of speculation. Two years earlier he had met Lord Edward Fitzgerald, and some years before that—perhaps as early as 1787, in London—he had made the acquaintance of Lord Edward's mother, the Duchess of Leinster.[110] Her sister was Fox's mother, so Fitzgerald and Fox were first cousins. Lord Edward and O'Connor rapidly became close friends and political collaborators, so it may well have been that O'Connor and Fox were first introduced by Fitzgerald or his mother.

The intimate friendship of Fitzgerald and O'Connor began in the early summer of 1793. Lady Lucy Fitzgerald later wrote that her brother was thirty-one years of age when he met O'Connor, whom "he ever after called the twin of his soul . . . because each breathed and loved alike, and their object Ireland!"[111] It was O'Connor's refusal to dress in mourning for Louis XVI that first caught the rebellious aristocrat's attention. According to Lord Edward's most recent biographer, O'Connor "denounced the government with an articulate vehemence that overwhelmed and impressed Lord Edward." Fitzgerald

> was dazzled by O'Connor and felt that . . . he had at last found a male friend he could trust with his secrets. The two were soon seen together everywhere, and Lord Edward was especially delighted that his new companion seemed to be able to express so eloquently and succinctly his own political views.[112]

O'CONNOR'S SPEECH ON CATHOLIC EMANCIPATION

The culmination of O'Connor's parliamentary career was a passionate speech he made on the floor of the Irish House of Commons on Monday, 4 May 1795, calling for Catholic emancipation—full political rights for everyone regardless of their religion. In it he exceeded the bounds of accepted political discourse in the eyes of the Protestant establishment, rendering his continued membership of the Irish parliament untenable. His speech and subsequent resignation caused his final estrangement from Lord Longueville and thereby ended any possibility of advancement in a conventional political career. Just three years later the uncle who had previously had such high hopes for him wrote: "Of all the bad men I ever was acquainted with, he is the worst."[113] In another letter he declared, "I really think Mr. A. O'Connor merits the worst fate that can befall him. Kindness has ever been misplaced and thrown away on that entire family. I speak from sad experience of them."[114]

On the other hand, O'Connor's speech "seized fast hold of the hearts of the people of Ireland," and thereby laid the basis for a revolutionary political career.[115] Its author immediately became widely renowned as a champion of the downtrodden Irish Catholics. Wolfe Tone told General Hoche he thought it was "the ablest and honestest speech ever made in the Irish parliament."[116] John Knox wrote to O'Connor to congratulate him for delivering a speech that "contained more boldness than any ever delivered in a House of Commons."[117] When Lady Lucy Fitzgerald first met O'Connor she identified him in her diary as "the man who made the famous speech."[118] Wherever he traveled from that time forward—from the salons of the social elite in

London to the governmental centers in Paris—Arthur O'Connor needed no further introduction.

Formally, the speech was in favor of a bill before the Irish House of Commons that would grant Catholic emancipation, but both he and his immediate audience knew full well that the bill had no chance whatever of passing. He utilized the occasion, therefore, not to solicit the votes of his fellow members of parliament, but as a forum to address the nation and present a case for resolving Ireland's social ills by revolutionary means. He was challenging his opponents, not appealing to them, when he declared that "your adoption or rejection of this Bill must determine in the eyes of the Irish nation, which you represent, the Minister of England, or the people of Ireland."[119]

He characterized "the gentlemen of the opposite side of the House" as "those men who have been nursed in the lap of venality and prostitution—who have been educated in contempt and ridicule of a love for their country."[120] He accused them of "bartering an unqualified sacrifice of Irish trade, of Irish industry, of Irish rights, and of Irish character, at the Shrine of English domination, and of English avarice."[121]

Those who opposed Catholic emancipation, O'Connor charged, were guilty of "a criminal attempt to exclude three-fourths of their countrymen from the blessings of freedom, for no other purpose than to perpetuate a system in which a few families are unnaturally exalted at the expense of millions of their countrymen."[122] He even attacked his former patron, Lord Kingsborough, by name.[123]

The political context of O'Connor's speech was created by a pivotal event that had occurred a few months earlier. An apparent reversal of English policy toward Ireland had been signaled by the appointment of Earl Fitzwilliam as viceroy. Fitzwilliam's arrival in January 1795 generated widespread jubilation among the disaffected majority, which expected him to swiftly bring about Catholic emancipation and parliamentary reform. However, the joy was short-lived. Fitzwilliam's efforts were bitterly resisted by the old-guard politicians of the Protestant Ascendancy, and in February he was recalled by Pitt, destroying all hopes for progressive change. The English prime minister, O'Connor charged,

> has sported with the feelings of a whole nation—raising the cup with one hand to the parched lip of expectancy, he has dashed it to the earth with the other, in all the wantonness of insult, and with all the aggravation of contempt. Does he imagine that the people of this country, after he has tantalized them with the cheering hope of present alleviation and of future prosperity, will tamely bear to be forced to a

*re-endurance of their former sufferings, and to a re-appointment of
their former spoilers?*[124]

O'Connor stopped short of openly calling for the separation of Ireland
from Britain, but he did explicitly raise the prospect of French military
assistance in the liberation of Ireland. "France must have lost her senses if she
hesitates what part she will take," he told his fellow MPs;

> *if you shall have once convinced the people of this country, that you
> are* traitors to them, and hirelings to the Minister of an avaricious
> and domineering nation . . . *you shall have driven the people of this
> country to court the alliance of any nation able and willing to break the
> chains of a bondage not more galling to their feelings than restrictive
> of their prosperity.*[125]

"I am aware," he continued, that "in the eyes of weak and timid men
. . . I shall appear as one who has had entered on a delicate subject with
too much freedom—as a dangerous man—as a Jacobin." But, he told the
legislators, if a revolution occurs it will be their fault, not his, because "abuses
are the parent of revolution," and "a timely and national reform of those
abuses . . . is the only security against those convulsions which shake society
to its foundation."[126] Be that as it may, this speech is clear evidence that by
4 May 1795 Arthur O'Connor had been transformed from a reformer to
a revolutionary. If he was not yet formally a member of the United Irish
Society, he was certainly one in spirit and he had gained the attention of the
Irish people.

PART II

The United Irishman
1795–1798

4

Seventeen Ninety-Five and Ninety-Six

IN HIS MEMOIRS O'CONNOR points to "Pitt's breach of faith with Lord Fitzwilliam and the Irish nation" in early 1795 as the act that created a revolutionary situation in Ireland by utterly destroying the people's illusions that a peaceful resolution of their grievances was possible.[1] It was Fitzwilliam's recall and the subsequent rejection of Catholic emancipation, he says, that prompted him to "examine the state of things," and the more he did so, "the firmer the conviction I acquired, that every right, every principle of law and justice, sanctioned the most vigorous resistance to this state of misery and oppression."[2]

He embarked upon a study of "the state of the public mind" in all parts of Ireland and although he discovered an unmistakable yearning for freedom in the capital, in the south, and in the west, he was most impressed with what he encountered in the north. "I went to the north," he reports,

> and here I found a public spirit, an ardor for liberty, a love of independence accompanied with an intelligence that was not to be found in any population of Europe except that of the lowlands of Scotland. This decided me to fix my hopes of being able to establish a republic in Ireland in the north among the Presbyterians.[3]

It was in Belfast that he met "the patriotic men . . . who have taken the lead in promoting Ireland's liberty and independence"—the founders of the United Irish Society.[4]

BECOMING A UNITED IRISHMAN

Although Theobald Wolfe Tone is traditionally hailed as the father of the United Irish Society, it was O'Connor's opinion that "the real fathers were the editors of the *Northern Star* in Belfast—the two Simms [William and Robert], [Samuel] Neilson, [William] Tennent, etc." In 1791 Tone "had immense success in promoting the cause of Union," but "from the beginning of 1793 the United system languished until 1795," when the political crisis sparked by Fitzwilliam's recall gave it new life.[5] In fact, the original organization— which had been dedicated to public agitation for political reform—had been effectively destroyed by government repression in 1794 and had resumed its existence in 1795 as an underground, oath-bound revolutionary association.

The instability of Irish society in the 1790s was largely, though not entirely, a product of sectarian strife that pitted Catholics against Protestants. The religious identifications were surrogates for social divisions; the well-to-do landlords were mostly Protestants and the most impoverished segment of the rural population was Catholic. Furthermore, the polity was entirely composed of Protestants, while Catholics composed the vast majority of the population. The Protestants protected their political monopoly by legally disenfranchising the Catholics. With Protestants wielding a vastly disproportionate share of economic and political power, Catholics were understandably resentful. The United Irishmen, however, called on Protestants and Catholics alike to put aside their differences and join forces in struggle for their common interests as Irish people in breaking the British stranglehold on their country.

The possibility of achieving such unity was grounded in the fact that the Irish Protestants did not constitute a homogeneous social entity. A sizable proportion of the population of the northern province of Ulster were Presbyterians, or Dissenters. Although they were Protestants, they were not of the established church, the Church of Ireland. Dissenters were subjected to legal and political discrimination which, though not nearly as severe as that imposed upon the Catholics, was a source of constant irritation. They also loathed being legally forced to pay tithes to support a church that regarded them as heathens. Ulster's Dissenters thus provided a social base for the dissident political movement that inspired O'Connor's paeans to the patriotic spirit he found among the Presbyterians of the north.

There was, however, a decided lack of symmetry in the United Irishmen's appeal for unity. The organization's mostly Protestant leaders—some of whom, including O'Connor, were wealthy landowners—avoided taking a position on the crucial issue of land reform.[6] The land-hungry Catholics wanted more than mere political equality; they yearned for a *social* revolution that would bring about economic equality as well. Above all, they wanted the land to be equitably distributed. The United Irish leaders perceived this as a utopian "leveling" demand that was unachievable and could lead only to a communal bloodbath. Their ambivalent stance on the issue that mattered most to the Catholic population—and their hesitance to mobilize the full power of the Catholic poor—undermined the United Irishmen's ability to offer revolutionary leadership in the struggle for national liberation.

Nonetheless, between 1791 and 1795 the efforts of Tone and O'Connor on behalf of Catholic emancipation lent credibility to the United Irishmen's appeal for nonsectarian unity. Meanwhile Catholic resistance to oppression had taken the form of a plebeian organization called the Defenders, which had spread rapidly throughout Ireland. As the social crisis deepened, Defenders and United Irishmen alike were driven toward seeking a revolutionary solution, and as their interests converged, Defender militants began to join the United Irish underground army in ever-growing numbers. The amalgamation of the Defenders and the United Irishmen was far from seamless, but from 1795 to 1798 the level of collaboration between Catholic and Protestant revolutionaries reached a height never before and never since attained.

THE LEINSTER DIRECTORY

When O'Connor arrived in Belfast in 1795 he found that his radical reputation had preceded him. "I found no difficulty," he says, "in gaining the entire confidence of the men who composed the Northern Executive." Although he and Lord Edward (whom O'Connor introduced into the United movement[7]) did not become formal members until the following year, they entered into close collaboration with the organization: "It was agreed between me and the Northern Executive that they should continue their most strenuous efforts and that Lord Fitzgerald and I should propagate the union in the other three provinces and particularly in Leinster."[8]

O'Connor later insisted that when he joined the United Irish Society he was not required to take the oath, or "test," of membership.[9] The implication is that because he was of the landowning gentry his high social status automatically conferred a guarantee of integrity that obviated the need for the oath.[10] Fitzgerald's first biographer assumed that the usual initiation by oath must also have been waived for Lord Edward in recognition of his "high honour and trustworthiness."[11] It seems likely, however, that O'Connor did take the oath; he explicitly told Fox in a 1796 letter that he had.[12]

At the end of 1795 O'Connor left Belfast and went to London to lobby on Ireland's behalf: "The account I gave to Fox, Sheridan, Grey and the opposition caused them the greatest sorrow and made them loud in the execration of Pitt's wantonness and bad faith that had brought the Empire to such jeopardy."[13]

The chronology at this point in O'Connor's memoirs is somewhat unclear, but it seems that during this trip to London urgent news from Ireland recalled him to Belfast in early 1796, where he found the United Irish leaders overwhelmed by the sudden explosive growth of their movement: "The Union spread like fire through all Ulster and the same spirit pervaded north and south, east and west."[14] O'Connor claims that the executive committee at that time "made me the President of the Union and Commander in Chief."[15]

From Belfast O'Connor went to Dublin to confer with Lord Edward and "to organize our Union agents." Together they formed the Leinster directory of the United Irish Society and were for some time its only members. (O'Connor later dated its official inception at December 1796, but it is evident that he and Lord Edward had been functioning as a *de facto* executive committee several months earlier.) William James MacNeven, Richard McCormick, Oliver Bond, and Henry Jackson were subsequently added to the Leinster directory. According to an account that O'Conner wrote to Dr. Madden in 1842, he invited Thomas Addis Emmet to join that leadership body but Emmet declined and only entered it later, in 1797, when O'Connor was in prison.[16]

There was a military aspect to the United movement from its inception; as one historian notes, "The United Irishmen were the offspring of the Volunteers."[17] In 1792 a revival of the Volunteers under the aegis of the United Irish provoked government anxiety over the prospect of a radical political organization building an armed wing. Within a year the Volunteers had been disarmed and suppressed. By 1796, however, the reborn United Irish Society had again superimposed a military organization onto its civilian structure and was training its troops in clandestine nocturnal drilling sessions throughout the country. Lord Edward was an obvious candidate for leadership of the United Irishmen's military forces. Previously, as an officer in the British army, Fitzgerald had served with distinction in North America and the West Indies, although he had been dismissed for taking part in a notorious Republican banquet at White's Hotel in Paris on November 18, 1792.[18]

It was undoubtedly the promise of arms, training, and military leadership that attracted Catholic as well as Protestant rebels to the United movement in large numbers. O'Connor believed that the former Volunteers of the Belfast area could furnish him with "some fifty thousand men trained to marching in line and passing into column."[19] In February 1798 a United Irish assessment of its own troop strength counted 279,698 men in arms in three of Ireland's four provinces (no figures were given for Connacht).[20] Even allowing for exaggeration, it is evident that the underground rebel army under United Irish command was immense and ubiquitous.

Meanwhile, O'Connor's stay in Dublin was prolonged by a few days because he had to sell his house and furniture there, together with his carriage and horses, "to defray the considerable expense I might have to incur after visiting the South." Then he once again returned to London, where his friends "perceived I had become thoughtful and lost much of my usual gaiety."[21]

In early May 1796 O'Connor was called upon by two gentlemen who said they had been officially mandated by the "society of United Scotchmen" to approach him with an offer. "Hearing from their friends in the north of Ireland that I was President of the United Irish, they came to request I would accept the command of the United Scotch," a revolutionary organization claiming 45,000 members. But he felt he had to regretfully decline: "I frankly told them I had already more than I could well perform, and entreated them to tell their friends how deeply sensible [I was] of the confidence they reposed in me."[22]

O'Connor's survey of the state of affairs in Leinster, Munster, and Connacht convinced him that although the Catholic peasants in their vast majority were ready and willing—indeed aching—for revolutionary action, long oppression had rendered them incapable of achieving liberation by their own hand: "It was not difficult for me to comprehend that of all necessity we should be driven to seek for foreign aid." It was at the beginning of May, he says, that "my determination was firmly taken to take the decided step of negotiating foreign alliance."[23]

It is necessary to look beneath the surface of O'Connor's words and consider whether his social position as a wealthy landowner influenced his judgment with regard to revolutionary strategy. Was an appeal to French armed support necessary because the Catholic poor were not powerful enough, or was it rather that they were potentially *too* powerful? Elsewhere O'Connor wrote that he sought French intervention in order that the separation from England "might be effected without bloodshed."[24] Without questioning the sincerity of O'Connor's statements on a conscious level, it must be suspected that he and other United Irish leaders subconsciously feared releasing the unpredictable, pent-up revolutionary fervor of the Catholic peasantry, and looked to the French army as a means of implementing a *controlled* revolution that would not ultimately result in the Irish social structure being turned completely upside down.

NEGOTIATIONS FOR A FRENCH INVASION

Later in the month of May 1796 O'Connor and Lord Edward traveled to the continent to explore the possibility of securing French military assistance in freeing Ireland from English control. O'Connor eventually succeeded in meeting and parleying with the celebrated French general Lazare Hoche, who agreed to undertake an invasion of Ireland. Their discussions, O'Connor says, "were known only to General Hoche and to me. He is no more. They now rest solely with me." It was this consideration that O'Connor says prompted him to write his memoirs in the first place, because "without them the history of these events must remain incomplete."[25] His recollections are indeed of historical value and interest, but they are not entirely reliable and must be weighed carefully against existing documentary evidence.

Lord Edward, according to his biographers, left Dublin for London in April for the express purpose of proposing to O'Connor that they open negotiations with the French Directory. O'Connor's account does not dispute this, but claims that he had anticipated his friend's idea. Just before Lord Edward's arrival O'Connor had received a letter from Belfast about the rapidly deteriorating political situation there that had prompted him "to lose no time in setting out for France." He had already made preparations for the trip, and to disguise his true intentions had drawn up some documents that made it appear he was going to Switzerland. And then:

> I was surprised by the sudden visit from my beloved Edward. He entered with a serious look quite unusual, and without embracing me, asked me if we were without the hearing of anyone, for he had something of the highest importance to communicate. Here I stopped him. "I see by your face you are come to tell me that you have seen the Northern Executive and that they have sent you to tell me the time is come for me to negotiate an alliance with France." "In the name of God," said Edward, "Who could have told you? On my sacred honor, not one tittle of it has ever escaped my lips."[26]

O'Connor answered, "It was impossible for me not to see that at the rate the Irish government were goading the people, the same idea of the necessity of resistance must strike everyone," and so he had gone ahead and prepared for the inevitable approach to France.[27]

Lord Edward proposed that they begin by contacting a French diplomat, Charles Reinhard, whom he had met in London several years earlier. Reinhard had in the meantime become the official French representative to Hamburg, an independent city that maintained diplomatic neutrality between England and France. Hamburg would therefore be the first stop on Fitzgerald and O'Connor's voyage. Their visit to that city initiated a pattern of United Irish diplomacy in which Hamburg would retain a major role for several years to come.[28] O'Connor and Fitzgerald's "famous journey of 1796 represented a turning point" by paving the way "for Irish radicals using the continental route via Hamburg."[29]

Lord Edward also needed a cover story for his trip to the continent, so his wife Pamela, Lady Fitzgerald, was traveling with him. They were ostensibly on their way to Hamburg to visit her mother, Madame de Genlis,[30] and to attend the wedding of her cousin Henriette on 19 May. The Fitzgeralds set off for Hamburg first and O'Connor joined them on 5 June. "When I arrived at Hamburg," O'Connor says, "I found Edward had got into a difficulty which might have ruined our project." On 18 May Fitzgerald had "opened a communication with the French agent at Hamburg, the Reinhard who was afterwards Minister of the Interior in France under the auspices of Tallyrand."[31]

O'Connor claims that he quickly became suspicious—"Every word he had uttered convinced me this Reinhard was sold to the British minister"— and that he persuaded Lord Edward they should cease dealing with him.[32] On 6 June they met with Reinhard together. At that meeting, O'Connor later recalled,

> *I lost no time in breaking off all conference by declaring that it would be the greatest madness for the Irish to contend with the colossal power of England and that on so poor a support as the French. . . . To this Edward acquiesced and was delighted to get out of a* faux pas.[33]

This account sharply conflicts with Reinhard's positive report to Charles Delacroix, the French foreign secretary. According to Reinhard, far from immediately "breaking off" the meeting O'Connor told him:

> *We only want your help in the first moment; in two months we should have 100,000 men under arms; we ask your assistance only because we know it is your own clear interest to give it, and only on condition that you leave us absolute masters to frame our government as we please.*

Reinhard described O'Connor in glowing terms ("one of the best orators in the House of Commons of his country") and declared that his representations on behalf of the United Irish cause had been considerably more effective than Fitzgerald's:

> *Mr. O'Connor has confirmed word for word what Milord Fitzgerald has told me. He has spoken even more positively and decisively about the general disposition of the people, the means of invasion, and the infallibility of success if the French government will lend support. . . . The assurance with which he speaks has removed a great deal of the doubt that I would have retained had I only been dealing with Milord Fitzgerald.*[34]

There is no evidence to substantiate O'Connor's suspicions that Reinhard was untrustworthy; to the contrary, he seems to have been a sincere advocate of the Irish cause. It is peculiar that O'Connor, in his memoirs more than three decades later, continued to express such hostility toward Reinhard.[35] O'Connor's caution in 1796 was not entirely unwarranted, however, because Hamburg was teeming with British spies, but they seem not to have detected O'Connor and Fitzgerald's mission until after the fact.[36]

The Directory instructed Delacroix to tell "these two plenipotentiaries . . . to proceed to Switzerland, where they will receive passports."[37] From Hamburg O'Connor and Fitzgerald went to Basel, where on 19 June they called on the French ambassador, François Barthélemy, and gave him a letter to be transmitted to the Directory. In that letter, according to O'Connor, "we addressed ourselves to the generosity of the French nation to aid us to liberate our country from an unsupportable thralldom and establish our independence."[38]

The following day Barthélemy sent a report on the meeting to Delacroix and enclosed the letter the Irishmen had given him. Unfortunately that letter is not in the French archives, but its contents were made known to Tone, who summarized it in his private journal. It described the great organizational progress that the United Irishmen had made: "Fourteen of the counties, including the entire North, were completely organized for the purpose of throwing off the English yoke and establishing our independence," and "in the remaining eighteen the organization was advancing rapidly." It also called attention to the weakness of Ireland's military defenses, reporting that "the militia were about 20,000 men, 17,000 of whom might be relied on," in addition to "about 12,000 regular troops, wretched bad ones, who would soon be settled in case the business were attempted."[39]

Barthélemy's accompanying report said that the detailed information the two Irishmen had given him indicated "there has never been a more favorable moment for rendering Ireland its total independence and separating it completely from England, which would deal the latter a mortal blow. This truth is incontestable." But although a "very numerous and very powerful" part of the Irish population was prepared to rise in insurrection, it would be unable, without the aid and support of the French republic, to sever the connection with England. Such a severance, Barthélemy added, "would be very useful to us." The French ambassador felt that the full impact of O'Connor and Fitzgerald's facts and observations could not be adequately conveyed in writing. He therefore endorsed their request that they be allowed to present their case in person to the Directory.[40]

Barthélemy's reports to Paris on his dealings with O'Connor and Fitzgerald were entirely positive, and even enthusiastic. In later years when he wrote his memoirs, however, his outlook had so changed that he falsified his account of the encounter. The fact that he had transmitted their requests to the Directory was explained away by declaring, "It wasn't up to me to deter these revolutionaries." But personally, he claimed in retrospect, he felt "a vivid sense of horror for the schemes of these two young madmen."[41]

Meanwhile, as they awaited the Directory's answer, O'Connor and Lord Edward embarked upon a tour of the western part of Switzerland because, according to O'Connor, Swiss regulations prohibited foreigners from staying in Basel for more than three days at a time. For two weeks they were sightseers: from Basel they traveled to Bern, then to Fribourg and Lausanne, then on to Lake Geneva and back to Basel by way of the Lake of Neuchâtel.[42]

Shortly after their return to Basel at the beginning of July the reply from the Directory (transmitted by Delacroix) arrived. Barthélemy summoned O'Connor and Fitzgerald and read the letter to them several times.[43] It informed them, according to O'Connor's memoirs, that General Hoche had been designated to negotiate a treaty, but O'Connor's memory was faulty on that point; he did not learn of Hoche's role until several weeks later.[44] The Directory's letter stated that it was "convinced by the reports it had received that Ireland was ripe for a rebellion." But the message to be given to O'Connor and Fitzgerald was not what they had hoped for: only *after* an insurrection had broken out in Ireland—and not before—would the French support the rebels by sending 15,000 troops and "the arms and ammunition necessary for a vigorous attack." It was stipulated "that the Irish *first* expel the English from their own island; *then* the Directory will recognize and support the proclaimed independence with all its power."[45]

The Directory indicated a willingness to continue discussions with the Irish rebels, but Fitzgerald was refused permission to enter France, so O'Connor would have to negotiate alone. The reason for Lord Edward's exclusion, Barthélemy told O'Connor, was "a report which had been circulated in France that a member of the Directory [Barras] had been in treaty with the Duke of Orléans to be King of France."[46] Lord Edward's wife, Pamela, had long been rumored to be the illegitimate daughter of the Duke's father, Philippe-Egalité. Whether that rumor was true or false, the perceived ties to the house of Orléans were enough to prevent him from entering the country. Furthermore, Fitzgerald's connections to the émigré General Valence, husband of Pamela's half-sister, most likely added to the suspicions. When Valence introduced Lord Edward to Reinhard in 1792 the general was still in the service of the French Revolution, but in 1793 he defected and followed Dumouriez into exile.

Although doubts as to Fitzgerald's trustworthiness figures in Delacroix's correspondence,[47] it was not the reason explicitly stated by the Directory for barring him from France. At first the Directory told Barthélemy to discourage both O'Connor and Fitzgerald from traveling to Paris, on the grounds that the Irishmen had already successfully made their case in writing, and appearing in person would only serve to compromise the secrecy of their mission if they were to be recognized by Pitt's agents. O'Connor, however, continued to insist on face-to-face negotiations. For one thing, it was obvious that the Directory had not yet been convinced of the crucial need for French military support as a precondition of a successful insurrection. Barthélemy wrote again to the Directory, repeating O'Connor and Fitzgerald's argument that because the British government's brutal disarming of the Irish people had left them virtually defenseless, an insurrection without prior French aid would be suicidal. He also conveyed the two Irish negotiators' acknowledgement that

> their proceeding to Paris could create some inconvenience and danger for the glorious enterprise they are planning, due to the risk of their being recognized. But on the other hand, they consider it impossible to bring such a great and useful project into being without explaining it in person.[48]

As a compromise, Lord Edward "gave up, for the good of his country and for the cause, his intention of entering France. He will immediately return to Hamburg." O'Connor, however, "being completely unknown, believes that he could stay a short time without causing the least suspicion." He also volunteered to take rigorous measures to avoid detection while in France including, if necessary, remaining confined to his room during daylight hours.[49]

O'Connor and Fitzgerald wrote a report that had the character of an ultimatum and Barthélemy again transmitted it to the Directory. "We have definite instructions not to be departed from," they declared, and then stated two nonnegotiable demands. The first was that no partial agreement was acceptable; they would "undertake nothing without having made complete arrangements for the project." The second reiterated that the United Irishmen had no interest whatsoever in French military support that would arrive after the outbreak of an uprising: It was essential "that the arrival of French aid shall be the *signal* for the *breaking out* of the insurrection." If the Directory could not agree with these demands, they added, Irish revolutionaries would have no choice but to await some future time when changed conditions would allow the Irish people to arm themselves by some other means.[50]

This take-it-or-leave-it declaration apparently triggered a fundamental change in the French government's strategy toward Ireland. The Directory acquiesced and began making arrangements for O'Connor to proceed to France to meet with General Hoche.[51] Well before that meeting occurred, however, the French leaders sent Hoche new instructions on 19 and 20 July that represented a dramatic shift toward the kind of military support that the United Irishmen had been seeking all along.[52]

On 10 July, four days after the final encounter with Barthélemy, Lord Edward returned to Hamburg. In a letter to his mother, Fitzgerald utilized carefully coded language to report to her about the negotiations in Basel:

> *I left my friend O'Connor in Switzerland taking another tour. There never were two persons who more thoroughly admired Switzerland than we did; we say it with the true Rousseau enthusiasm. He is as fond of Rousseau as I am so you may conceive how we enjoyed our journey. He entered completely into my way of travelling, which was walking most of the way, getting into a boat when we could, taking our dinner in some pretty spot etc, swimming when we could. In fact we agreed in everything, and if it had not been time to come home I should have been very sorry to leave him.[53]*

Fitzgerald's biographer assures us that the Duchess of Leinster would have equated her son's references to Rousseau with republicanism and to walking with democratic activities, and would have understood "we agreed in everything" as signifying the success of the negotiations with the French government.[54]

On 22 July the Directory ordered that O'Connor was to be escorted by a General Crublier to Rennes, where he was to meet with General Hoche.[55] Elaborate precautions were taken to disguise the nature of his voyage and "avoid all the suspicions to which he could be exposed." O'Connor was to be given an American passport; he and Crublier would leave Basel at daybreak on 31 July from different gates and rendezvous later outside the city. "In this way," Barthélemy reported to the Directory, "Mr. O'Connor will enter France without being recognized." O'Connor was informed that he would not be told beforehand exactly where he was going or whom he would be meeting there, and he did not object. "These precautions," Barthélemy wrote, "seemed very wise to him; far from exhibiting any sort of unease or curiosity to General Crublier, he applauded them."[56]

With Lord Edward unable to participate, O'Connor had requested of Lazare Carnot, one of the Directors, that Wolfe Tone—"this distinguished hero, noble and highly talented man"—be sent to join the negotiations.[57] Tone had already been engaged in diplomacy with the Directory since February, but to little avail. Hoche knew Tone; in fact, he had made inquiries of Tone concerning O'Connor. Tone, in his memoirs, says Hoche "asked me, 'Did I know one Arthur O'Connor?' I replied, I did, and that I entertained the highest opinion of his talents, principles, and patriotism." Hoche commented favorably on O'Connor's "*explosion* in the Irish parliament," and Tone concluded that "O'Connor's speech is well known here."[58]

However, when O'Connor arrived at Hoche's headquarters at Rennes, he was "astonished and disappointed" to find that "instead of Tone they had sent a low-lifed presumptuous blowhard of the name of Duckett."[59] William Duckett was a dedicated Irish patriot and probably did not deserve the harsh evaluation that both O'Connor and Tone made of him, but he was certainly not the right man for the job of negotiating with Hoche.[60]

From O'Connor's point of view Duckett was too radical; he was still attached to the pre-Thermidor phase of the French Revolution. O'Connor tells of a conversation wherein Duckett boasted to General Hédouville, Hoche's chief of staff, "that at a dinner of patriots at Killarney they all got down on their knees to the memory of Robespierre, Couthon and St. Juste." O'Connor was horrified by this impolitic blunder. "I passed for an American," he says, "and observed that I had traveled through Ireland during two years, yet I never had met an Irishman who did not execrate these three men."[61] O'Connor vehemently complained to General Hédouville about "this wretch who had been substituted to Tone," and declared that "with such mistakes it was impossible the expedition could succeed." Hédouville "assured me I should never see this fellow more and that the mistake was inexplicable to him."[62]

MEETING GENERAL HOCHE

O'Connor waited for Hoche at Rennes for almost two weeks before receiving word, in the second week of August, that their meeting would instead be held at Angers, about sixty miles away. After a trip over bad roads O'Connor arrived after midnight and was introduced to Hoche. O'Connor, at thirty-three, was a young man, but France's leading general (he had "made a name for himself in the Republic when Bonaparte was still unknown"[63]) was even younger: Hoche was only twenty-eight years of age. "Our first interview," O'Connor says,

> *was the most cordial, and I believe never did two diplomats ever meet with more frankness or with a more firm inclination to act with the most sincere good faith. After some general desultory conversation it was agreed I should give Hoche a clear idea of the state of things of the country he was to succor.*[64]

Caveat lector: When reading the following narrative of the O'Connor–Hoche negotiations, keep in mind that it is entirely based upon O'Connor's memoirs and is for the most part uncorroborated by other sources. A critical analysis of its essential claims will follow below.

Their first meeting was brief, but O'Connor says he immediately realized that he would have to disabuse Hoche of the notion—held by so many French officials—"that Ireland was a second La Vendée" populated only by a backward, ignorant Catholic peasantry.[65] The significance of this misperception can hardly be overstated. It meant that the aim of French military strategy in Ireland was not to assist a progressive republican revolution, but to create a *chouannerie*—that is, to disrupt and paralyze Irish society by fomenting pillage, rape, arson, and generalized terror on a massive scale.[66] The invasion force that Hoche and the Directory originally had in mind was not to be made up of regular French soldiers inspired to help liberate an oppressed people, but of prisoners (including those condemned to death), deserters, and incorrigible troublemakers that the government wished to rid France of.

Another problem was that Hoche perceived the invasion of Ireland as merely a small, secondary adjunct to a larger invasion of England. Hoche let O'Connor know that

> *an invasion of England had been resolved on of 25,000 and that at the same time a smaller one of 5,000 might be sent to Ireland, where it was presumed very few troops would be left from the necessity of sending all against the invasion of England.*[67]

At that point O'Connor saw that he would have to convince Hoche of the futility of a direct assault on England and of the wisdom of concentrating French forces in Ireland instead. Ireland, he explained, was ripe for rebellion but England was not. England "was an independent nation proud of the immense domination she exercised over her extensive possessions all over the globe." If Hoche attempted to land in England he would find there was "not a man in all the country who would not risk his life and his last shilling to repel the invader."[68] Those Englishmen who were the most adamant opponents of Pitt's war against France—he named Fox, Sheridan, Grey and Whitbread—would be the staunchest defenders of their country against an invasion.

O'Connor continued his argument by analyzing the two parts of a successful invasion: the landing and the subsequent occupation of territory. He estimated the odds against a successful French landing on the coast of England at ten to one, "and it is fifty to one that before the whole can be debarked the English fleet do not arrive to attack it." O'Connor pointed on a map to Falmouth, Plymouth, Dartmouth, Weymouth and Portsmouth, and asked Hoche whether "from all these places enough of English ships should not come in time to attack the invading fleet before she could disembark her troops, her horses, artillery and ammunition?" And yet, he declared, "without all these the expedition must fail."[69]

However, what if by some miracle a successful landing were to be realized. What then? What could 25,000 French troops expect to accomplish in England? The closer to Lands End in Cornwall you disembark, he told Hoche,

> the less chance you run of being intercepted, but also the longer when landed must be your line of operation, supposing London your object. Look at the immense space you would have to traverse between the Lands End and London, and that in a country where every inch of ground would be contested with the most desperate valor, the roads broken up, the bridges destroyed and every possible embarrassment thrown in your way.[70]

In the unlikely event that the invading army should make its way to London, it would certainly have lost at least half of its numbers, "and what is 12,000 men to invest a capital of 1,200,000 souls with all Scotland and nine tenths of England to conquer?" To gamble "25,000 men and the last fleet of France" on such a venture, O'Connor concluded, would be "folly and even madness."[71]

Ireland, by contrast, presented nothing but advantages for a French invading army: "Here the strong west wind that wafts your fleet from the French coast by a parabolical course falls on the western coast of Ireland, while the same wind blocks up every English vessel in the channel." And once you land, he told Hoche, "what a difference between a nation where every man will die to oppose you and where every man will support you."[72] According to O'Connor's reconstruction of the negotiations, this discussion took an entire day, at the end of which Hoche conceded that "from the unanswerable reasons I had given he was perfectly satisfied that [a strike] against England presented too little chance of success to be hazarded."[73]

CATHOLICS AND PROTESTANTS

The following day, O'Connor says, he proceeded to educate Hoche about the state of Irish society: "I began by making him clearly understand that the men of Ireland on whom we could depend to join us were divided into two populations diametrically opposite in mental qualities; the one the Presbyterians of Ulster, the other the Catholics of Leinster, Munster and Connaught." The Presbyterians of the north were among "the best informed people in Europe and of the best public spirit and independence," while the Catholics of the rest of Ireland were "generally uneducated, without any manufacturing industry, and entirely restricted to seek their living in cultivating lands."[74]

Nonetheless, O'Connor contended, it would be a "gross error" to underestimate the Catholics of rural Ireland by equating them with the Catholic peasants of the Vendée. "When I tell you," he said to Hoche, "that even the Irish papists have a considerable advantage over the very best part of the French population in the article of fitness for liberal institutions you will be astonished, and yet nothing is more true."[75] Although denied the benefits of democracy, the Irish Catholics were keenly aware of their value and had long been engaged in struggle to attain them. In France before 1789, he declared,

> *the people had no experience in representative government, nor in civil liberty, nor in the principle of all classes contributing according to their fortunes to the support of government. Now in all these vital points even the Irish Catholics have had for centuries intimate knowledge of all those vital institutions.*[76]

Furthermore, despite the burden of legal discrimination, the Irish Catholics appreciated the importance of the rule of law. In Ireland there was "no *lettre de cachet*, no Bastille; every man in prison can by the law demand to be tried and if acquitted be set free."[77] As for the notion that the Irish Catholics, like the *chouans* of the Vendée, were completely dominated by a reactionary priesthood, O'Connor responded that in Ireland "the priests have not the twentieth part of the influence of those in La Vendée."[78] The purpose of this argument was to convince Hoche that a purely destructive *chouannerie* in Ireland would be counterproductive.

Perhaps O'Connor was more eloquent on behalf of the Catholics than he had intended, because when the discussion turned to the formation of a provisional government in a liberated Ireland, Hoche suggested that the Catholic Committee described to him by Tone might provide a good basis. O'Connor demurred. "With the Catholics," he said, "I found the as yet indelible mark of the long and cruel tyranny they had endured. This made them timorous, indecisive, underhanded, intriguing." The Catholic leaders, he predicted, "would seek domination and a monopoly to the exclusion of the Presbyterians and Protestants and seek support in working on the bigotry of the papist people." The only hopes for establishing liberty in Ireland, he maintained, "lie in the enlightened independent minds of the Presbyterians and Protestants . . . . I did not conceal from Hoche that if Ireland contained but the papist population I never would have attempted separation from England."[79]

The apparent contradiction in O'Connor's attitude toward the Catholics is explained by his distinguishing between those at the lower end of the social spectrum and those at the top: "I counted infinitely more on the zeal and courage of the lower papists than the higher." Although "the papist aristocracy" was "bigoted and timid," he declares, "I placed the greatest reliance on the bravery of the papist peasant in which there was the making of the best troops in Europe."[80] It is difficult to avoid the conclusion that O'Connor wanted the Catholic poor to do the fighting and then leave the governing to the Presbyterians.

At the end of this discussion, O'Connor says, Hoche "confessed to me he had the firm conviction he had attained as perfect knowledge of the land it was possible to give him." O'Connor was likewise impressed with Hoche's perspicacity: "I never conversed with any man who had a clearer comprehension or one that made more pertinent remarks."[81]

THE TERMS OF THE TREATY

The next day O'Connor and Hoche discussed the role France would play in an Ireland she had helped to liberate. Hoche began by saying he assumed that a grateful Ireland would grant France a monopoly of its commerce. Again O'Connor demurred:

> *I observed that would be usurping an immense power not a particle of which belonged to me; that the first thing to be done would be to*

elect the representative body that should make laws for Ireland, and an executive. These only could decide what laws were most advantageous for the country, those to regulate her commerce with the others.[82]

Hoche did not protest, but asked O'Connor for his own opinion of the matter. O'Connor replied that he was in favor of Ireland's commerce enjoying "the utmost freedom as in everything." Thinking that he detected "a shade of mistrust" in Hoche's face, O'Connor hastened to expand upon his answer. "I see your military occupation has prevented you from cultivating the economical science," he told the General.

What you demand is the greatest cause of Ireland seeking separation with England, for the monopoly she makes of all our commerce is the greatest cause of our misery, as will remain if we were to exchange an evil for as great a one. To free our industry from England to fall into the same dependence on France would be a silly object for which to make a revolution.[83]

O'Connor explained that the freer Ireland's ports, "the greater the number of foreign vessels which would frequent them." This would create great competition, "and consequently all foreign produce Ireland might want would be furnished at the lowest price." At the same time, "Ireland would sell the produce of her industry at the highest price of competition."[84] By O'Connor's account, his arguments were completely persuasive, because at the end of this exposition

Hoche embraced me and acknowledged that when I had refused to grant France the monopoly of Ireland's commerce . . . he had no idea of the economical science; that from what I had said he was convinced that if we were to sacrifice the benefit of free ports and free trade with all the world we should sacrifice the great advantages of separation and independence, adding that he hoped when we were in Ireland and had some leisure I would teach him this fine science, for never did I meet a man who had a greater thirst of knowledge than Hoche or a mind more worthy to receive it.[85]

With that business concluded the negotiators tackled the more immediate issues of where in Ireland the French troops should land, and the strategic operations that would follow. O'Connor proposed Galway Bay in the west as the targeted landing place "because it was most central, gave the shortest line of operation to Dublin," and was "in the midst of a well affected population. This met the entire approbation of Hoche."[86]

For his part, the French general promised to begin immediate preparations to send 15,000 men and 80,000 guns to Ireland. The surplus weaponry was to be distributed to the Irish insurgents who greeted them. Hoche told O'Connor to organize a United Irish corps in the vicinity of Galway Bay to reinforce the French troops, and another in the north. O'Connor—who would then himself bear the rank of general—was to make his headquarters at Belfast, "from whence at the head of thirty thousand old Volunteers, I was by a rapid march to move upon Dublin and from thence to the Shannon to put the enemy between Hoche and me."[87] It was expected that as soon as Hoche landed at Galway most of the British army would rush to the west, leaving Dublin virtually undefended. The plan called for General O'Connor to quickly capture the capital and then head west to attack the English forces from the rear.

O'Connor claims that the treaty he negotiated with the Directory explicitly stated that it was equivalent to the earlier pact between the French and the Americans, "where Hoche should stand in the place of Rochambeau and I in Washington's." He told Hoche, however, that in the interests of the success of the expedition, "I would most willingly yield him the command of the two armies and would think it a high honor to serve under him." But, O'Connor insisted, "I should exercise the chief command . . . in all that concerned the administration and civil government of Ireland, where I must be supposed to have more knowledge than him."[88] He was presumably alluding to his role in a provisional government that would supervise democratic elections for a more permanent regime.

At the end of their deliberations, Hoche promised O'Connor "he would accelerate the expedition by all the means in his power," and O'Connor promised "to lose no time in returning to Ireland and in putting it in the best state to receive him." O'Connor says that he and Hoche "parted with the most perfect mutual esteem."[89] Hoche's report to General Clarke on the meeting seems to confirm this estimation: "I was very happy with this person," he wrote. "He is talented, loyal, and truly patriotic. We agreed on all the facts. Ireland wants a revolution; the Defenders are well organized."[90]

One incident, however, led O'Connor to speculate that Pitt's efforts to exhaust France's finances were meeting with some success. Although the Directory had ordered that all of O'Connor's traveling expenses be paid, Hoche told O'Connor that he simply did not have the funds to do so and apologetically asked O'Connor not only to pay his own expenses, but those of Crublier as well![91]

EVALUATING O'CONNOR'S NARRATIVE

Although O'Connor's account of his discussions with Hoche may accurately reflect the way he remembered them, certain of its main elements are seriously misleading. Hoche perhaps played the standard diplomatic game of allowing O'Connor to believe that the proposals they agreed to had been initiated by the Irishman himself, but that certainly was not the case.

First of all, it is not true that O'Connor had to convince Hoche to change the focus of French invasion plans from England to Ireland. On 19 June, some two months before O'Connor and Hoche met, the Directory had issued a lengthy directive to Hoche instructing him to concentrate on preparing to invade *Ireland.* Consideration of simultaneously sending a small force to England "as a useful diversion" was relegated to a postscript appended to the orders, an apparent afterthought.[92]

Secondly, if O'Connor played a role in persuading Hoche to abandon the strategy of mass terror in favor of promoting a revolutionary republican uprising, it did not occur during their rendezvous at Angers in August. The Directory's instructions to Hoche on 19 and 20 July already clearly reflected that important change in policy, as will be demonstrated below.

O'Connor's claim that he and Hoche negotiated a secret treaty cannot be confirmed; no such document has been found in the French archives or among his personal papers. The idea that Hoche would enter into the kind of detailed discussions of specific military plans that O'Connor reports is extremely unlikely, given the high degree of secrecy that characterized French military operations in general and this one in particular. The fact that Hoche knew O'Connor was planning to return to Ireland makes it all the more improbable that he would have shared sensitive military information with him. On the other hand, Hoche's 29 August report to General Clarke suggests that the discussions were substantial enough to satisfy O'Connor's prior insistence that nothing short of "complete arrangements for the project" would be acceptable as a basis of agreement.[93]

THE SIGNIFICANCE OF THE MEETING WITH HOCHE

Recognizing the limitations of O'Connor's account of the negotiations should not be taken to mean that his personal impact on the course of French policy toward Ireland was unimportant; to the contrary, it was crucial. A close examination of the chronology of the diplomacy bears that out. The Directory's decision to change the invasion target from England to Ireland was first made known in its 19 June directive to Hoche. O'Connor's August meeting with Hoche obviously could not have influenced that decision, but the representations he and Lord Edward made to Reinhard in May and early June almost certainly did.

That the Directory's receptiveness toward proposals to invade Ireland increased dramatically and suddenly at that time is clearly demonstrated by Wolfe Tone's journal. In mid-April, after two and a half months of his own diplomatic mission in France, Tone recorded the observation that "Altogether things cannot look worse."[94] Two weeks later he had an audience with one of the Directors, Lazare Carnot, who was anything but encouraging, leading him to lament:

> This was a staggering blow to me, to find myself no farther advanced at the end of three months, than I was at my first audience. . . . *I am utterly ignorant whether there is any design to attempt the expedition or not; I put it twice to Carnot, and could extract no answer. My belief is that as yet there is no one step taken in the business, and that, in fact,* the expedition will not be undertaken.[95]

Three weeks later his pessimism continued unabated: "I am almost worn out of hope; I act now without expectation."[96] But after O'Connor and Fitzgerald made contact with the Directory, Tone found that suddenly, for reasons unknown to him, he was at last getting a positive hearing. On 23 June he wrote:

> *Called on Clarke in the morning, and found him in high good humour. He tells me he has mentioned my business to Carnot, and that within a month I may expect an appointment in the French army. This is glorious! . . . the business, and even the time, were determined on by the Directory.*[97]

O'Connor and Fitzgerald's initial representations did not, however, convince the French officials to change the *character* of the invasion. As late as 9 June Hoche continued to plan a *chouannerie* and was still proposing to inflict this "terrible kind of war on our enemies."[98] The Directory's 19 June directive was somewhat ambiguous on this score; it proposed assisting "a revolution for independence and freedom" in Ireland, but in reality did not abandon the *chouannerie* perspective. The composition of the forces it planned to send "will be such that it can purge France of many dangerous individuals," including "foreign deserters" and "former *chouans*."[99]

The French government's decision to organize the supportive invasion requested by the United Irishmen was first evidenced in its revised instructions to Hoche of 19 and 20 July. Although that, too, was before O'Connor met Hoche at Angers, it came directly after his correspondence with the Directory through Barthélemy and Delacroix. Although O'Connor and Fitzgerald were not mentioned by name, their influence was alluded to in the directives of 19–20 July: "According to reports that the Directory has received, the inhabitants of Ireland seem to strongly desire to live from now on under a republican form of government."[100] The strategy was transformed accordingly: Rather than unloading the dregs of French society onto Irish shores to wreak havoc, an invasion force of fifteen thousand well-disciplined regular troops under seasoned commanders was to be sent to Ireland.[101] Care would be taken not to alienate the Irish population, but rather to help it in its quest for liberation. The diligent lobbying efforts of Tone and Duckett over the previous several months had prepared the ground for this policy change, but it was O'Connor and Fitzgerald's intervention that apparently proved decisive in convincing the French officials of Ireland's genuine revolutionary potential.

The directives of 19–20 July also reflected another highly significant reversal of policy: the Directory's agreement to send troops and arms before rather than after an insurrection had broken out in Ireland. That change occurred immediately after it received O'Connor's 6 July letter firmly rejecting its offer of a French intervention following an uprising. The chronological table on the next page outlines the evolution of the French decision to aid Ireland.

The centrality of O'Connor and Fitzgerald's diplomatic efforts in bringing about and shaping Hoche's expedition to Ireland has not generally been credited by historians. Wolfe Tone's role has tended to dominate the historiography. In 1888 Edouard Guillon established the pattern for later scholars by concluding that Tone's "personal initiative had more of an effect than Fitzgerald and O'Connor's official mission."[102] A rare dissenting opinion was registered in 1966 by William B. Kennedy who, after a thorough analysis of the material in the French archives, concluded that "insofar as any Irish emissaries influenced the French decision, O'Connor and Fitzgerald did."[103] Kennedy's study has been acknowledged in the bibliographies of subsequent researchers but unfortunately his cogent argument and conclusions have for the most part been ignored.

Chronology of
French–United Irish negotiations,
1796

Wolfe Tone's diplomatic
mission in Paris begins. . . . . February

April 18 . . . . The Directory proposes to
Hoche that he create a
chouannerie in England.

Fitzgerald meets with Reinhard
in Hamburg. . . . . May 18
O'Connor and Fitzgerald
meet together with Reinhard. . . . June 6
O'Connor and Fitzgerald
meet Barthélemy and give
him a letter for the Directory. . . . June 19

June 19 . . . . The Directory changes the
primary target of the *chouannerie*
from England to Ireland.

June 22 . . . . . The Directory says it will only
send aid to Ireland after an
uprising has occurred.

June 23 . . . . Tone's journal indicates a
sudden change for the better in the
Directory's receptiveness toward
his proposals to invade Ireland.

O'Connor and Fitzgerald meet
again with Barthélemy; they send
an ultimatum to the Directory
demanding aid prior to
an uprising. . . . . July 6

July 19 . . . . The Directory drops the
chouannerie strategy in favor of
aiding a democratic revolution,
and agrees to send aid prior
to an uprising.

O'Connor and Hoche meet
at Angers. . . . . mid-August

Guillon and those who followed his lead noted that the French government eventually followed the course of action urged by Tone and therefore assumed that a cause-and-effect relationship connected Tone's words and the Directory's deeds. Kennedy demonstrated, however, that the Directory was in fact very wary—even distrustful—of Tone's representations and demanded further corroboration before making a commitment to invade Ireland. On 27 May it ordered the gathering of "intelligence entirely different from that communicated by citizen Wolfe Tone, all of which can be culled from the English gazettes." General Clarke was instructed to send an agent, Richard O'Shee, to Ireland, insisting that he should "be in every way on guard against the reports of citizen Wolfe Tone, in order to better verify the truth."[104] O'Shee did not return before October, however, so the Directory's strategic *volte-face* of 19–20 July must have been based on information from another source that it considered trustworthy. That source could only have been O'Connor and Fitzgerald. Their written communications in June and July, it seems, were of much greater consequence than O'Connor's personal negotiations with Hoche in August. The August meeting served mainly to ratify decisions that had been made earlier; it may have been organized by the Directory to reassure O'Connor that his demand for "complete arrangements" was being taken seriously.

RETURNING TO ENGLAND AND IRELAND

After concluding his negotiations with Hoche at Angers, O'Connor left France. "Night and day, without stopping, I went, passing by Pays Bas, Holland, Westphaly, Luxembourg, to Hamburg, where I met my beloved Edward, who was overjoyed at my complete success. We lost not an instant in going to England."[105] It was toward the end of September that O'Connor and Fitzgerald left Hamburg. In London O'Connor paid brief visits to his "beloved friends," including the Duchess of Devonshire, to whom he gave a box of minerals he had gotten from a professor at Lausanne he had called upon at her request, "and some beautiful landscapes of Switzerland."[106]

Some of O'Connor's politically prominent friends—especially Fox— would later be accused of having known about O'Connor's negotiations with France, and therefore of sharing the guilt of his treasonous actions. O'Connor declares that "the truth and the whole truth" is that "I never told Fox I had made a treaty with France." He did, however, tell Fox he "had had an occasion to dissuade the French government from attempting to invade England with an army of 25,000 men." In response to the latter revelation, Fox agreed that French troops were unlikely to succeed in reaching London, but if they did, "the evil they might do to England was incalculable." What O'Connor had not told Hoche was that "there were 200,000 men in London so wretched that in rising in the morning they were not sure to find a dinner in the day." If an invading French force had encouraged the London poor to riot, "there can be no doubt the horrors these men would commit would bring England to her ruin." O'Connor says that Fox told him "I had rendered him and his country the greatest possible service."[107]

O'Connor's accounts of his conversations with Hoche and Fox may not have been deliberately falsified, but they surely do not represent the whole truth about the United Irish plans with regard to England. The United Irish strategy depended on a threefold simultaneity; in addition to the French invasion and the insurrection in Ireland, it also called for diversionary uprisings in England. The purpose of the latter was to tie up British troops at home to prevent them from being sent to Ireland to repress the rebellion there. Whether or not O'Connor himself was directly involved in encouraging sedition among the London poor (and there is some ambiguous evidence suggesting he may have been[108]), he was certainly aware that such activity was being carried out by United Irish agents in London.

It was not "want of confidence" in Fox that prevented O'Connor from telling him of the arrangements for a French invasion of Ireland: "Oh, no—I knew his noble, generous soul too well to hesitate." He kept it from him because telling him "would place Fox in a disagreeable situation as the leader of opposition or if he should become Prime Minister of England and Ireland." He had no doubt, however, that if he had disclosed the invasion plans, Fox would certainly have approved:

> I have the firm conviction that not only Fox but men a thousand times less generous and liberal than him would admit that if it was the degree of oppression and misery that could give a nation the right of resistance, there never was a people in the world whose oppression and misery had arrived at a higher degree to warrant it.[109]

There was, O'Connor says, only one Englishman to whom he told the whole story, and that was Sir Francis Burdett. After the short stopover in London O'Connor and Burdett set out for Belfast in early October. "I had an immediate meeting with the Northern Executive," he says, the purpose of which was to make "every arrangement for all that would be necessary to meet the arrival of the French." As part of the preparations, O'Connor publicly proclaimed himself a candidate to represent the county of Antrim in parliament—a rather peculiar announcement because the next elections were ten months away. Then he left for Dublin, "where I had all to organize for hitherto all was done by Edward and me."[110]

In Dublin, the first person he told of the invasion plans was Henry Jackson, "one of the frankest and bravest men I ever knew."[111] Then he spoke with Thomas Addis Emmet, "but from knowing the extreme timidity of his character I addressed him with reserve."[112] When reading what O'Connor says in his memoirs about Emmet it is necessary to bear in mind that the two became bitter, lifelong enemies after 1798. O'Connor claims that when he told Emmet the situation was so far advanced that a rising was inevitable, Emmet responded that "neither his disposition nor his habits led him to think he would have the firmness to engage in a revolution; that he imagined he could speak his opinions at a public assembly but that he was not a man of action." (This assessment is corroborated by William Drennan, a close friend of Emmet's, who described him as having "more eloquence than energy, more counsel than action."[113]) O'Connor adds that he applauded Emmet's frankness and "told him we should make use of his talents later."[114]

The United Irish Society was put on a military footing and its leadership was reorganized. A national executive committee was established that consisted, at first, of O'Connor and Fitzgerald plus McCormick and Robert Simms; it was later expanded to nine members.[115] O'Connor then set off on an organizational tour. First he and Burdett traveled to Cork, where O'Connor told a gathering of United Irishmen organized by his brother Roger to put themselves in a state of military preparedness because the French would be coming soon. Timothy Conway, a leading local member who later turned government informer, provided a detailed account of what transpired. From small beginnings in Cork in the summer of 1793 the United Irish Society had increased rapidly in numbers and influence. In late November 1796 Roger O'Connor, in spite of having been arrested, got word to another local leader, Edmund Finn, "that his brother Arthur was to be in Cork upon business of *importance* and that it would be necessary to speak to a few men who may be confided in . . . . Accordingly a select few were summoned of the members."[116]

The meeting that O'Connor addressed consisted of seven or eight people. Conway was unable to attend, but as soon as it was over he was immediately "informed of its purport." O'Connor had reported "that he was just returned from the Continent" and declared

> that there was not a moment to be lost in opening a communication with the Executive Directories of Dublin and Belfast as an invasion of this country would to a certainty be attempted, and that it ought to be a primary object to have the whole country in a state of the most perfect organization.[117]

O'Connor "recommended the forming of an Executive Directory in Cork." There was no time to hold elections—"the urgency of the moment" made it necessary to create a self-appointed leadership body. A five-man committee was thus established, and according to Conway, who was one of the five, "From this period a regular correspondence was kept up through the medium of Oliver Bond." Whenever the national leaders in Dublin had something important to communicate to the Cork executive committee, Bond would write a business letter to one of its members, John Swiney, telling him "he had just received a large assortment of goods" and urging him to come to Dublin to choose the articles he wanted. "This business being accomplished," Conway concluded, "A. O'Connor immediately set off for Dublin and informed the Executive there how far he had succeeded."[118] O'Connor's later contention that he had personally participated in organizing the people of the countryside adjacent to Bantry Bay was not an empty boast.[119]

O'CONNOR AND THE LADIES

It was toward the end of November when O'Connor returned to the capital to confer with Lord Edward. They stayed in a small lodge rented by Fitzgerald on the edge of the Curragh of Kildare. On 27 November Edward's wife, Pamela, and his sister Lucy joined them. According to the Duchess of Leinster's biographer:

> Because Arthur O'Connor was Edward's great friend, with a soul "twin to his own", and a great democrat, the excitable Lucy had immediately proceeded to fall in love with the wild young Irishman. . . . all her thoughts were with Edward and Arthur O'Connor, and with the cause of Ireland, of Democracy.[120]

The four of them—Edward, Pamela, Arthur, and Lucy—formed, in Pamela's words, "our beloved Quoituor."[121]

> They went for ten-mile walks on the Curragh. They rode; Edward and Lucy keeping together, Pamela and O'Connor talking to each other for hours about French friends they had in common. Arthur O'Connor read aloud to them Julius Caesar. (Edward loved Shakespeare.) In the evening a piper came and they danced jigs.[122]

The entry in Lady Lucy's diary for 3 December 1796 reveals her amazement and fascination with O'Connor's deistic religious views, which denied immortality of the soul. After Edward had gone to bed early, she reports,

> *Arthur, Pamela, and I had a conversation I never shall forget. I never heard anything of the kind before. I was very much amused and interested, lost in admiration of such superior talents, but not convinced, and grieved to Tears at such a mind supposing itself perishable.*

He apparently took pleasure in startling her with his radical opinions; on 14 December she wrote, "Arthur shock'd me by a thing he said; he is so odd one must not judge him by other people."[123]

The precise nature of O'Connor's relationship with Lady Lucy, who was then twenty-five years old, is unclear, but there is evidence that her friends and relatives did indeed believe that she was in love with him. She undoubtedly encouraged that perception—up to a point. In 1798 when O'Connor was on trial at Maidstone, her uncle, the Duke of Richmond, "went to her in the most affectionate manner, and proposed, if she would confide in him, to obtain O'Connor's release, and assist their marriage."[124] She assured her uncle, however, that her feelings toward O'Connor went no farther than friendship. The letters they exchanged during his later imprisonment at Fort George indicates that theirs was a warm but platonic relationship.[125]

O'Connor greatly enjoyed the rituals of courting aristocratic women, but not all of the social butterflies of the Devonshire House set were vulnerable to his charms. One of the most prominent of them, Lady Elizabeth Foster (who for more than twenty years lived with the Duke and Duchess "in a jealous and uneasy ménage à trois, during which both women bore the Duke's children—as well as those of other men"[126]) recounted her impressions of O'Connor in unflattering terms:

> *His countenance, when I first saw him in 1794, appeared to me gloomy and designing. He supped at D[evonshire] House and I have seen him in our box at the Opera—but I dislike a vulgar familiarity in his manner and a want of openness in his countenance, and I begged of my dear G[eorgiana, Duchess of Devonshire] not to see him often.*[127]

William Drennan thought the casual way O'Connor spoke about the women he courted "showed somewhat of the character of Don Mathias in *Gil Blas*."[128] O'Connor's pledge to himself to remain unmarried was certainly not a vow of celibacy; a passage in Lady Lucy's diary refers to an illegitimate child he fathered.[129] According to this account, O'Connor did not try to hide the fact; Lucy says the four-year-old boy was at Lord Edward's house in March 1797.[130] Perhaps that is one reason why Lucy, though infatuated with O'Connor, had no intention of marrying him.

In his memoirs O'Connor neglects to mention the "natural son" or any romantic feelings he may have had for Lady Lucy Fitzgerald or any other woman. Either there had been very little emotional attachment on his part, or he felt it would be improper to reveal such sentiments to his wife and children.

LORD EDWARD'S GREEN CRAVAT

One day during their stay at the lodge on the Curragh, O'Connor and Lord Edward attended the races at the famous racetrack nearby and afterwards, galloping home, they were accosted by about twenty cavalry officers. The officers blocked their way and demanded that Lord Edward remove the green cravat he wore as a symbol of his republican sympathies. Fitzgerald's biographers say that he angrily refused, declaring, "Here I stand. Let any man among you, who dares, come forward and take it off," and O'Connor backed him up.[131] "I told them their conduct was neither that of soldiers or gentleman," O'Connor says, and "if they would select two from their number we would speak to them." This challenge, however, went unanswered. "Whether from shame or a sense of the gross impropriety of their conduct, they left us free to continue our road."[132] O'Connor says that even his brother William, who commanded a regiment in the same camp, stood up for him on this occasion in spite of their opposing political views.

This story of how the two United Irish leaders faced down twenty officers has a mythological quality. Regardless of its historical accuracy, however, the heroic tale of the green cravat was historically significant because it became known throughout the country and contributed to the romantic legend of Lord Edward Fitzgerald.

GETTING BACK TO BUSINESS

On 4 December it was time for O'Connor and Lord Edward to return to the business of preparing for the French invasion. Lady Lucy's diary reports that Edward was "very angry with us for sitting up" in conversation until all hours of the night; "he and Mr. O'Connor set off on a tour" to Galway.[133] O'Connor describes their mission:

To leave nothing undone that could prepare support for the arrival of our allies, we went to Connaught to examine the line of operation from Galway Bay, and see ourselves the state of the people's minds. We went on horseback to be better enabled to examine the country, first to Athlone, then to Banaker [Banagher], which has two bridges over the Shannon.

They spent some time examining ways to get an army across "this fine river."[134]

In passing through Roscommon he and Edward, in their desire to sound out "the people's minds," struck up a conversation with six peasants. "Have you not heard within this year there was something doing for Ireland?" they asked the men. One of them allegedly replied:

Oh, yes, we have heard of it. It goes that we are all to be one, Protestant and papist, and join against the Saxons. The story is rife that the old chiefs are stirring, and who are they? Why, they talk of an O'Connor and a Fitzgerald, and that the French will be with Ireland. For see you, we have an old prophecy that as Ireland was lost under an O'Connor, it can never be gained but by the same. This is all the talk in Connaught these months past.[135]

Although O'Connor would generally look upon talk of prophecy as worthless superstition, he surely must have been gratified by this particular forecast. The "peasant," in passing, quoted a Latin proverb. "I see you are a scholar," O'Connor remarked. "I was the master of scholars," the man responded, "but the people are too poor to pay for the education of their children and I was forced to abandon my school."[136] On parting, O'Connor and Fitzgerald gave the men some money to drink to the freedom of Ireland.

They then made a visit that apparently possessed a great deal of symbolic significance for them. Lucy wrote in her diary that they later gave her an account "of their reception at the King of Connaught's. His name is O'Connor also, so he address'd them: 'Arthur O'Connor, you are welcome. House of Leinster, I am proud to see you within my doors.' "[137] In his description of the encounter in his memoirs, Arthur mentioned having been there previously, as an infant:

We went to O'Connor of Belanagare where I was received as a child of the family. Nothing could be more affectionate or more hospitable when I recounted to them the meeting between my father and theirs and his taking me at his arms, blessing me—prophesying I would be the friend of my country. They were deeply affected. The most active of this estimable family was Charles who has written the memoirs of his family.[138]

One family member—"a son-in-law, a Dr. McDermott, a clever and truly patriotic man"—was especially happy to see them. They told McDermott, a United Irishman, about the imminent arrival of the French expedition and sent him on a mission to "sound the best men of his acquaintance and know if we could rely on their joining"; that is, to determine how far the Catholic gentry could be depended upon in a revolutionary situation. Alas, McDermott returned after a few days to report that he had met with no success at all. O'Connor's assessment of the "papist gentry" is rather bitter:

The debasement into which oppression had sunk that class of men, [and] the dread of the people on whose mercy they fattened and the profit they made of it, made them such heartless, selfish, timid beings that nothing could be expected from them, even for their own liberty.[139]

O'Connor claims that Lord Edward shared his disgust, and quotes him as exclaiming, "What a vile set these men must be not to have the courage to join us in fighting for their liberties."[140] In any instance, however, where O'Connor attributes anticatholic sentiments to Fitzgerald, his assertions should not be accepted without corroboration.

Meanwhile, during their wait for Dr. McDermott to return they had embarked on a mission of their own to canvass the Protestant gentry of the area. O'Connor reports that they were received with warm hospitality. More significantly, however,

in all these visits we could easily perceive by the looks and the officious attention of the servants, who were for the most part papists, that we were more in their thoughts than their masters', and as these had all been in Dublin, knew what was passing and were United Irishmen.

These servants spread the news of their presence throughout the countryside and before long, O'Connor says, there was a sort of competition among them as to "who should show us the greatest marks of their affection."[141]

On 11 December Arthur and Edward returned to Pamela and Lady Lucy at the lodge in Kildare, but their stay was very brief. On the 15th they were off again for more meetings in Dublin.[142]

CAMPAIGNING IN THE NORTH

At the end of November, O'Connor's memoirs tell us, "a messenger arrived from Hoche to me saying that all would be ready to put to sea in six weeks or two months."[143] His account of this incident reflects the deep mistrust he felt toward the Catholics among the leaders of the United Irishmen. O'Connor alleges that Hoche's emissary, Captain Bernard MacSheehy, "fell in the hands of McNeven and two other Catholics," who for factional reasons tried to block MacSheehy from seeing Fitzgerald and himself. "Already those Catholics we had initiated," O'Connor charges, "began to intrigue and to form a Popish party against Edward and me, but infinitely more against me."[144]

O'Connor, however, was seriously mistaken as to the nature of MacSheehy's mission—especially in the belief that Hoche's agent had come to inform him of the time and place of the landing. MacSheehy was not entrusted with that top-secret information. His voyage to Ireland was primarily to gather up-to-date information for Hoche about the state of the rebel forces. The "message" he was carrying was nothing more than vague assurances of continuing French support. Furthermore, O'Connor was not deliberately shunned, but simply overlooked. Tone, at Hoche's request, provided MacSheehy with names of people to contact for information and Tone directed him to see Oliver Bond and Richard McCormick, which he did.[145] O'Connor was not named because Tone did not know him personally.[146]

Nonetheless, the news of MacSheehy's visit eventually reached O'Connor—probably by way of Bond—and prompted him to go north to begin making the final preparations for Hoche's arrival. He left Fitzgerald in Leinster and moved into a country house about a half mile from Belfast; the house was lent to him by John Magee, editor-publisher of the *Dublin Evening Post*. Upon his arrival in the north, O'Connor began to actively carry out the election campaign that he had launched in October. Martha McTier opined that "the election apathy" might well "be blown up by such a spark as this."[147]

Although ostensibly seeking to represent County Antrim in parliament, O'Connor's intention was not to win votes but to use the forum provided by the electoral process as a legal and efficient means of spreading the United Irishmen's message, and as an organizing tool to rally their forces. Being a candidate gave him a legitimate reason to address large public rallies, to organize groups of supporters, to publish and distribute "campaign literature," to give interviews to newspapers, and to raise funds. It was a brilliant tactic, and in retrospect he judged it successful: "Never was time better employed in preparing the minds of the people for the arrival of our allies." In less than two months, O'Connor claims, "everything was arranged for all the old Volunteers marching on Dublin."[148]

The first of O'Connor's two major addresses to his Antrim constituents had been published earlier, on 22 October. Its verbal assault against the established authority was so passionate that Lady Lucy commented, "it is glorious, but I think Government won't let it pass."[149] O'Connor's old friend John Knox feared for his safety: "In the name of God, what put it into your head to propose yourself a candidate for Antrim—& with that mad address. Take my advice—postpone politics till the sober time of peace. The present times are dangerous."[150]

On 24 December O'Connor wrote a letter to Fox that revealed no hint of knowledge that the invasion had actually begun; the United Irishmen, he said, "are waiting patiently" until some time in the obscure future when they "have a decided majority of the Nation with them."[151] This was not entirely a feint; O'Connor was genuinely unaware that the French were already on the sea. In fact, the operation had commenced eight days earlier and some of the French ships were at that moment already in Bantry Bay attempting to land. Not until he received a letter dated 27 December did O'Connor learn that the expedition had reached the southern coast of Ireland.[152]

When that news became known at Belfast the high sheriff called a mass meeting of all the inhabitants with the purpose of having them take an oath to fight against the French. The Northern executive committee assigned O'Connor to go to the meeting to counter that proposal. It took place "in a vast room and densely crammed." After the sheriff had spoken, O'Connor rose to reply, but the sheriff stopped him, saying that as a stranger O'Connor had no right to address the assembly. O'Connor responded by reading the sheriff's own printed notice of the meeting, which invited "all the inhabitants in and about Belfast." Being an inhabitant, O'Connor declared, he was at the meeting by the sheriff's "own express invitation." He then called on the assembly to decide whether he should be allowed to speak or not, and was given the floor by acclamation.[153]

O'Connor demanded to know what law gave the sheriff the right to swear the citizens of Belfast into an army to fight a foreign enemy. Was he not aware that there had previously been such a citizens' army a hundred thousand strong—the Volunteers—which had defended Ireland "from within and without"? Was he not aware that the legislature of Ireland had disarmed and outlawed the Volunteers, and prohibited all such self-defense corps? Was he not aware that in place of the Volunteers had come "20,000

English mercenary soldiers" who "forced upon us those laws that disarmed us like slaves"? Why would he think that "the slaves of English and Irish government oppression" would have any interest in fighting to maintain that oppression?[154]

After an hour of O'Connor's spellbinding oratory the crowd had been whipped into a frenzy against the sheriff.

> *The agitation was so violent that the High Sheriff was visibly alarmed for his personal safety. I saw I had completely defeated the attempt of this magistrate, and fearing the indignation of the people might lead to some unhappy violence, I changed my tone and appealed to the good sense and love of order of the people, that the Sheriff had seen his mistake and that this magistrate invested with the highest power should be treated with respect and reverence even in his errors. . . .*
> *The Sheriff, in a short speech, thanked me for my love of order and the support I had given to his authority, and dissolved a meeting he well wished he had never assembled.*[155]

After the meeting the crowd gathered around O'Connor to applaud him, but he left as quickly as he could to rejoin the executive committee, which was deliberating "on what measures the crisis demanded." When the news arrived that the French fleet had been unable to land and had left Bantry Bay, O'Connor says, "this made great circumspection a rule for us."[156]

THE ATTEMPT AT BANTRY BAY

At Angers in late August General Hoche had promised O'Connor that approximately 15,000 French troops and 80,000 weapons would soon be on their way to Ireland, and he kept his word. On 16 December 1796—less than four months after their deliberations—a fleet of forty-eight ships carrying 14,450 men and more than 40,000 weapons departed from Brest. The rest of the promised armaments had been shipped separately, prior to the expedition.[157] It was evident that a major invasion effort with a reasonable expectation of success was under way. Instead of Galway Bay in the west, however, the expedition entered Bantry Bay in the south and endeavored to land there. With O'Connor awaiting Hoche in Belfast as instructed, it was ironic that the French forces arrived at a place very close to his home in County Cork.

O'Connor thought that the attempt to land at Bantry Bay was a spur-of-the-moment expedient prompted by bad weather conditions. What he did not know, however, was that Hoche—believing that British spies had learned of the Galway Bay destination[158]—had changed his mind and before leaving Brest had issued orders to land at Bantry Bay instead.

The operation was irreparably weakened when on the first day at sea Hoche's frigate, the *Fraternité*, became separated from the main body of the fleet and remained out of contact for the duration of the expedition. The primary leadership role then of necessity fell to Hoche's second-in-command, Emmanuel de Grouchy. Only thirty-five of the vessels of the original fleet reached the mouth of Bantry Bay, and only fifteen, carrying 6,400 troops, succeeded in entering the bay. One of them, however—the *Immortalité*—carried the acting commander, General Grouchy. On the day before Christmas 1796 Grouchy ordered the invasion to proceed and began preparing for an immediate landing. As they tried to reach shore, however, the winds built up against them and kept them at sea.

The weather worsened into a major storm that thoroughly disrupted the operation. On the day after Christmas Grouchy abandoned the invasion plans and the *Immortalité* left Bantry Bay. The retreat was extremely disorganized— some of the ships lingered in the area as late as 6 January—but by 13 January the thirty-five remaining vessels, many badly damaged, had returned to France. The episode, which had cost the lives of more than 1,500 French soldiers and sailors, had come to a definitive end. The first attempt to liberate Ireland had ended in failure.

O'Connor—together with Tone and many other commentators since— attributed that failure to the bad luck of hostile weather conditions. It was, he opined, "the winds which dispersed the French fleet and that separated its general from his army," and "the terrible storm of Christmas 1796" that were "the natural cause of Ireland's adverse fortune."[159] Poor seamanship, however, is a more likely explanation than bad weather for the early separation of Hoche's frigate from the expedition. Furthermore, Thomas Bartlett has argued persuasively that "the poor weather conditions were an asset not a hindrance to the French," because better weather would have allowed the far superior British navy to quash the attempt long before it reached Bantry Bay.[160] A careful analysis of the weather encountered by the expedition indicates that there were several "moments of opportunity" for a landing in Bantry Bay of which the French commanders did not take advantage.[161]

Some contemporaries and subsequent commentators blamed the failure on Grouchy's indecisiveness,[162] an evaluation that, if justified, would be somewhat ironic in light of O'Connor's future relationship with Grouchy. Later, in France, they were to become good friends and Grouchy's niece would become O'Connor's wife and the love of his life. However, the negative assessment is probably unfair. Grouchy did make a difficult decision to proceed with the invasion, and called it off only under pressure from Admiral Bouvet, the naval commander upon whose cooperation he depended. Although Hoche would have had a better chance of prevailing against Bouvet, the difference was not a matter of decisiveness but of "clout"; the celebrated General Hoche possessed a degree of personal authority that Grouchy did not.

Even Hoche, however, was severely frustrated by what he called "the navy's scandalous struggle against the government," which had earlier almost led him to abandon the invasion plans altogether.[163] As late as 8 December he had written in anger to the Minister of War: "I find myself obliged to renounce this enterprise. Our detestable navy cannot and will not do anything."[164] Although he changed his mind and proceeded with the expedition, the internal political obstacles that hampered it are evident.[165] The blame for its failure certainly cannot be attributed to Grouchy.

What would have happened if the French forces—even the smaller number that were able to enter Bantry Bay—had been able to successfully go ashore? The answer depends, of course, on how they would have been received. Would the Irish people have greeted them as liberators and risen to join them, or would they have remained loyal to the local government and military officials?

Some contemporary observers noted that the inhabitants of the area around Bantry Bay were quiescent while the French warships were offshore and made a great display of their loyalty after the ships had gone—an indication, it was said, that the people would have resisted rather than joined the French invaders. To O'Connor, however, this assertion was but an example of "how easily men believe what they wish," and he claimed firsthand knowledge to the contrary. "When I went to the south with Burdett," he says, "I took particular care that all the people of this coast should be well organized." The great zeal with which the local inhabitants professed their loyalty after the French departure "was but a veil to cover themselves from suspicion." Nowhere in Ireland, he declares, "were the people more resolute to second the expedition than those at Bantry and all along the coast."[166]

O'Connor was hardly a disinterested observer, but his assertions on this score have been corroborated by others. Many contemporary defenders of the status quo feared that "Ireland could not have been saved if the French had landed."[167] Most modern students of the period, moreover, would agree with the historian Lecky that the French would have had little difficulty in gaining control of Cork had they been able to land, "and a nation-wide rebellion might well have ensued."[168]

But the French did not land and the people did not rise. The attempted invasion had powerful effects nonetheless, both in England and in Ireland. The English policymakers were shocked and dismayed by the demonstration of how thoroughly the French fleet had breached their reputedly "impregnable" naval defenses. And in Ireland the rebellious population, far from being discouraged by the French failure to land, was invigorated by the expectation that its powerful military ally would surely return soon for another try. But as the spirit of revolution rose among the people, so did the determination of the authorities to crush that spirit with all the repressive means at their disposal. The appearance of the French at Bantry Bay served to sharpen social tensions and bring them to the point of crisis throughout Ireland—especially in Ulster, where martial law was soon to be proclaimed and the population systematically terrorized in an effort to disarm the United Irish army.

5

Seventeen Ninety-Seven

O'CONNOR UTILIZED HIS ELECTION campaign to send a message to the United Irish ranks and to their French allies. On 20 January 1797 he published a second campaign statement, entitled *To the Free Electors of the County of Antrim*, which he describes in his memoirs as "the means of carrying intelligence to Hoche that we were not disheartened" by the failure of the French expedition to land at Bantry Bay.[1] The *Northern Star*, he says, printed it on a single sheet and circulated hundreds of thousands of copies, which were framed and hung in houses throughout the country.[2] A police spy reported: "It appears now that O'Connor's letter has been printed off privately by the journeymen of almost every press in Dublin."[3]

With regard to its publication in the *Northern Star*, Martha McTier declared her surprise "that two such quiet, prudent men as the Simms would have printed that paper." She had heard that the Simms brothers had "clipped a good deal that O'Connor struggled to have stand."[4] Nonetheless, she predicted, "His paper will indeed be a touchstone, and must have effects of importance. . . . it's the subject everywhere," and she related an anecdote by way of illustration:

> *In compliance with Lord Londonderry's example, J. Kennedy of Cultra forbade the* Star *coming into his house. On going into the stable he found one of his eleven sons of twelve year old, mounted in the manger and proclaiming to all the listening servants, O'Connor at full length—the printers of which cannot get it ready fast enough.*[5]

O'Connor's statement was a declaration of war against the ruling establishment. The candidate explained why he was participating in an electoral system that everyone knew to be hopelessly corrupt: "I have offered my services to use every means in my power to effect its destruction." He railed against the "contemptible" Irish government and against the "disgraceful and ruinous vassalage" that subordinated Ireland to England: "Too long her slaves, we must shew her we are resolved to be free." And he recited a long litany of the government's "crimes" that justified the recent French invasion.[6] His formulations were carefully fashioned, however, to remain technically within the law.

A letter from Lady Sarah Napier to Lord Edward's sister Sophia provides a contemporary account of how O'Connor's agitational efforts were viewed in aristocratic circles. "I am out of the way of hearing news, but even here the public talk is so great about O'Connor's Letter of Confinement that one hears of nothing else," she wrote. "In the ministerial circles I believe it would be almost dangerous even to name such a wicked treasonable rebel's name, but out of that circle, people venture to think and speak from reason." She referred to a mutual friend as "an admirer of O'Connor's & a man of great sense & judgement," and told Sophia that "I listen with great respect to his opinions." Lady Sarah, however, did not share his admiration for O'Connor because she abhorred the idea of revolution, and "the whole bent of the letter is to preach one to all Ireland."[7]

O'Connor wrote *To the Free Electors of Antrim* in answer to an anonymous pamphlet attacking him that had been widely circulated through the post office by the Irish government; he called it "the most virulent diatribe filled with the most unfounded calumnies with a view to blacken my character with the people." It claimed that as a member of parliament O'Connor had been a government supporter and only went into opposition because he had been refused certain sinecures that he had asked for, and that he had "broke faith" with his uncle, Lord Longueville. The attempt to discredit him backfired, however; according to O'Connor "it considerably augmented the people's love for me throughout all of Ireland."[8] This so enraged the government, he says, that when he arrived in Dublin on 2 February he was arrested "on the pretext that in answering them I was guilty of high treason."[9] McTier believed he had wanted to be "taken up" to force a judicial showdown with the authorities,[10] and one historian has likewise suggested that in jailing him, "the government played into O'Connor's hands,"[11] but there is no evidence to support that hypothesis.

Simultaneous with O'Connor's arrest in Dublin the authorities in Belfast were ransacking his house and confiscating his private papers. The next day the offices of the *Northern Star* were raided and a number of United Irish militants were taken into custody. The previous September Samuel Neilson, Thomas Russell, Charles Teeling and several others had been arrested and charged with high treason. By June 1797, 103 of the leading United Irishmen of the north were in prison.[12]

THE "FLOATING REPUBLIC"

Meanwhile, even though the attempted French invasion at Bantry Bay failed, it had exposed the vulnerability of British defenses. At the beginning of 1797 the military threat France posed to England was more menacing than ever. The powerful coalition that had earlier opposed the French revolutionary armies crumbled as one after another of Britain's allies deserted the fight. In 1795 Prussia and Spain had made peace with France, and Holland had become the Batavian Republic, leaving Austria as Britain's only significant ally on the continent. When Bonaparte's triumphs in Italy forced Austria to sue for peace in April 1797, Britain stood completely isolated against the French juggernaut. It was at this critical moment of maximum peril that England's defensive shield—the mighty British navy—was convulsed by a series of mutinies. The sailors' committees that led them proclaimed the creation of a "floating republic."[13]

On April 16, 1797 the sailors of the Channel Fleet at Spithead, off Portsmouth, ran the red flags of mutiny up the masts of every ship. Intolerable conditions, including low pay, abominable food and arbitrary floggings, had provoked the revolt. The discontent derived in large part from the fact that a large proportion of the sailors had been coerced into the service against their will. The war with France had stimulated an immense upsurge in forced recruitment. During the war's first year the size of the navy more than quadrupled, from about 16,000 men to almost 70,000. By 1797 the number had surpassed 114,000.[14] By Wolfe Tone's reckoning, two-thirds of them were Irishmen.[15]

The Irish government routinely used the Fleet as a repository for suspected subversives. Fifteen thousand United Irishmen and Defenders had been forced between 1793 and 1796 to serve the English crown at sea, according to a British official's estimate.[16] Whether this was an exaggeration or not, the massive presence of Irish rebels in the navy certainly had a major impact on the events of 1797. Generally speaking, the larger the number of Irishmen in a given ship's crew, the more solidly supportive that ship was of the mutiny. It was not coincidental that the mutineers utilized oaths like those of the Irish secret societies and that their public statements echoed the language of United Irish manifestos.

By mid-May the mutiny had spread from the Channel Fleet at Spithead to a detachment of the North Sea Fleet based at the Nore, at the mouth of the River Thames. By the end of the month it had grown to include the main base of the North Sea Fleet at Yarmouth. The Channel Fleet's mission was to counter the French naval forces stationed at Brest, and the North Sea Fleet was depended upon to keep the Dutch navy at Texel in check. With these two fleets immobilized Britain and Ireland were completely vulnerable. If a significant French force had been sent to Ireland in the spring of 1797, the British government would have been helpless to resist it.

At the beginning of June the rebel sailors embarked upon their most audacious operation. They sent ships up the Thames to blockade London, cutting off all commerce and threatening to starve the metropolis into submission. It was a dramatic demonstration of their power, but the mutineers had miscalculated. The government succeeded in removing the navigation buoys from the lower Thames, effectively trapping the blockading ships and preventing them from being resupplied. As the rebels' rations ran low, so did their morale, and eventually it was they who were starved into submission. On June 14 most of the ships capitulated and by the following day the floating republic had come to a definitive end. Four hundred or more sailors were arrested and at least thirty-five identified as leaders were executed. Some three hundred and fifty were flogged or sentenced to a lifetime of servitude in colonial forces.

The harsh punishments did not succeed in restoring peace throughout the fleet. In 1798 during the rebellion in Ireland one of the flagships of the Spithead mutiny, the *Defiance*, would again be taken over by its crew and there would be rumblings and plots on virtually every ship with a large component of Irishmen. Nonetheless, the British navy would never again be immobilized to the extent that it was from April through June of 1797. Throughout the crisis the United Irish leaders, through their representative Edward Lewins, continued their urgent requests for French assistance but the French military planners, with the Bantry Bay debacle fresh in their minds, were hesitant to act. They realized too late the irreplaceable opportunity the mutinies had offered to separate Ireland from England.

O'CONNOR'S ARREST AND IMPRISONMENT

Wolfe Tone, noting reports in English newspapers of O'Connor's detention in February, commented, "It seems he was walking with Lord Edward Fitzgerald when he was arrested. It is not for nothing that these two young gentlemen were walking together!"[17] Tone had not met them but was well aware of their activities on behalf of the United Irishmen. The morning after the arrest Lord Edward woke Lady Lucy to tell her the bad news. "Eddy and I lamented together all day," she wrote in her diary, "I never saw Eddy so unhappy. It really is too shocking."[18]

"When I was arrested," O'Connor says, "I was sick in bed with a violent fever from a cold I caught at the meeting in Belfast," where he had foiled the high sheriff's plans to mobilize the population against French invaders. "In this condition I was kept from early in the morning until the evening, when I was taken to council chambers." There, at a hearing presided over by the viceroy, Lord Camden, O'Connor was told by the chancellor, Lord Fitzgibbon, that he was being charged with high treason.[19]

He responded that the charge was transparently false. They all knew him, he avowed, and "knew that I lived but for the liberty and prosperity of my country." Was it treason to proclaim Ireland's right to make treaties with whatever nation she thought fit? No, it was treason to deny that right. "I never took a shilling for betraying my country's rights to England or to France," he declared. "Let those who owed all their rank and honors to the selling the rights of their country to England answer for their treason!" Camden had heard enough; he made a signal to Fitzgibbon and the hearing was ended. O'Connor was sent to prison.[20]

O'Connor describes his incarceration in Birmingham Tower of Dublin Castle as very harsh: "I was imprisoned in an ancient tower which had not been inhabited for centuries. The walls were twelve feet thick and so full of fleas that the moment I got into bed I was devoured and tortured by them." He soon recovered from "the vile fever" he had when put in prison, "notwithstanding the torture the multitude of vermin made me suffer."[21]

O'Connor's prison conditions were milder, however, than those experienced by other United Irish leaders, who were held in Kilmainham and other jails. O'Connor had his "poor faithful dog" to keep him company and his personal servant, Jerry Leary, was allowed to visit and bring him books to read.[22] That is not to say that O'Connor deliberately exaggerated his prison hardships. He abhorred confinement and his subjective sense of suffering could hardly have been greater. He was deeply aggrieved at being cut off from the rest of the world, and at being forced into idleness when there was important work to be done. Apparently discounting his teenaged servant's visits, O'Connor lamented, "Not a soul but my jailer were suffered to approach me for the six months I was incarcerated in this dungeon."[23]

The contact with his jailer turned out to be a major asset, because O'Connor says he was able to make a United Irishman of him. That allowed O'Connor to engage—very cautiously—in secret communication with Lord Edward. And although his friends were not permitted direct contact with him, he was able to see them and exchange waves with them from his window. A week after his arrest, Lady Lucy appeared below. "Saw poor dear Arthur at the window of his prison," her diary entry for 12 February reports. "He look'd very melancholy. We kiss'd our hands to each other."[24]

O'Connor and Lucy also carried out a lively correspondence by means of notes written in the margins of the books carried in and out by Jerry Leary. Two days after Lucy's first appearance below his window, he wrote to her:

> I saw my dear beloved friend from my grat'd prison, alas, she looked pale, she grieves for her friend. . . . The dear song, & the old dance, the conversation, the humble meal & the jug of native punch, accompanied with social friendship. Shall we ever pass those days again? I am becoming weaker and weaker every day from want of exercise, and am now busy inventing some way of taking much exercise in a small space.[25]

When the stagnant air in his cell gave him headaches, his sympathetic jailer allowed him to leave his cell and go to the top of the tower for some fresh air. O'Connor's enemies noticed him taking these fresh-air breaks. One day the jailer was on top of the tower and one of the sentries below fired at him; the ball grazed his cheek. When questioned about the incident, the sentry declared that he thought it was O'Connor he had fired at. On another occasion O'Connor was standing near the window in his cell and reading when a shot was fired at him; the ball struck the wall beside O'Connor's head. After a third such incident O'Connor was able to turn them to his advantage to secure his release.

In Ireland the United Irishmen had been waging a vigorous war of words against the government for holding O'Connor indefinitely without trial, and in England O'Connor's allies had been doing the same. Sir Francis Burdett devoted his very first speech on the floor of parliament to a passionate defense of O'Connor:

> One person now immured within the walls of a dungeon in Dublin, I have the honour of being connected with—for an honour as well as a happiness I shall ever esteem it—by the strongest ties of friendship and affection, whom I know to be incapable of treason to his country. Good God! that treason to Ireland and the name of O'Connor should be preposterously coupled together!—as he is capable of every thing that is great, generous, and noble, for his country's good; a man whose whole conduct delineates the exact line of rectitude and honour; whose private virtues equal—they cannot surpass—the integrity of his public

*conduct; who is indeed endowed with every good as well as every great
qualification, and of whom it may fairly be said, "Nil non laudandum
aut dixit, aut sensit, aut fecit." When such men become the objects of
fear and hatred to government, it is not difficult to ascertain the nature
of that government.*[26]

O'Connor's Foxite supporters publicized a statement he wrote that cited
"the three attempts which had been made to assassinate me" and blamed them
on the government. Lord Camden, he later maintained, was so embarrassed "at
seeing such a well-founded accusation brought against his administration, he
insisted that either I should be tried or bailed; in consequence I was liberated
on bail at the end of July 1797."[27] In fact, Camden had been pressured by the
British government to release O'Connor as a result of the effectiveness of the
agitation on his behalf. Once free, O'Connor proclaimed that his release was
a tacit admission that the charge of treason had all along been "but a pretext
to deprive me of my liberty."[28]

O'Connor's bail was posted by Lord Edward and Thomas Addis Emmet.[29]
William Drennan called on him very soon after his release and found him "in
good spirits, and tolerably healthy." His "paleness was pathetic," however, as a
result of his confinement. "I believe he goes into the country immediately to
drink the spirit of the mountain breeze."[30]

THE PRESS

"On regaining my liberty," O'Connor says in his memoirs, "my first
business was to inform myself of the progress the Union had made and here
I found nothing had been done. I had to set the machine in movement."[31]
He made a similar claim in August 1798 in a prison conversation with a
government official, Alexander Marsden. According to Marsden, "O'Connor
said that it was by his sole exertion that Leinster was organised. When he got
out of prison he found that everything had gone back, and for five months he
stuck to it and effected more than all the others put together."[32]

The United Irishmen's primary organ, the *Northern Star*, had been
forcibly suppressed at the same time O'Connor was arrested, and it had not
resumed publication. O'Connor established a new journal, *The Press*, to take
its place and once again the movement had a coherent voice. Its dual purpose
was organization and agitation—in O'Connor's words, "spreading the Union
and animating the minds of the people."[33]

The success of the venture, O'Connor says, "passed my most sanguine
hopes."[34] He was elated by "the astonishing influence of *The Press*, which
so engrossed the journalism of the capital that not another journal could

find readers while *The Press* lasted."[35] His assessment was corroborated by a government report that admitted the paper "was distributed throughout all parts of the kingdom, and . . . had immediately a more extensive circulation than any paper long established." The same report described the content of *The Press* as highly seditious:

> *Every species of misrepresentation and sophistry was made use of to vilify the government, to extend the union, to shake the connexion with Great Britain, to induce the people to look to French assistance, to exaggerate the force and numbers of the disaffected, and systematically to degrade the administration of justice in all its departments.*[36]

The popularity of the newspaper was evidenced by the crowds that gathered outside the printshop awaiting its publication, creating what its enemies viewed as "a revelry of sedition," and by its street vendors "bellowing at every corner their treasonable publications."[37]

As an example of its influence, O'Connor claims that two "papist priests" of the "higher order" called on him to complain that his newspaper attacked their religion. O'Connor says he assured them it did no such thing: "I had particularly forbidden that any religious controversy should be admitted in my journal." The priests nonetheless informed O'Connor that they intended to ban *The Press* in their parishes. "Go then," O'Connor replied, "and by and by you will give me news of your success." That same night he dispatched two United Irish organizers to these parishes "to inform the people of the insolent menaces of their priests to destroy the liberty of the press." Two weeks later the priests returned with "their tone and assurance . . . totally changed." None of their parishioners, claims O'Connor, would have anything to do with them; "not a soul had come to mass." O'Connor further states that the priests asked him for forgiveness and promised "they not only would abstain from opposing the circulation of *The Press* but would do all they could to promote it." And that, O'Connor exults, shows how "thoroughly had the line of political liberty got the upper hand of priestly ignorance."[38]

The Press was printed in Dublin because the government's campaign of military terror throughout Ulster in 1797 made publishing it in the north impossible. To finance it O'Connor solicited funds from men of means who were United Irish supporters—Valentine Lawless (later Lord Cloncurry) was the principal "investor." Its editorial office was at No. 4 Church Lane and it was produced at a printshop in Upper Exchange Street owned by a Mr. Whitworth. After just seventeen issues, however, government persecution caused Whitworth to abandon the job; John Stockdale of Abbey Street took it over and continued printing the newspaper for the duration of its existence.

On several occasions thugs ("low Orangemen") attacked workmen carrying the papers from the printshop to Church Lane; the workmen had to form a defense guard to protect themselves and the papers.[39]

The first issue appeared on 28 September 1797; it came out thrice weekly, on Tuesday, Thursday, and Saturday evenings. Its press run was about 3,000 copies at first, and rose to about 4,500 by the end of the year. (By way of comparison, the *Times* of London's circulation was about 4,800 in 1800.[40]) A man named O'Flanagan who worked as a typesetter for the newspaper recalled the first editor, Charles Brennan, as "a very able writer, but a man of questionable integrity." Brennan was jailed on account of some personal debts and attempted to resolve his difficulties at the expense of the proprietor of *The Press*. He threatened O'Connor that if his debts were not paid immediately he would turn over all the manuscripts in his possession to the authorities at Dublin Castle. O'Connor, according to O'Flanagan, replied:

> *If you wish to act a base, dishonourable part towards us and the righteous cause you have engaged to sustain, we must regret it, we must likewise regret having been associated with a man capable of such baseness. Do your utmost. Posterity shall decide upon the rectitude of the cause you have expressed your intention of betraying.*[41]

Brennan was released from prison a few days later and apparently had no further association with the United Irishmen.[42]

Although *The Press* in fact belonged to O'Connor, it was considered prudent to legally register its ownership under a less notorious name; one of the editors, a United Irish stalwart named Peter Finnerty, was thus originally made its official proprietor. On 26 October, however, an anonymous letter attacking the viceroy, Lord Camden, appeared in *The Press* and the government seized upon the occasion to charge Finnerty with seditious libel. He was held in jail for two months and then sentenced to the pillory in front of Newgate prison on Green Street in Dublin. While Finnerty was in the pillory O'Connor and Lord Edward went at the head of a mass demonstration to stand in solidarity with him. O'Flanagan, the typesetter, gives this account of what transpired:

> *There were several thousands present, and the people seemed much excited. When they reached the guard of soldiers, Lord Edward endeavoured to pass one of them. The soldier raised his gun, and was about to strike him, when the high sheriff (Mr. Pemberton) immediately advanced, and ordered him not to act without orders.*

*He then gave directions to the officer in command of the guard to
allow Lord Edward Fitzgerald and Mr. O'Connor to pass. They both
continued near Finnerty during the time he was suffering the penalty.
The high sheriff seemed puzzled how to act; but owing to his mild and
conciliatory conduct to the people, all passed off quietly.*[43]

As a result of a law that required Finnerty to forfeit ownership of the
newspaper when he was convicted of libel, it became necessary to name
someone else as proprietor. O'Connor laments, however, that "no one at the
moment could be found to assume a position which exposed him to the
persecution of the tyrannical government."[44] To prevent *The Press* from being
shut down he had to take the legal responsibility upon himself. Beginning
with the 30 December 1797 issue, "A. O'Connor" took the place of "P.
Finnerty" as the owner of record. The change gave an immediate boost to the
paper's circulation. According to O'Flanagan,

*the day that Arthur O'Connor's name was announced as printer, it
got a rise of 1,500, and increased to 6,000, which was the utmost
that could be printed in time by the presses of that period. The name
of Arthur O'Connor was everywhere received with enthusiasm by the
people, particularly in the counties of Kildare and Meath.*[45]

O'Connor complains in his memoirs that the responsibility of legally
owning *The Press* was made particularly "dangerous and disagreeable" because
of the impetuousness of some of the newspaper's contributors—"violent,
gross and brutal men" who took every opportunity to misuse its columns
"to satisfy their infernal passions." On one occasion, "one of these wretches
bribed a compositor to insert an article" stating that Lady Fitzgibbon, the
Lord Chancellor's wife, was bald and wore a wig.[46] O'Connor had this fellow
"literally kicked out" of the newspaper's office and fired the compositor. (They
may have been government agents deliberately planting libelous material in
The Press to justify outlawing it.[47]) He then immediately paid a visit to Lady
Fitzgibbon to apologize. "She knew me too well," he told her, "to imagine I
could have authorized what I knew was the most gross falsehood from the
ocular knowledge I had that she had a most beautiful and abundant flock of
hair."[48] O'Connor's account of this incident—told without a hint of humor—
leaves no doubt of the sincerity of his apology to the lady, and illustrates his
peculiar duality as a revolutionary democrat with patrician sensibilities. His
primary concern, of course, was to avoid unnecessary provocations that could
damage the United Irish cause, but his aristocratic sense of propriety had also
been genuinely offended.

THE REPRESSION INTENSIFIES

The Press was still in operation when O'Connor left Ireland in the first week of January 1798. He handed over the reins of control to a United Irish lawyer, William Sampson. The newspaper survived until the government seized its sixty-eighth issue and finally suppressed it on 6 March 1798. On that morning, O'Flanagan reports, "a guard of the Cavan militia, under the command of a rampant Orangeman, Maxwell, came and seized the office, carried away all the newspapers that had been printed, and destroyed the type, presses, etc., in a wanton manner."[49]

This represented the southward extension of the campaign of terror that the British military had unleashed against the Irish population in March 1797, when General Gerard Lake put the province of Ulster under martial law. "You may rest assured," Lake declared,

> *that nothing but coercive measures in the strongest degree can succeed in this country, the lower order of people & most of the middle class are determined republicans, have imbibed the French principles & will not be contented with anything short of a revolution.*[50]

Lake and his second-in-command, O'Connor's former friend John Knox, sought to systematically disarm the rebels in Ulster. A policy of collective punishment, including torture and executions, was implemented to compel the surrender of hidden pikes and firearms. British army units encouraged local gentry and yeomanry to draw up long lists of "suspects" whose homes then were burned and who were tortured to extract confessions and to force the naming of friends and neighbors as rebels.

A hundred years later Lecky gave a famous description of the suffering thus visited upon the Irish nation: "It was a scene of horrors," he wrote, "hardly surpassed in the modern history of Europe."[51] Two particular instruments of torture—"triangles" and portable gallows—became symbols of the savage repression. The triangles were three-sided frameworks to which suspects were tied as they were publicly flogged with a fiendish whip called a "cat-o'-nails"—a cat-o'-nine-tails with barbwire tips. The portable gallows were wooden apparatuses upon which suspects were subjected to a procedure known as "half-hanging": they would be hung by the neck until almost unconscious, then let down, requestioned, and if their answers were still deemed unsatisfactory the procedure would be repeated. A third form of torture that also became emblematic of the period was known as "pitch-capping," whereby a cap of coarse cloth or paper filled with boiling tar was forced onto the victim's head and held until it cooled.

The brutality of "Lake's reign of terror"[52] generated intensified resistance on the part of the outraged population, finally culminating in the Rebellion of 1798. This violent and chaotic scene was the general context of O'Connor's departure for England at the beginning of 1798, but the specific circumstances are unclear. He certainly intended to go from England to the continent, where he planned to continue lobbying for a French invasion of Ireland. The timing of his journey, however, may have been prompted by an explosive factional struggle within the United Irish leadership.

FACTIONAL STRIFE: O'CONNOR VS. EMMET

One of the first people O'Connor met after his release from prison in July 1797 was Thomas Addis Emmet, who had become a member of the national executive committee while O'Connor was in jail. Emmet told him that on the committee "there had been violent divisions between those who desired an insurrection and those who opposed it." O'Connor says that Emmet informed him that he himself had been one of those who opposed an insurrection and only prevented the others from instigating one by threatening to go to the government and disclose their plans. "It is not possible," O'Connor says,

> to express the indignation I felt at hearing this account from Emmet. I reminded him of the confession he made me of his want of nerve to engage in a rising. Why, then, had he in despite of his acknowledged timidity [engaged] in a situation [in which] he knew he was incapable of discharging the duties?[53]

"The cowardice of Emmet and some others had paralyzed the Union movement," O'Connor concluded.[54] That, in his opinion, was the cause of the bitter factional struggle within the leadership of the United Irishmen that would outlive the organization itself, echoing among their respective partisans—and among historians—long after both O'Connor and Emmet were dead. The division would seriously weaken the United Irishmen by discrediting the organization in the eyes of its ranks and its potential French allies.

The exact nature of the dispute as it stood in 1798 before O'Connor left Ireland is not easy to determine. The claim that one side—O'Connor's—"desired an insurrection" and the other side—Emmet's—opposed it is probably not untruthful, but it certainly oversimplifies the conflict. Both sides attached conditions to their support for, or opposition to, insurrection, but precisely what those conditions were is uncertain. Most commentators have relied on the reports of spies and police informers that have survived in government archives, but these provide only a garbled description of the contending positions.

Leaving aside his attribution of motives, O'Connor's account seems generally accurate in portraying the division as a struggle between a militant faction impatient for revolutionary action and a moderate faction that wanted to proceed more cautiously. Although he was unable to participate in the initial stages of the dispute, as soon as he emerged from prison he aligned himself, predictably, with the more militant group that had coalesced around Lord Edward. The militants among the foremost leaders of the movement were O'Connor, Fitzgerald, and Henry Jackson and the moderates were Emmet, MacNeven, and McCormick. (It is possible that O'Connor was not at this time formally a member of the executive committee; he later insisted that he and Emmet had never been members at the same time.[55])

Another member of the executive committee, Oliver Bond, was placed among O'Connor's opponents by a police spy report,[56] but O'Connor, in his correspondence with Madden, says he had "implicit confidence" in Bond.[57] The confusion of the spies' reports is evidenced by the observation of one, Samuel Turner, that "Macnevin and Lord Fitzgerald are of the moderate party."[58]

After his initial confrontation with Emmet in late July or early August, O'Connor attempted to rally support for the militant position by means of an organizational tour in September that took him to Cork and to Belfast. The police spy reports indicate that he and Lord Edward then confronted the moderates at a meeting of the leadership in December and argued in favor of calling an immediate insurrection. When they were defeated, O'Connor allegedly left in a huff for England. The spies' reports, however, are so riddled with inconsistencies and improbabilities that it is impossible to know what really transpired.

One of the government's most important paid informers was a man who had earlier ranked high in the United Irishmen's leadership and was the organization's chief attorney, Leonard McNally. McNally had defended many United Irishmen in court and was looked upon as a highly trusted ally. Only long after his death did historians examining government archives discover the shocking evidence that for payment of "two hundred pounds a year for the life of myself and children" he betrayed his comrades for many years.[59] It was McNally's copious letters to the authorities—signed "JW"—that reported most fully on the factional strife between O'Connor and Emmet.

McNally's characterizations of O'Connor are rendered suspect by his evident bias in favor of the moderates' political views; his secondhand information certainly came from one or more of their partisans. In a report dated 26 December 1797, "JW" stated: "Lord Edward, under the influence of Arthur O'Connor remains of opinion that violent measures should be immediately adopted. O'Connor is in a state of impatience amounting to frenzy, and it is with the utmost difficulty that the more moderate of his party keep him within bounds."[60]

In another report, McNally wrote of O'Connor's "intent to promote an immediate rising of the people." But he added that the difference between O'Connor and his opponents

> *is merely on two points—the time to act—and the manner of acting. He [O'Connor] was for an immediate exertion without waiting the event of an invasion—and severity that would strike terror. They are for patiently waiting the result of the French preparations—and securing life and property.[61]*

This makes it seem that O'Connor and Fitzgerald wanted to call upon the people to rise without French assistance, while Emmet and his allies were insisting on waiting for the French to arrive. A few days earlier, however, a contradictory report from "JW" had said that "Arthur O'Connor has softened down his mind, or pretends the conviction, that no popular attempt should be made previous to a landing."[62] It also seems paradoxical that O'Connor would be denying the necessity of French assistance just before leaving for Paris to solicit it.[63]

The most outlandish claim in McNally's reports is that O'Connor and Fitzgerald were promoting a plot to spark an uprising by having O'Connor's "immediate confidential associates of the mechanical class" disguise themselves as Orangemen and attack Catholic chapels during mass on Christmas morning. The moderates allegedly foiled this plot by alerting the Catholic bishops, who postponed early mass on Christmas. Fitzgerald's most recent biographer has pointed out that any such attempt to inflame hatred between Catholics and Protestants "would have been anathema to Lord Edward."[64] It would likewise have been utterly out of character for Arthur O'Connor. And finally, there are suggestions in these reports that O'Connor's interest in promoting an immediate rising in Ireland was to create a diversion to aid a French invasion of England, which is at odds with his commitment to the opposite course of action.

Were the militants against French assistance? Were the moderates in favor of it? Such simplistic notions are not of much value in comprehending the complex political positions that divided O'Connor and Emmet. Nonetheless, it seems that however the issues were posed O'Connor did indeed lose the argument and found himself outvoted, which may have prompted his departure.

Another factor was information that O'Connor had received from Walter ("Watty") Cox that the authorities were searching diligently for a pretext on which to imprison him. O'Connor was at that time staying with Lord Edward at a Fitzgerald family villa named Black Rock, about three miles from Dublin. Cox, the former publisher of the ultraradical *Union Star*, went to Black Rock to tell them that government spymaster Edward Cooke had offered him a bribe of £10,000 and passage to America to provide incriminating evidence against O'Connor. Cox related a conversation he had overheard between Cooke and another top government official, John Beresford, wherein the latter "declared that if O'Connor was not arrested the revolution must succeed."[65] Although all of this is hearsay, it accurately reflects the essential historical truth that O'Connor was at that time public enemy number one in the eyes of the Irish government.[66]

When bailed out of prison by Fitzgerald and Emmet the previous July, O'Connor had not been unconditionally freed; he was required to make himself available for trial at any time. He was not prohibited from travelling, but could do so only with official permission. After receiving Cox's disturbing warning O'Connor immediately paid a visit to Undersecretary Cooke at Dublin Castle and told him he had "urgent business in London and wished to know if my appearance would be called for by my prosecutors." Cooke gave him permission to leave, "assuring me I may go when and as long as I like to, so rejoiced was he to be able to tell the government they were rid of me."[67] Although Cooke and his superiors would undoubtedly have preferred to put O'Connor behind bars, they believed the "disadvantage of taking up persons without bringing them to trial" made it "inexpedient to take up the ringleaders of the conspiracy at present."[68]

That same evening, O'Connor says, he attended the final stormy meeting of the executive committee, and from that meeting went directly to the boat that took him to England. McNally reported his departure to Cooke somewhat differently: "O'Connor left Dublin without notice to even many of his most intimate friends. The last person he conversed with was Stockdale of Abbey Street, his printer, and that was on Tuesday night [2 January 1798] when he said he was going for England."[69] Two days later he added, "O'Connor is undoubtedly gone for France via London and Hamburgh."[70] Word of O'Connor's departure spread rapidly. "I hear," Drennan commented, "that a warrant was out for O'Connor, and that he has been missing these two days. . . . He is the news maker of the day."[71]

It was to be a very ill-fated voyage. As his boat pulled away from the coast of Ireland, O'Connor could not have known that he would never again live in his homeland.

6

Seventeen Ninety-Eight

IN HIS *ADDRESS TO the Free Electors of Antrim* O'Connor had written, "I promise you, as soon as time will permit, that I will lay before you the best account of the state of our country my poor abilities will allow me to furnish."[1] Earlier, in January 1797, Martha McTier reported to William Drennan that O'Connor and Fitzgerald were then in Belfast and that "People who are with them say O'Connor is writing a book."[2] Later that year he no doubt took advantage of his six months in prison to complete it, and in the following year a well-argued 174-page pamphlet entitled *The State of Ireland* appeared under his name. Though set in type by February 1798, it was evidently not released for distribution until later. In a letter sent to Lord Edward in mid-February,[3] O'Connor—then in England with the intention of going to France—made clear that he did not want it to be made public until he was beyond the reach of the English authorities:

> *I send two Copies of the Pamphlet, but they must not be let out of the room you and Pamela read them in, until you hear from me, as otherwise I should be in Limbo; there is not one out here, nor will there, until I can do it in safety,—you can have an edition printed in Ireland—shall send you 100 copies for the instant—They are to be sold at three shillings and sixpence, and of course not to be given to any that cannot be depended on, to avoid prosecution.*[4]

The State of Ireland is, according to a recent assessment, "without doubt [O'Connor's] most valuable and insightful work."[5] Because it presents his view of the situation in Ireland on the eve of the Rebellion—and is the most thorough exposition of his ideological outlook in his prime—it is worth a digression from the narrative of his voyage to England to examine the contents of this pamphlet.

In *The State of Ireland* O'Connor utilized the classical economics of Adam Smith to identify the root causes of Ireland's social ills. The central concept that he employed was what he called the "sacred funds" of a nation's industry. "Industry is the source of human prosperity," he declared. "In every civilized country, the wealth garnered by industry forms a fund for the employment of the industrious." In Ireland, however, "the Government and Legislature, by treason and plunder, have perverted this fund" to the advantage of England. "Every means by which Irish industry could acquire Irish capital has been sacrificed," he charged, "to promote the industry of Great Britain."[6] He castigated British imperialism for its crimes not only in Ireland, but "in every quarter of the globe; pillaging, starving, and slaughtering the unoffending inhabitants of the East Indies; lashing the wretches they have doomed to slavery in the West Indies."[7]

There are several sources, O'Connor explained, from which a nation can increase its capital fund. "The first, the most permanent and the most abundant source" is agriculture. But in Ireland:

> *Does the produce of the lands of Ireland go to supply the fund for the employment of its People? No! your corn, your cattle, your butter, your leather, your yarn, all your superfluous produce, and much more . . . are all exported without a return to pay the rents of Irish Landlords who do not think the country worthy of their residence.*

The "forsaken, plundered People of Ireland are left to languish in famine and misery, for want of that wealth" originally produced by their own labor, thus "exhaling the sap and moisture of the Irish soil to fertilize Great Britain."[8]

The second source from which a nation might generate its "sacred funds" is commerce. But how can Ireland become commercially successful, he asked, when "the Legislature has thrown open every market in Ireland to every species of British manufacture, whilst every market in Britain is shut against every species of Irish manufacture" (with the sole exception of Irish linens)?[9] The unfairness of these terms of trade rendered Irish commercial development hopeless.

A third possible source is "the profits of the national capital employed in Manufactures." But again, with Ireland's home market inundated with relatively cheap British manufactured goods, and with markets in Britain closed to Irish products, how would it be possible for Irish manufacturing to even get started? "Thus famished, manacled, and in infancy, it is thrown a prey to the monster of mercantile avarice."[10]

A final potential source of national capital might be "savings made from the wages of the Industrious." But, O'Connor protested, "how can I insult you by talking of savings from wages, in a country where the nation has been converted into an almshouse, and the industrious into beggars?"[11]

"It is not enough," he continued, "that you should know the manner by which you have been deprived of the means of acquiring wealth: You should, also, be informed of the various ways by which the pittance of wealth your industry has acquired under its mutilated means, has been robbed and plundered." First was "the enormous drain which is extorted from industry" to support the clergymen of the established church—an annual expense of half a million pounds. "By what title," O'Connor demanded, "does one class of Irish Protestants, not one tenth of the nation, arrogate the power of appropriating such exorbitant funds for the ministers of its religion?"[12]

He also condemned "the enormous and growing land-tax" that was "levied on the poorest and the most oppressed part of the nation for making and mending the bridges and roads, the new establishments of the cavalry constables, and, in short, all the money raised by grand-jury assessment." It is the height of injustice, O'Connor said, to impose these taxes on the poor tenants rather than on the wealthy landlords whose property the revenues improve.[13]

But the most damaging deduction from the national wealth was "the enormous expense at which your Government is supported." If the government served the interests of all of its citizens those expenses would be justified. The Irish government, however, was "a system of supporting the few in oppressing the many." The consequent "smothered war between the oppressors and the oppressed" required "sanguinary laws and military outrage, the expenses of which are endless."[14]

The strangulation and robbery of Ireland's "sacred funds," O'Connor charged, had created numerous social evils, including alcoholism and crime. When industriousness brings no reward, a man's mind "flies to the oblivion of intoxication, to relieve it from the torture of thought." Furthermore, "compelled by his own and his children's wants, the calls of nature convert crime into duty. Without property, comforts, or rights to require protection, he regards laws as restrictions, which prevent him from seizing the means of relieving his wants."[15]

To remedy these ills, O'Connor argued, it would not be sufficient to replace the corrupt men who govern with a new group; the entire system of government must be abolished and replaced. Even political reform creating genuinely democratic elections would not solve the problem as long as the economic structure of society remained based on "monopolizing laws of primogeniture, entails and settlement" that kept all power in the hands of a few hereditary noblemen.[16] "As long as those laws of monopoly exist," universal suffrage "under the appearance of Democracy, renders Aristocracy omnipotent."[17] As for how the laws of monopoly could be abolished, he pointed to the French Revolution as the example to be emulated.

O'Connor responded to the accusation that he was instigating rebellion by turning it back against his accusers:

> *Away with the charge of a whole people rebelling! The minor parts are the rebels: a decided majority can never rebel: usurpers and tyrants only can commit rebellion. If not, what are the liberties of Europe but rebellion? . . . What are the liberties of England but rebellion, aided by foreign assistance, against the bigotry and tyranny of Stuart? What are the liberties of America but rebellion, aided by France, against the tyranny of Britain?[18]*

The pointed references to foreign assistance were an implicit defense of the United Irish alliance with France. And in reply to the charge that he was a dangerous incendiary, O'Connor declared:

> *The Minister and his accomplices will tell you that I am exciting you to revolution. I answer, the revolution has been made already by the inflexible progress and order of human nature. They will tell you that they are endeavouring to save you from the horrors of revolution. I answer, there is nothing horrible in the revolution, it is the means which have been employed to obstruct and retard it which have caused all the horrors.[19]*

No matter how defensively O'Connor crafted his formulations, however, he knew that *The State of Ireland* could certainly lead to another prosecution, which accounts for his leaving Ireland and taking the precautions outlined in the letter to Lord Edward quoted above.

FROM DUBLIN TO LONDON

In the first week of January 1798 O'Connor boarded a boat bound for England. He went into his berth before any of the other passengers had arrived, so none of them knew he was on board. Most were Englishmen, he tells us, "hastening out of Ireland from the agitated state of the people." From inside his cabin he could hear them talking, late into the night, and he found that he himself was a central topic of their conversation; they "gave me many a hearty curse and in terms very little measured." The next day when he came out on deck many of them seemed "a little confounded at finding the person of whom they had been so lavish of their imprecations." An Irishman who was enjoying the Englishmen's embarrassment asked O'Connor if all the talking had prevented him from sleeping. "I assured him," O'Connor responded, "I had slept so sound that I did not hear a word of it, and I said it with such good humour looking on the Englishmen that I could perceive I had disarmed a good part of their anger."[20]

This anecdote illustrates another aspect of O'Connor's peculiarity as an Irish revolutionary. His "good humour" toward these hostile Englishmen was not insincere. O'Connor was not anglophobic; in fact, it would be more accurate to describe him as an anglophile. As much as he hated the Pitt ministry and its policies, he loved the nation that to him was epitomized by Fox and Sheridan. When he arrived in England, he says, "I was received with the warmest tenderness and affection by my beloved friends and the joy and pleasure I felt was the most exquisite of my life."[21]

By contrast, he describes his experience with many of his fellow Irish revolutionaries as a descent "from this heaven into a gutter so low that it seemed to me another world." His dedication to liberating Ireland, he laments, forced him "to associate with men with all the vices of the slave, whose minds had been emasculated of all the noble, generous sentiments which belong to conscious freedom and independence." These ingrates (he clearly had Emmet and MacNeven in mind) were too mean-spirited to appreciate men like Lord Edward and himself who dared "to risk their lives and fortune to rescue their enslaved countrymen."[22]

O'Connor arrived in London "some time about the 7th of January."[23] Although he had left Ireland with the intention of going to France, once in the company of Sheridan, Fox, and Lady Lucy he seemed in no hurry to leave England. But eventually "the time arrived when I was to tear myself from the exquisite happiness I enjoyed in this society." The repression in Ireland had reached a critical point: "The whippings, picketings, torturings, burnings, imprisonings so goaded the people that I dreaded nothing could restrain them from breaking out." If the Irish people rose, he feared, it would be "a war of pikes against muskets, balls and powder, and stones against bullets and grapeshot" that could only result in a bloody massacre of the patriots. Therefore, he concluded, "I saw I had not a moment to lose in ascertaining what we had to expect from French assistance."[24]

Some historians have suggested that O'Connor's voyage to France was motivated by a desire to replace Edward Lewins as the United Irishmen's chief representative to the Directory.[25] In early 1797, in the wake of the Bantry Bay debacle, the organization's executive committee had sent Lewins, "carefully briefed" by O'Connor, to reopen negotiations with the French government.[26] In his memoirs, however, O'Connor described Lewins as having "set himself up as a sort of ambassador for Ireland," and attributed the idea of supplanting him to the low intrigues of the Reverend James O'Coigley, who wanted "to get the place of Lewins."[27] O'Connor's assertion is corroborated by the recollections of Benjamin Binns, a United Irish stalwart in England: "The object of Coigly's going to France, as he proposed doing . . . was to displace Lewins. I heard from himself, and one of the Irish Executive, that he was commissioned by the Executive to supersede Lewins in Paris, whom some suspected of betraying the interests of Ireland."[28] But a well-placed informer's report on the subject should also be noted: "Edward Fitzgerald . . . said he would prevail on O'Connor, or some such, to go to Paris. If not, he would have to go himself in order to have Lewins removed."[29]

Whatever O'Connor's intentions may have been vis-à-vis Lewins, his primary purpose in going to France was to once again seek military support for a United Irish uprising. The timing of his departure from England, however, was also influenced by an important personal consideration. He learned that the Irish authorities were falsely claiming that he had jumped bail and consequently were seeking his arrest and extradition to Ireland. O'Connor's Foxite friends, including Thomas Erskine, one of England's most celebrated attorneys, advised him to leave England for the continent as quickly as possible.[30]

He decided to go directly to France rather than taking the more roundabout route via Hamburg. For that purpose he asked "an honest Irishman, John Binns" (who like his brother Benjamin resided in England) to make the travel arrangements. O'Connor was anxious to rebut later gossip to the effect that Binns had betrayed him: "Nothing can be more false," he declared. "A more honorable man it was not possible to see, and in all I had to do with him, never did a man conduct himself with more zeal and fidelity than John Binns."[31]

O'CONNOR AND THE "ENGLISH JACOBINS"

O'Connor's connections with John and Benjamin Binns lead naturally to the assumption that he was involved with London's revolutionary underground. The Binns brothers were United Irishmen who had moved to London in 1794 and had become leading activists in a conspiratorial organization known as the United Englishmen or the United Britons.[32] As United Irish agents, they were presumably seeking to implement the strategy of encouraging diversionary insurrections in England to coincide with a French invasion of Ireland.

O'Connor, in his memoirs, vehemently denies any complicity with the English revolutionaries, whom he unkindly characterizes as "a very small knot of miserable starry visionaries."[33] He says that although he was aware Binns "belonged to some English societies," he himself had absolutely nothing to do with them. Pitt, he says, published "a most calumnious accusation" against him: "that I frequented assemblies of English societies where it was debated to assassinate the King." He declares that "in all my life I never attended a single one of those English societies, nor was I ever in the Furnival's Cellar, where my calumniators assert I frequently was; nay, I never knew where this cellar is."[34] Elsewhere, O'Connor also denied any association with Colonel Edward Despard, one of the primary United Irish agents working among London revolutionaries.[35] Despard was hanged in 1803 for allegedly plotting to assassinate George III.[36]

There is some evidence that contradicts O'Connor's denials, but it is circumstantial evidence based on the uncorroborated reports of police informers. The spies who had infiltrated meetings of the United Englishmen at Furnival's Inn Cellar did not place O'Connor there, but they reported that John Binns and the Reverend James O'Coigley met with Despard at Furnival's, and that Binns then shared lodgings with O'Connor at the house of Thomas Evans, a leading figure in the United Englishmen.[37] Another spy report suggested that O'Connor deliberately avoided Furnival's Inn Cellar, but met Despard at an apartment rented by the latter at Osterly in Middlesex.[38] This informant's credibility is weakened by his further claim that Despard met at the same time with Archibald Hamilton Rowan, who had been in exile in America since 1795.[39]

Although the precise truth of the matter is impossible to discern, it is possible that O'Connor's denials are factually accurate. Nonetheless, they are certainly misleading. O'Connor may never have attended a meeting of the United Englishmen, and he may never have actually met Colonel Despard, but it is impossible to believe that he was unaware of the United Irish plans to organize diversionary uprisings in England.[40]

John Binns, in his memoirs, records that he first met O'Connor when Sir Francis Burdett introduced them at Burdett's house in Piccadilly in early February 1798. Binns says that because he and O'Connor were engaged "in a common cause, and for a common country," *we at our first interview became entirely confidential. He mentioned his anxiety to get to France to see Napoleon Bonaparte and General Hoche, who, it was understood, was to command the army which was expected to invade Ireland, the movements of which O'Connor expected to hasten, and in some measure direct.*[41]

If O'Connor in February 1798 was depending upon Hoche to lead an invasion of Ireland, he was to be disappointed because Hoche had died of consumption (tuberculosis) the previous September at the age of twenty-nine. Henceforth French aid to the Irish cause would lie in the less trustworthy hands of Napoleon Bonaparte.

O'CONNOR AND O'COIGLEY

While not blaming Binns in the least, O'Connor bitterly laments: "The whole of my plan for getting to France was an egregious *faute* from first to last."[42] The principal cause of his misfortune, he says, was allowing the Reverend James O'Coigley to accompany him. O'Coigley (whose name is often rendered variously as O'Quigley, Quigley, Coigley, or Coigly) was an Irish priest who had embarked upon a conspiratorial career on behalf of the United Irish cause.[43]

O'Connor says that his involvement with O'Coigley came about as a result of "a letter from an Irish Lord, an United Irishman, who strongly recommended him as a persecuted man and entreated me to let him go with me."[44] The unnamed intermediary was probably Valentine Lawless, Lord Cloncurry. Dr. Madden corroborates O'Connor's report of his initial encounter with O'Coigley:

Coigly, on his way to France, passed through London. He brought a letter of introduction to an Irish gentleman, then residing in London. . . . The account I am now giving was related to me by the gentleman in question. . . . Coigly was in great distress; he was assisted by this gentleman, and invited to his house on two or three occasions. Arthur O'Connor, who had recently arrived in London, dined with this gentleman, when Coigly and O'Connor met at his house, at dinner, for the first time. They had no previous acquaintance, and, at this casual meeting, the purpose of both, with respect to their intended visit to France, led to the proposal of Coigly's accompanying O'Connor to that Country.[45]

Although O'Coigley was undoubtedly sincere in his devotion to the cause of liberating Ireland, his talents as a conspirator evidently left much to be desired. According to O'Connor, "Never was indiscretion more extravagant than that of O'Quigly. . . . nothing could equal the babbling, extravagant conversation he held right and left with all he met."[46] John Binns succinctly confirmed that assessment; O'Coigley, he wrote, "has been a damned blab."[47] Compounding the problem, O'Coigley "had the misfortune to be given to spiritous liquors."[48] In retrospect O'Connor lamented that if he had suspected "the thousandth part" of O'Coigley's carelessness, "no consideration could have induced me to have suffered him in my society."[49]

O'Coigley's most flagrant indiscretion—the one that would prove fatal to himself and almost fatal to his companions—was to be carrying in his pocket a document "every word of which was rank English high treason."[50] It was a communiqué from an unknown (and perhaps nonexistent) revolutionary organization called the Secret Committee of England that appealed to the French government to invade and conquer England: "With the tyranny of England," it read in part, "that of all Europe must fall; haste, then, great nation! Pour forth thy gigantic force: let the base despot feel thy avenging stroke."[51]

In addition to O'Connor and O'Coigley there were two other members of the party—young Jerry Leary, O'Connor's personal servant, and a United Irishman named John Allen who came with a recommendation from Lord Edward. For security reasons most of them adopted false names and identities. O'Connor took the pseudonym "Colonel Morris" (perhaps in tribute to his first military instructor), O'Coigley traveled under the name "Captain Jones," Allen posed as the servant of "Captain Jones," and Binns presented himself as a gentleman named "Williams." The only one who did not adopt a fictitious identity was Jerry Leary.

O'Connor apparently intended to stay abroad for an extended period of time; he took with him an extraordinary amount of luggage. Unfortunately, Binns says, "the immense quantity of baggage, mahogany cases, swords, pistols, military accoutrements and equipment of all sorts, which O'Connor had brought with him" attracted attention and suspicion to the group.[52] This was not, however, the cause of their downfall. Neither Binns nor O'Connor ever knew it, but they had been betrayed to the English authorities by Samuel Turner, a prominent United Irishman who had become an informer.[53] The government had also placed O'Connor's friend and business advisor Hugh Bell under surveillance and was intercepting and reading his correspondence.[54]

ARRESTED AT MARGATE

Binns's memoirs, based on a journal he kept while in Maidstone jail, provide a detailed account of O'Connor's failed attempt to leave England. On 21 February 1798, Binns reports, "I left London in a Gravesend packet" and went "to the several towns in the county of Kent which were opposite to the coast of France." At Whitstable, among other places, he found no one in whom he felt he could confide, but finally, in Margate, he met some boatsmen he thought he could trust. He made an agreement with them and returned to London on 25 February, only to find that O'Connor and O'Coigley had "that morning at six o'clock, embarked in a hoy for Whitstable—that very town, some of the inhabitants of which I had sounded, and found unworthy of trust. This information filled me with sad forebodings."[55]

Binns then turned around and tried to catch up with the others. After an overnight stop at Canterbury he set off on foot toward Whitstable, looking for O'Connor and O'Coigley. "On the road, about five miles from Canterbury, I met O'Connor on his way from Whitstable to Canterbury in search of me."

> On our arrival in Canterbury, we ordered a post-chaise and posted to Deal, where we slept that night. The next morning we posted to Sandwich, where we discharged the post-chaise and walked a few miles across the country to the town of Margate.[56]

At Margate they were reunited with O'Coigley, Allen and Leary, who were accompanying a cart heavily laden with O'Connor's baggage. They checked into the King's Head inn where Binns, O'Connor, and O'Coigley "supped together and retired to bed early." At dinner Binns told the other two that everything was arranged for them to leave for France the next afternoon in a first-rate boat captained by a trusty friend. However, his memoirs say, "I was sadly mistaken."[57]

The next morning, 28 February, Binns was descending the stairs from the bedroom when he was seized by the collar by a police officer backed by "a party of dismounted light-horsemen, who had been stationed on the stairs with their swords drawn."[58] The officer demanded Binns's name, but he refused to say anything. He was taken downstairs into a room where he saw Allen and Leary with O'Connor's luggage. O'Connor and O'Coigley were then brought into the same room by another policeman accompanied by troops.

They were all arrested and loaded into four post-chaises to be conveyed under military guard to London. At four o'clock in the afternoon they reached Canterbury, where they were to spend the night in the town's main hotel. They had been kept separate during the trip, and at the hotel soldiers and constables continued to prevent them from speaking to each other.

The prisoners had become objects of public curiosity. "There was a vast crowd of people in the yard and in the street, more especially at the street windows of the hotel," says Binns. When the entourage left Canterbury on Wednesday, 1 March, at six o'clock in the morning, it encountered a "multitude of people" that "at every favorable position, gathered together to see the procession." A government courier sent ahead to announce their approach gave time for "great numbers" of people to assemble all along the way.[59]

They reached London at about 3:30 in the afternoon. When they arrived at the police office in Bow Street, O'Connor, O'Coigley, and Binns were put in a large back room where they finally found themselves alone and able to talk together. It was then, Binns says, that O'Coigley, "in a tone and with a look of the deepest concern," gave him and O'Connor the bad news: "In his greatcoat pocket, which had been taken by the officers at Margate, there was a treasonable address to the Executive Directory of France."[60] This account is supported by O'Connor, who quotes O'Coigley as saying that if that document were found, "they would hang us all."[61] And indeed, it was not long before they learned that all five of them—O'Connor, O'Coigley, Binns, Allen, and Leary—were charged with the capital crime of high treason for conspiracy to solicit a foreign invasion of England.

They were sent to Cold Bath Fields jail—popularly known among the London poor as "the Bastille"—to await questioning by the privy council. O'Connor says only that he was then "taken to Downing Street to be examined by [Richard] Ford, chief of the police, and after by Pitt and [Henry] Dundas," the Secretary of War.[62] Binns's account of his own interrogation provides more detail:

> *I was shown into an apartment where there were from fifteen to twenty Privy Councilors, seated at the Council Board, which was a long table covered with green cloth, on which were writing materials, papers, maps, charts, and books, of various kinds and sizes. . . . The room was perfectly quiet; whoever spoke, spoke in a low voice.[63]*

Finding himself confronted by Pitt, Dundas, Ford, the Duke of Portland, the Lord Chancellor, and the Attorney-General, among others, Binns says he was momentarily awed but managed to pull himself together. When told he was being charged with high treason, he refused to answer any questions and was returned to prison. O'Connor similarly declined to incriminate himself.

At Cold Bath Fields jail, O'Connor felt he had not been accorded the respect his social status merited. "Of all the furies I ever met," he says, "the wife of the gaoler was the greatest." When he asked her for a cup of tea, "the volley of ribaldry this simple demand called forth" wounded his dignity. She tried to have him put in the same cell with a murderer, but to avoid that indignity, he says, "I passed the night on a chair."[64]

On 7 March the state prisoners were transferred to the Tower of London. O'Connor was put in a room on the ground floor of a house close to that of the governor of the institution, Colonel Smith. Fox visited O'Connor there and wrote to a friend: "When I saw him, he appeared to me to be in a great degree an altered man from what he had been, owing, as I suppose, to his long imprisonment having shaken his health and shattered his nerves, for he seemed exceedingly nervous."[65]

Although the Tower was legendary for harsh treatment of those confined therein, O'Connor was happy to report that "the barbarism of the feudal times . . . has been softened down by modern manners." The two beefeaters assigned to keep their eyes on him were "the civilest guardians I ever met." In contrast to the "fury" at Cold Bath Fields, "the wife of the yeoman where I lodged was the kindest of women." She allowed her six-year old daughter to play in O'Connor's room, which delighted him.[66]

O'Connor and the other inmates remained in the Tower exactly a month. On Saturday, 7 April, they were transferred to the county jail at Maidstone, thirty-six miles from London, to await trial there. The government's desire to hold the trial anywhere but London reflected its resolve to win a conviction against O'Connor, the revolutionary leader it feared most. Martha McTier reflected a widespread opinion when she wrote that "O'Connor has certainly got the worst county and the worst judge in England and I dare say they will if possible hang him."[67] In the previous three years the government had been repeatedly embarrassed when prominent radicals charged with treason had been acquitted by sympathetic London juries. Pitt was determined not to let O'Connor escape his grasp. With regard to the ministry's prosecutorial efforts, Fox commented: "It must be owned they are as unrelenting hunters of lives as ever lived; and I suppose they will have as much pleasure the first time they hit, after so many misses, as ever had the most eager shooter."[68]

Binns provides this account of the journey from London to Maidstone, the county seat of Kent:

> *About half-past six o'clock [in the morning] the whole cavalcade moved slowly forward, and passed the outer gate of the Tower, the other state prisoners, Coigly and O'Connor, being accompanied and disposed of in separate post-chaises. At the outer Tower gate we were received by*

fifty of the London Yeomen Cavalry. . . . The concourse of people was prodigious, considering that our removal was intended to be kept secret, and the early hour at which it had been got under way.[69]

All of this fanfare, Binns realized, was designed "to prejudice and poison the public mind, and especially the minds of those who were to be our jurors."

About fifteen miles from London, we were met by a troop of the Kent Co. Cavalry, to whom we were given in charge; and nine miles further, they were relieved by another party of the same corps. Thus men from every part of the country, farmers and others, were taken from their usual occupations to guard us in prison; these men, on their return, through every part of the country whence our jurors were to be selected, would spread abroad exaggerated accounts of our guilt, and the clearness of the proof against us. It is a fact not unworthy of note, that the two captains who commanded the two divisions of the Kent Yeomanry, which formed our guard, were both on the grand-jury which found the bill of indictment against us.[70]

The procession of prisoners reached Maidstone at four in the afternoon, and there, too, large crowds lined the streets. Inside the jail Binns was led though narrow passageways to a small, dark room where he was locked away. "To get to this very mean habitation I had passed through five heavy doors, all of them strengthened and fastened by iron bolts and bars, chains, and locks."[71]

Binns estimated the room to be about fourteen by twelve feet, with an eight-foot ceiling, and with walls four feet thick. In the door there was a small hinged opening about six inches tall by four inches wide. "Through this little door I sometimes received my victuals and sometimes other communications, and held short conversations and exchanged notes with Coigley and O'Connor, who were each confined in rooms about the same size and on the same platform." They were kept in these cells "22½ hours in every 24."[72]

In that jail at Maidstone, O'Connor says, "new means were resorted to" to torment him in his "secret dungeon, where the light of heaven entered so sparingly" that he could hardly tell night from day. Sleep became all but impossible when the colonel of the regiment on duty "gave an order the sentinels should walk around the prison every five minutes crying as loud as they could, 'All's well.' "[73]

ON TRIAL AT MAIDSTONE

On 11 April a grand jury indicted O'Connor, O'Coigley, Binns, Allen, and Leary on charges of high treason for violating a law that "during the present War between Great Britain and France" prohibited "all traitorous correspondence with, or aid or assistance given to, his Majesty's Enemies."[74] They were arraigned on 30 April and all pleaded not guilty. The trial was postponed for three weeks, apparently to allow the government more time to strengthen its case against O'Connor. Sheridan, in the House of Commons, said he regretted the delay "because I am convinced that Mr Arthur O'Connor is not a traitor, and is incapable of acting hostilely against this country or its constitution."[75]

The trial began on 21 May 1798. Lady Lucy wrote in her diary: "The Tryal at Maidstone (Arthur O'Connor's) came on this day. . . . a kind of melancholy feel came over me which I never had before experienced anything like." The following day she added: "I sat all the evening in painful anxiety. I thought the fate of poor O'C. was then at the point of being decided."[76]

At first glance, the prosecution's case appeared quite strong. The five defendants had been apprehended in highly compromising circumstances. Numerous witnesses confirmed that the men had been travelling under false names and identities and were attempting to illegally hire a boat to take them to France. When arrested, they had told a number of easily disproved lies: they initially claimed not to know each other and all had disclaimed ownership of the luggage, which was found to contain a very large amount of cash—nearly £1,000. The most damaging piece of physical evidence was the treasonous message found in the pocket of O'Coigley's greatcoat, but other suspicious documents were found as well, including some that appeared to incriminate O'Connor.

In his memoirs O'Connor seems to attribute his not being caught red-handed to luck: "By a strange accident my tailor forgot to make pockets to my coat, so that when I was arrested I had not even pockets to contain any papers, nor had I a single scrap of any kind."[77] Nonetheless, a "cypher" was discovered in a razor case in O'Connor's luggage; it was a key to a code he used in corresponding with Lord Edward. A coded letter from O'Connor found in Fitzgerald's possession clearly implied some sort of conspiracy involving France and Ireland. In spite of all this, O'Connor wrote to a number of his friends telling them not to worry because in his opinion the government had no solid evidence against him.

The trial began on a note favorable to the defendants when one of the defense attorneys, Mr. Plumer, revealed a "wicked attempt . . . to tamper with the Jury." As evidence he presented a letter written by a clergyman named

Arthur Young, the son of a well-known author of the same name. In the letter Reverend Young said he had "dined with three of the jurymen of the Blackburn Hundred, who have been summoned to Maidstone, to the trial of O'Connor and company." On that occasion, he wrote, "I exerted all my eloquence to convince them . . . that the felons should swing." He told the prospective jurors that "they should go into Court avowedly determined in their Verdict—no matter what the evidence."[78]

When confronted with the letter Young admitted to having written it, but refused to name the three men he had tried to influence. The government's chief spymaster, William Wickham, opined that O'Connor's eventual acquittal was "entirely due" to the jury's disgust with this flagrant misdeed.[79] Although Wickham overstated its importance, the revelation did create sympathy for the defendants as victims of a campaign to deny them a fair trial.

The government's case centered on the explicitly seditious document discovered in O'Coigley's coat pocket. Although that piece of paper could be directly connected only with O'Coigley, the prosecutor charged that all five men were engaged in a conspiracy to deliver it to the French government, and therefore all were equally guilty of high treason. The "cypher" and the coded letter from O'Connor to Fitzgerald, the prosecutor said in his opening statement, "connect Mr. O'Connor beyond doubt to the treasonous appeal found on O'Coigly."[80]

The code key found in O'Connor's razor case contained forty paired items, including these:

France → Williams
Holland → Gray
England → Richards
Brest → Lisbon
Texel → Embden
Belfast → Boston
L. Swilly → Rhode Island
R. Shannon → New York
Galway → Philadelphia
Shannon → Delaware
Bantry → Chesapeak
Cork → Charles-fort
Wexford Coast → Newfoundland
Wicklow Coast → New England
Dublin Bay → Honduras Bay
Houth Bay → Campechy
1000 men → £1000

Ship of line ➔ A Hogshead
A Frigate ➔ A Tierce
Ireland ➔ Patrickson
A Musket ➔ A Nail
A Cannon ➔ A Jarr
A Six Pounder ➔ Six Quarts[81]

This key was not of much use in decoding some passages of O'Connor's cryptic letter to Lord Edward. For example: "The black terrier and his little brother, are but forty curs; the latter has become a Land-Broker, and, if I am rightly informed, has found the little Priest, and the Sugar Baker, and many others have sent him their money to lay out for them." One line, however, was easy to interpret: "The instant I get to Williams you shall hear from me, I mean to be as active as I can."[82] The very first entry in the key revealed that "Williams" meant "France."

Attorneys Plumer and Dallas did not deny most of the government's allegations, but they offered explanations for their clients' suspicious actions to make them seem reasonable under the circumstances. Why had the defendants been trying to arrange illegal passage to France (a misdemeanor, not high treason)? Because they had fled unjust persecution in Ireland and felt they were in danger of being extradited from England. Sheridan and Erskine both testified that they had personally advised O'Connor to flee the country. Why had the defendants used false names? Because they knew they were committing a misdemeanor. Why had they resisted arrest? Because they feared being sent back to Ireland—O'Connor's experience of having thrice been shot at in prison proved that his life was in danger there. Why had O'Connor written coded letters? Because he was the publisher of an important newspaper—*The Press*—and had to send confidential news reports to his editors. Why was he carrying a large amount of cash in his luggage? Because he had intended to stay abroad for a long time.

O'Connor's lawyers did not even deny that the coded letter found in Lord Edward's possession showed their client promoting a French invasion of Ireland. They insisted, however, that it was irrelevant because the charges in the current trial concerned a French invasion of *England and England alone*, about which the letter said nothing at all.

Mr. Plumer and Mr. Dallas focussed their case on arguing that O'Connor, Binns, Allen, and Leary had no knowledge whatsoever of the seditious document allegedly found in O'Coigley's possession. That contention was almost certainly true. Although O'Connor's intentions were in fact treasonous according to English law, unless he could be connected with the appeal to the French Directory, the prosecutors would lack the necessary proof to convict him.

The defense strategy on behalf of Allen and Leary amounted to manipulating the jurors' class prejudices to convince them that the two lower-class youths lacked the mental capacity to participate in a sophisticated international conspiracy. Allen was described by his lawyer as "a poor, ignorant, uneducated man."[83] Is Allen, another defense lawyer asked the jury, "a person whom you can for one moment believe to have received the wages of treason? Why, the evidence on the part of the Crown informs you what is the miserable condition of this wretched man."[84] (In later life, it should be noted, Allen proved himself a highly competent military leader, rising to the rank of colonel in the French army.[85])

Leary's lowly status as O'Connor's servant was exploited to the hilt. "Gentlemen," one of the defense lawyers declared to the jurors, "you know perfectly well, that we are not in the habit of communicating our plans, even upon ordinary occasions, to those who are in the capacity of domestics about us."[86] Another attorney added: "Good God! Gentlemen, what is his crime? That he is a servant; and for this is that boy now standing at your bar, trembling for his life. Gentlemen, this is my case; it is very plain and very short."[87] The jury apparently accepted this rationale, but ironically it may have been Leary's quick thinking that saved O'Connor from the gallows. Leary later boasted that he dumped O'Connor's incriminating documents in the toilet at the King's Head inn at Margate while the police were in the next room.[88] Leary's claim is uncorroborated but some historians, unwilling to cast doubt on a good story, have simply repeated it without qualification.

The prosecutors inadvertently weakened their case against the defendants by calling ineffectual witnesses, as the following excerpt from the trial transcript demonstrates:

Mary Lemon testifies, examined by Mr. Garrow. She is a servant to Mr. Cloke at the Sun Inn.

Q. Do you remember upon a Sunday night any person whom you now see in Court sleeping at your master's house?

A. Yes.

Q. Which is the person?

A. That man, Binns, (Pointing to Mr. O'Connor).[89]

The witness exhibited further confusion in identifying other people she said she saw, so at the conclusion of her testimony Judge Buller announced, "I have struck her evidence out of my notes."[90]

O'COIGLEY'S DEFENSE

A token effort was made to assert O'Coigley's innocence by suggesting that the incriminating document might have been planted in his coat pocket by persons unknown—perhaps the arresting officers. Although O'Coigley was not wearing the coat when he was arrested—it was found in another room—its pockets also contained French passports in his name and papers identifying him as a Catholic priest. Neither the defendants nor their lawyers held out much hope that O'Coigley would be acquitted.

The same lawyer, Mr. Plumer, was officially representing both O'Connor and O'Coigley, but his four-and-a-half-hour speech to the jury was almost entirely devoted to O'Connor's defense. At one point during the examination of a witness, O'Connor intervened in the questioning, attempting to disassociate himself as much as possible from O'Coigley. The witness was O'Connor's friend, Hugh Bell, at whose home in London he had stayed just before embarking on the journey that ended at Margate:

Mr. O'Connor. Had you any reason, from any thing you heard me say, to suppose that there was any sort of intimacy between Mr. O'Coigly and me, that I should commit myself in any dangerous way with Mr. O'Coigly?

A. I understand not, but that he was entirely a new acquaintance.

Mr. O'Connor. Do you believe that I had any other object in having Mr. O'Coigly with me, than from a good-natured motive to relieve a distressed countryman, from what I told you in confidence as a friend?

A. No motive whatever, except the desire you might have, from good nature, to assist him.

Mr. O'Connor. I will put it stronger. Did I not tell you I was averse to it?

A. Yes, you lamented it.

Mr. O'Connor. Lamented that I was grieved I had allowed Mr. O'Coigly to go with me out of the country?

A. Yes.

Mr. O'Connor. Did I assign any reason for that?

A. Yes, you assigned a reason, you was afraid Mr. O'Coigly had been very indiscreet in mentioning your intention of going out of the country.

At this point Judge Buller interrupted, saying, "Mr. O'Connor, do you not see how much this is at the expence of the other prisoner?"[91] Although O'Connor was later accused in some quarters of selfishly saving his own neck by sacrificing poor O'Coigley,[92] neither Binns nor Allen, nor even O'Coigley himself, seem to have interpreted O'Connor's actions that way.[93]

They apparently recognized that O'Coigley's carelessness had put all of them in danger of hanging, and that the others had no choice but to distance themselves from the treasonable document attributed to him.

In court, and later on the scaffold, O'Coigley vigorously proclaimed his innocence and insisted that the notorious document must have been put in his coat pocket to frame him.[94] As previously mentioned, however, both Binns and O'Connor state in their memoirs that O'Coigley apologetically confided his guilt to them, and their accounts perfectly corroborate each other.[95]

FOXITES TO THE RESCUE

O'Connor's greatest asset in his fight against the Pitt ministry's determination to hang him was the wholehearted support he received from his many friends among the Foxite opposition, and especially from Charles James Fox himself. "It was Fox," O'Connor says, "who conducted all the arrangements of my defense."[96] The list of powerful men who took the stand to swear that they knew O'Connor well, and that they knew him to be completely incapable of any treasonous act or intent, could hardly have been more impressive: Fox, Sheridan, Erskine, the Earl of Suffolk, the Earl of Moira, the Earl of Thanet, the Earl of Oxford, the Duke of Norfolk, Henry Grattan, Michael Angelo Taylor, Lord John Russell, and Samuel Whitbread.[97] As an example of their testimony, here is an excerpt from what Fox said under oath:

> *I always thought Mr. O'Connor to be perfectly well affected to his country; I have always considered him to be a very enlightened man, attached to the principles and the constitution of this country, upon which the present family sit upon the throne, and to which we owe all our liberties.*[98]

After Whitbread stepped down O'Connor's lawyer said that "Mr. Grey, my Lord Lauderdale, and several other gentlemen," were waiting "to give the same testimony." One of the prosecutors challenged the necessity of further encomiums, saying that "it will be understood, from your stating it, that there are many more gentlemen equally respectable."[99] The judge agreed and the parade to the witness stand came to an end.

The testimony of these men was especially relevant in light of the contents of the seditious document at the heart of the prosecution's case. The address from the "Secret Committee of England" included a lengthy diatribe against the Foxites that belittled them as "some few of the opulent" who have "by speeches professed themselves the friends of democracy," and blasted them as "political imposters."[100] The evidence of O'Connor's intimate personal and political relationship with Fox and his friends made it seem obvious that he could have had nothing to do with a document so hostile toward them.

Sheridan almost failed to make it to the trial in time. In a letter to his wife Hecca he said that when he stopped to change horses at Wrotham, ten miles from Maidstone, he heard that the trial was almost over. "In my Life I never spent a more miserable half hour," he wrote to her, "but when I arrived the first thing I saw was a group of my Friends who gave me a welcome that convinced me I was in Time." The prognosis was not completely dismal: "Matters we think look well for O Connor—but I am resolved not to be too sanguine. I got to speak to him this morning—his mind is composed—but his Nerves sadly shaken."[101] O'Connor describes the same encounter:

> On the second day of my trial, as I was entering the court Sheridan and Burdett placed themselves in my passage. I could see the strong apprehensions they entertained for me. Tears started in their eyes. Their fears arose from having heard the address to the Directory brought against me and that the ministers would find some means or other to implicate me in [it]. I shook their hands and entreated them not to affect themselves, that all would be dissipated that day.[102]

Roger O'Connor had traveled from Ireland to aid in Arthur's defense, but he was arrested as soon as he arrived in London and rather harshly returned to Dublin. Then the British authorities issued a warrant for his appearance at Maidstone as a material witness and had him transported back to England.[103] He was never called to testify but at the end of the trial was rearrested and once again sent to a Dublin prison.[104] "The usage of Roger O Connor," Sheridan wrote to Hecca, "has been merciless beyond example." Arthur, he said, "was greatly affected when his poor Brother was brought into Court yesterday, and when the other took his Hand he burst into Tears."[105]

Sheridan and Fox played a trick on the chief prosecutor that O'Connor says "had some influence on the trial":

> Sheridan observed to Fox that, as the Attorney General was excessively susceptible, if he should whisper a criticism it would disconcert him. Accordingly, when Scott had spoken some time, Fox whispered to Sheridan so that Scott might hear him, "This is wretched," which evidently had the effect desired, and when Fox some little time after whispered, "This is worse and worse," the Attorney General could hold no longer and called on the judges to protect him against Mr. Fox, who insulted him. Fox coldly replied he could not conceive why he

should take offense at his complaining of the excessive heat to his friend
Sheridan. This exposed Scott to the laughter of the whole court, and it
was evident he did not recover his aplomb for the rest of his speech.[106]

O'Connor recounts another stunt by the oppositionist politicians that
enlivened the trial. Following testimony concerning the treasonous paper
found in the pocket of a coat belonging to O'Coigley, but which he had not
been wearing,

> *Lord Stanhope in full court took a knife and cut off his pockets, saying*
> *he would not subject his life to the circumstance of any man's putting*
> *a scrap of paper in his pocket while his servant had taken his coat to*
> *brush at the other end of his house.*[107]

LORD MOIRA'S SURPRISING TESTIMONY

The only sour note in the Foxite chorus of tributes to O'Connor on the
witness stand was an exceedingly weak statement offered by the very first of
them to testify, the Earl of Moira. Moira, who had led a bold campaign in the
British and Irish houses of lords exposing the atrocities being perpetrated in
Ireland, was presumed to be well disposed toward O'Connor, but here is the
whole of his testimony:

Q. Has your Lordship any knowledge of Mr. O'Connor, now at the
bar?
A. But very little.
Q. Has your Lordship ever had occasion to converse with him upon
political subjects?
A. I think only once.[108]

This came as a shock to O'Connor because Fox and Sheridan had led
him to believe that all of the oppositionists were prepared to enthusiastically
defend him. He later learned that Fox, too, had been astonished by Moira's
inexplicable performance. O'Connor says that in 1802, when Fox visited
him in Paris, they discussed this incident. Fox told O'Connor that Moira
approached him before the trial and requested that he be the first of the
character witnesses called, because he had had "several important and
confidential conversations" with O'Connor and "his testimony would have
great effect with the jury." However, Fox told O'Connor, "when he appeared
and declared he knew *but very little* of you and that he never conversed with

you *but only once*, not I alone was confounded, but [so was] every man who had heard him declare his evidence was of the utmost importance."[109]

According to O'Connor Moira perjured himself:

> *When this Lord swore he had but very little knowledge of me, he forgot he had frequently invited me to dine at his house, that I as frequently accepted his invitation, that he was so generally regarded as intimate with me, that when Englishmen asked me to dine, Lord Moira was often asked.*[110]

On one occasion, when O'Connor and Moira were leaving a dinner at Lord Suffolk's together, "for more than two hours he ordered his coachman to drive to different places, taking advantage of the privacy his carriage afforded to speak with me of the state of politics in general and of Ireland in particular." Indeed, O'Connor declares, "I can affirm that of all the political men I ever met and knew in England, Lord Moira was the man with whom I had the most frequent and the most particular conversation about Irish politics."[111]

Moira's attitude toward O'Connor's arrest was indicated in a letter to a political ally, the Earl of Charlemont, at the time O'Connor was imprisoned in the Tower: "The persuasion here at present with regard to [Arthur] O'Connor is that nothing can be proved against him, though everybody is satisfied that he was attempting to get to France, and [that] necessarily infers a further guilt."[112] This, however, provides no clue as to Moira's motives for testifying as he did.

Why, O'Connor asks, did Moira "swear falsehoods in a case where my life was the stake?" He says he had once been warned by two leading members of the Catholic Committee in Ireland, Edward Byrne and Randall McDonnell, not to put any confidence in Lord Moira. According to O'Connor, these men told him they had offered Moira "the command of the Catholics in case of an insurrection, but they had the greatest difficulty to get him to decide." Moira was tempted by "the vanity of the command," but ultimately declined, apparently because he believed that any such insurrection was doomed to failure.[113] In retrospect, O'Connor thought that Moira had simply been "very curious to know what was going on" in Ireland, "and in order to pump me he sought every private occasion to confer with me."[114] No doubt O'Connor had been a key provider of "the ammunition for Moira's attack on Pitt's Irish policy,"[115] but that sheds no light on Moira's conduct on the witness stand.

THE VERDICT

Fortunately for O'Connor, the others whom Fox had organized to speak at the trial on his behalf performed according to expectations. The parade of important men had the desired effect: the jurors were awed and Judge Buller was sufficiently intimidated to assure O'Connor's acquittal. Responsibility for the treasonous address was pinned on O'Coigley alone, and the other four defendants were found not guilty.

Judge Buller's charge to the jury before their deliberations all but guaranteed the verdict. After summarizing the testimony against O'Coigley, Buller said, "You see this is extremely strong evidence; and, as I said before, what have you to contradict it?—Nothing."[116] On the other hand, he continued:

> *Before you can convict this prisoner [O'Connor], or Binns, I think you must be satisfied that they knew the contents of this paper [the address from the "Secret Committee of England"], because there is no evidence but that letter, from whence to impute any species of treason, or communications from England to France, to either of them . . . and as to O'Connor there is this circumstance also certainly in favour of him more than in favour of Binns, namely, that the paper, which is the principal thing in question, was not written till the 6th of February, but it is clear, by Mr. Bell's evidence, if you believe him, that Mr. O'Connor had made up his mind about quitting the kingdom and going out of the country so early as the 20th of January.*

Furthermore, Judge Buller said of O'Connor, "I think I may say, generally, that no man's character can be better established, or by men of more respectability and more honour than the witnesses who have been called for him."[117] It seems that Buller was not, after all, "the worst judge in England" for O'Connor, as Martha McTier had feared.[118]

When Buller concluded his summation at ten minutes before 1:00 AM, the jurors withdrew to begin their deliberations. They returned to the courtroom thirty-five minutes later with their verdict: O'Coigley—guilty; O'Connor, Binns, Allen, and Leary—not guilty. O'Coigley was sentenced to be drawn and quartered and the others were acquitted. As Buller read the sentences, pandemonium erupted in the courtroom. Sheridan, naturally enough, described the outburst in theatrical terms: "The whole Court was a scene of general tumult and a scene of panic."[119]

RIOT IN THE COURTROOM

The Pitt ministry had anticipated the possibility that O'Connor might be acquitted and had taken steps to block his release. The Duke of Portland had issued a warrant for O'Connor's rearrest and extradition to Ireland to stand trial there on yet another charge of high treason. As Judge Buller spoke, policemen were rushing to seize O'Connor.

Burdett and others, having received prior warning of this attempt to further detain O'Connor, had planned to offer resistance and if possible to thwart it. A noisy confrontation ensued that quickly escalated into a general melee. Some of the lamps were doused and the courtroom went partially dark. O'Connor was hustled over the bar and toward the door by some of his supporters. Fistfights broke out throughout the room, policemen began flailing about with their batons, a bailiff jumped onto a table wildly brandishing a sword, soldiers rushed in, and the judges hastily retreated through the passageway behind the bench. After several minutes of bedlam, however, the uproar subsided and O'Connor was led back to the bar.

Five men were arrested and later tried for instigating the riot, of whom two were found guilty: one of the defense lawyers, Robert Fergusson, and a young Foxite nobleman, Lord Thanet. According to O'Connor's version of the events, when the news circulated that he was about to be rearrested,

> I was advised to quit the court, but the crowd was so great I could not pass and two bailiffs seized me by the collar. Lord Thanet and Fergusson, who aided me in no act but standing in the passage in the way of the bailiffs, were prosecuted for a rescue and condemned to a year's imprisonment, though the real aggressors were the bailiffs who struck Lord Thanet and Fergusson with their bludgeons.[120]

At the trial of Thanet and Fergusson one eyewitness testified that the instant Judge Buller had stopped speaking,

> Mr. O'Connor raised himself upon the bar: he jumped with his left foot upon the bar; he put his hand upon the shoulder of Mr. [Dennis] O'Brien, and, I think, his right upon Lord Thanet's shoulder, jumped over the bar between Lord Thanet and Mr. O'Brien, passed Mr. O'Brien towards the door of the Court.[121]

Another witness, Thomas Watson, the warden of Maidstone Jail, gave a somewhat different account:

Q. Before [Judge Buller's] sentence was finished, did you say any thing to Mr. O'Connor?

A. I did: I said, "Mr. O'Connor, remember you are not to be discharged, though you may be acquitted." He said, "Why?" and I said, "Because I have no authority to discharge you, and therefore you must not go."

Q. Was any thing said after that to Mr. O'Connor by any body?

A. A person just below him, after sentence was passed, said to Mr. O'Connor, "You are acquitted; what do you stand there for? Why don't you jump over?"

Q. You don't know who that person was, I suppose?

A. No; Mr. O'Connor said, "Mr. Watson says I am not to go." The gentleman below said, "Pshaw! You are acquitted; what do you stay there for? Jump over." He instantly sprung, and I instantly caught hold of the skirt of his coat as he got over, and held him; I then cried out, "Stop him, stop him!" There were some of them shoving him behind to shove him through the wicket, and others shoving him back; but he was so secured, that they got him back into his place again.[122]

John Binns claims in his memoirs: "I had a commanding view of everything which was done in front of the bar. I was attentive to all that was said, and all that was done during the riot." Once O'Connor had jumped over the bar, Binns says, he

> *ran toward the hatch-door on his left hand, which, at a distance of twenty or thirty feet, opened into the audience part of the court-house. Midnight as it was, that portion of the house was crowded, and the large doors, or rather gates, opening to the street on each side, were open for the ingress and egress of the people, and to admit fresh air into the court-house. These gates were guarded by the Maidstone Infantry, some of whom were stationed between the gate and the hatch-door to which O'Connor ran, but through which he was unable to make his way. He was there seized, brought back, and replaced in the bar.*[123]

After O'Connor had been recaptured, but before the tumult in the courtroom had subsided, Sheridan intervened to help restore order, and afterward Judge Buller publicly thanked him for doing so. Sheridan was therefore not among those subsequently charged with causing the riot, but some contemporary observers who knew him well believed that he had in fact been the principal instigator. Lady Holland wrote in her diary that "those who were really the stimulators of the enterprise were Sheridan himself and Dennis O'Brien." (O'Brien, a close friend of Sheridan's, was among those charged in the incident but acquitted.) "Just before the scuffle," she continued, Fergusson

> *leaned across the table to whisper to O'Connor; the truth of the whisper was an endeavour to deliver unseen a note from S[heridan] to O'Connor, the words of which were as follows: "As soon as sentence is passed, leap over the bar, run to the right, and we will manage the rest."[124]*

Lady Holland's allegations may be nothing more than unfounded gossip. In a letter to his wife Hecca, Sheridan denied direct responsibility, saying that O'Connor "had no thought of escaping himself, but three or four injudicious Friends... endeavour'd to hustle him out of Court."[125] Nevertheless, Sheridan's most recent biographer has carefully sifted the evidence and concluded that there "was a plot to free O'Connor, and Sheridan was part of it." Sheridan, he added, "took extraordinary risks for O'Connor."[126]

In addition to O'Connor's upper-class friends, there may also have been more proletarian elements present in the courtroom with plans to help the prisoners escape if convicted. Rumors were circulating that members of the United Englishmen had come from London for that purpose. According to a memoir of John Binns's brother Benjamin, who was a leader of that organization: "The fact is, preparations were made for effecting the prisoner's escape, and post-horses were engaged, and in readiness on the road, to facilitate Coigly's flight."[127] During the courtroom ruckus, however, O'Coigley remained still and made no attempt to flee.[128] Furthermore, in the arrests that followed the incident, no working-class radicals from London were apprehended, so the rumors of their presence may have been false or exaggerated.

After order was restored and O'Connor was returned to the bar, he demanded to know by what authority he had been seized. The Duke of Portland's warrant, dated 22 March, was shown to him. Because the warrant charged him with high treason, O'Connor's lawyers argued that he had just been fairly tried and acquitted on that charge, and therefore should be immediately freed, but the judge said the court did not have the authority to do so. O'Connor then reportedly exclaimed: "I am not afraid of death. If I am to die, let me die here."[129] O'Connor "entreated Buller to interfere, and that if he was to endure the hardship of another confinement, at least allow him to be imprisoned with his brother. Buller behaved with humanity, regretting that the court had no power to interfere."[130] O'Connor was sent back to jail to await being transported to Ireland. Binns, Allen, and Leary were released the following morning.

"You may imagine," Sheridan wrote to his wife, "that Fox and all of us were in sufficient indignation at this horrible Persecution." He received permission from Judge Buller to see O'Connor alone in his cell. "By the Time I got to the Jail O'Connor was in Bed in the dark under a hundred Locks and Bolts." The jail was full of soldiers because they feared another rescue attempt would be made. "At last however I got to him and was with him alone an hour. Notwithstanding his renew'd imprisonment He was in extremely good Spirits tho' He had had nothing to eat or drink the Jail was in such confusion."[131] After visiting O'Connor again the following morning Sheridan returned to London to attempt to broker a deal that would allow Arthur and Roger O'Connor to go into exile in America in exchange for their promise never to "meddle again with either English or Irish politics," but nothing came of the effort.[132]

O'COIGLEY'S FINAL ACT OF RESISTANCE

On 7 June 1798 the Reverend James O'Coigley was executed at Pennington Heath. He was hanged and his body was beheaded, but he was not subjected to the medieval torture of drawing and quartering, "the King having graciously remitted the remainder of the sentence."[133] Before his execution, however, he had been subjected to such intense pressure to turn against his United Irish comrades that he told friends he would have committed suicide had his religion not prohibited it.

The English government routinely made use of clergymen to extract confessions or information from condemned prisoners.[134] Undersecretary of State William Wickham wrote a letter marked "Secret" to Edward Cooke on 21 April 1798:

> *I have the satisfaction to inform you, that Mr. Coigley has desired a Catholic Priest to confess him, and that he has declared that he shall have no objection to having one chosen by Government. Much will depend on the choice of the Person, and as pains are taken to make a good one, I have hopes that Quigley will make a full disclosure of every thing.*[135]

The man they chose was one Father Griffin (or Griffiths). O'Connor remarks that the priest had been "sent, [O'Coigley] said, by Pitt to make him the offer of his life on the condition he would inform against me."[136]

John Binns says that when they were all in Maidstone jail O'Coigley passed notes to him through the small opening in his cell door. The notes alerted Binns to the government's efforts to manufacture a case against him and O'Connor:

For some weeks a Catholic priest was closeted daily, and for hours,
every day, locked in the room with the Rev. Mr. Coigley, promising
him that his life should be spared if he would make a full discovery
of all he knew touching my brother's late visit to Ireland, and give
evidence against O'Connor and I.[137]

Binns quotes one of O'Coigley's notes as saying that Father Griffin

used every means that cunning, unbounded zeal, or pretended piety
and religion could invent to induce me to make an entire confession to
Government of everything I knew; asked if I would swear against my
fellow-prisoners, O'Connor and you in particular.[138]

According to a memoir written by O'Coigley himself, Father Griffin told
him the government "had no design upon my life, as their whole aim was
directed against Mr. O'Connor." He also said that Griffin not only offered
to spare his life if he would testify for the government, but threatened his
brothers and his elderly parents if he did not.[139] Despite his weaknesses,
O'Coigley exhibited an admirable strength of character in resisting the
government agent's harassment. Benjamin Binns reports that "though heavily
ironed, he pushed [Father Griffin] out of his cell."[140] O'Coigley went to
the gallows defiantly, becoming yet another martyr to the cause of Ireland's
freedom.

If O'Coigley had turned King's evidence and betrayed O'Connor and
Binns, would it have led to their conviction? In his memoirs, O'Connor
discounts that possibility, saying that O'Coigley "had no more to swear by
me than the man I never saw." Therefore, O'Connor concludes: "I declare
I had not the most distant obligation" to O'Coigley for refusing to testify
against him.[141] This sentiment seems not only ungenerous but naïve in its
apparent assumption that O'Coigley, with the government's prompting,
could not have invented false testimony that might have led the jury to find
O'Connor guilty.

The morning after the riot in the courtroom Fox, Sheridan, Grey, and
Whitbread visited O'Connor in jail, giving him "the exquisite pleasure of
seeing every mark of affection and expressing my love and gratitude" to
them.[142] Soon thereafter O'Connor was on his way to Ireland under a military
escort. "The first night," he says, "I was lodged in an inn, a sergeant placed
two dragoons at each side of my bed with pistols loaded and cocked with
orders to blow my brains out if I stirred." When he was left alone with his
sentinels, however, they assured him they would rather see the sergeant dead
"than touch a hair of my head." The following day, "four men of the regiment
[the Scotch Greys] offered to set me at liberty, so well was Scotland disposed

towards Ireland."[143] O'Connor reached Dublin without incident; he would pass the next few months in three of that city's penal institutions: Marshalsay, Kilmainham, and Newgate.[144]

IRELAND IN REBELLION

The Ireland to which O'Connor returned at the end of May 1798 was in the throes of rebellion, and by the time he arrived the revolt had already run much of its tragic course. Ferocious military repression in the north throughout 1797 had stimulated an escalating cycle of violent resistance and savage government reprisals that had spread beyond Ulster to engulf all of Ireland by early 1798. By March the campaign of military terrorism had sparked widespread uprisings in Kildare, Carlow, Wicklow, and Wexford.

On 30 March the government proclaimed the entire country in a state of rebellion and imposed nationwide martial law. As O'Connor and the other United Irish leaders had recognized, it would not be possible to restrain the justified wrath of the oppressed people indefinitely. With or without French assistance—and with or without United Irish leadership—the people were rising.

In addition to O'Connor, almost all of the other primary leaders of the United Irish Society were behind bars. The decisive blow had been struck by the government on 12 March when police, guided by an informer's tip, raided a meeting of the United directory at Oliver Bond's house and arrested all those present. After that, of the major leaders only Lord Edward remained at large. The organization then came under the control of second- and third-tier leaders who were less committed to the strategy of patiently awaiting the arrival of French troops. As the social crisis had obviously reached the point of spontaneous combustion, the remaining leaders felt they could hesitate no longer and issued a formal call to rise on 23 May.

On 19 May Lord Edward, betrayed by another informer, was arrested and wounded in a shoot-out.[145] The wounds Fitzgerald received proved fatal and he died on 4 June. Meanwhile the Rebellion had begun in earnest, releasing the repressed fury that had accumulated over decades of oppression. At the end of May and the beginning of June—at precisely the time when O'Connor was arriving in Ireland—an army of twenty thousand rebels took over the town of Wexford. By the beginning of June another massive rebel army in Wicklow was threatening to move against Dublin. The insurrectionaries, however, were at a significant disadvantage in arms. Fighting with pikes against British cannons, they were decisively defeated at Vinegar Hill. The delayed rising in Ulster finally began on 7 June, but it was crushed within a week.

The final scene of the Rebellion occurred in the west of Ireland when—at long last—the French arrived. On 22 August a force of about a thousand French soldiers under the command of General Jean-Joseph Humbert landed at Killala in the province of Connaught. By that time, however, the rest of Ireland had been brutally pacified and the full strength of the English armies could be brought to bear against Humbert's relatively small band of men. After some initial successes, Humbert surrendered at Ballinamuck, County Longford, on 8 September, and the Rebellion was over. In its aftermath the general populations of both north and south were treated with great brutality.

During these tragic events O'Connor remained behind bars, a helpless onlooker. "On arriving at Dublin," O'Connor says,

> I was assailed with every circumstance that could tear the heart.
> The chosen friend of my soul in the agony of death by the hands of
> the assassins that attacked him . . . and the people throughout all
> Ireland beaten after a contest without arms, ammunition, leaders,
> or discipline, pursued in every direction and butchered in cold blood
> without resistance.[146]

O'Connor characterized the failed rebellion as an "ill-fated, ill-concerted, wretchedly ill-executed attempt at emancipation from English tyranny." What he had dreaded most, he says, is what had come to pass: a rising without "enlightened tolerant leaders" had been doomed to "degenerate into papist bigotry by falling into the direction of papal priests."[147] It was a common misconception among O'Connor's contemporaries that the Catholic clergy had played a major leadership role in the Rebellion.[148]

In his memoirs O'Connor proclaims his intention to "give the public the true account" of the debacle. "I have read all the accounts which have [been] published of it," he says, "and I find them all written by men who knew nothing of the hand which had moved the affair of the Union from the day the separation was resolved on."[149]

The underlying cause of the Rebellion, he says, "lay in the six hundred years of English tyranny" that had left Ireland in "disorder, poverty, turbulence and wretchedness." But the *immediate* cause was the deliberate policy of Pitt "to madden the people" in order to draw them into open insurrection. "The rising on the 23 of May 1798 was wholly his doing," O'Connor declares; "If I could have prevented it, assuredly it would not have taken place." He further asserts that "had Edward not been arrested and killed . . . the rising could not have been forced on the people."[150] These categorical avowals—written many decades after the fact—must be balanced by the evidence that at the beginning of 1798 O'Connor and Fitzgerald represented the more militant faction within the United Irishmen that was prepared to initiate an insurrection without French assistance.

The government's success in beheading the movement by capturing its leaders resulted in an uncoordinated series of local risings in which, O'Connor says, no two "had the smallest understanding with another," and "no two men had the smallest confidence in each other, such was the absence of all discipline." Furthermore, "The sole force of the Irish peasants lay in their numbers but it never entered their heads to form an oblique to attack the enemy by its flank or in its rear. The army without its officers is a body without its eyes." Lord Edward's death was the final setback: "On him rested, and on him only, all the means of giving unity of action to the movement, and when this unity was totally wanting, every hope of success must vanish."[151]

By contrast, O'Connor describes how a well-coordinated insurrection could have been accomplished—if only the leadership had been able to remain intact. After Hoche's failed expedition to Bantry Bay, he says,

> *I had organized a plan. The organization of the United Irishmen was so perfect that in five days I could send a question to any part of Ireland and get an answer. By this means I knew the number of the government troops that were stationed in every part of Ireland. Our organization was by Baronies and Counties and Provinces. According to the number of the enemy, the attack was to be made by one, two or more Baronies. As the rising was to be simultaneous over the whole island, the order was that after the first day's attack, all the Baronial Corps, as well those who had been victorious as those that had not, were to assemble at the given point in the County, and march together against the corps of the enemy which had not been beaten. . . . The two first attacks, it was presumed, would enable the United force to have procured a considerable augmentation of arms and ammunition, so all those who were provided with them were to repair to the headquarters of the two armies of Ulster and Leinster commanded by Edward and me. . . . What is essential for the perfect understanding of this plan is the state the contending parties would have held after the armies of Ulster and Leinster were formed, both moving on the capital. It is not possible to conceive how the English government could have resisted two armies composed each of a hundred thousand men led by men who possessed their confidence.*[152]

However, the Rebellion did not proceed according to O'Connor's plan. Instead of being at the head of a liberated Ireland, he and his comrades found themselves in Dublin prisons with a decidedly reactionary Irish parliament loudly demanding their immediate execution.

PART III

Prison and Exile

1798–1852

7

From Kilmainham to Fort George

ONE OF THE MOST remarkable facts about Arthur O'Connor's life is that it did not end in 1798. At the beginning of 1799 O'Connor wrote that for the previous three years he had "lived in constant habits of intimacy with death." There had not been a night that the grim reaper "has not sat perched on my pillow, not a step have I taken that he has not walked by my side."[1] He was not being overly dramatic. The attempts to assassinate him when he was in Dublin Tower were genuine and his acquittal on capital charges at Maidstone had by no means been a foregone conclusion. But it was after his rearrest and forced return to Dublin that his life was in greatest danger. In the wake of the Rebellion the Protestant ultras were thirsting for vengeance, and O'Connor, their most notorious enemy, was apparently at their mercy.

With the insurrection crushed, an estimated 30,000 rebels already dead, and the surviving insurrectionists disarmed, local authorities throughout Ireland were carrying out wholesale executions of their vanquished foes with little pretense of adhering to the rule of law. In Dublin, however, the imprisoned leaders of the United Irishmen were in an international spotlight that required the government to at least pay token respect to legal formalities before hanging them. In July 1798 a series of trials began with John and Henry Sheares as the first defendants. The Sheares brothers were believed by the government to have been central leaders of the United Irishmen, but O'Connor wrote to the historian Madden in 1842: "You seem to think the Sheares were leading men in the Union, whereas I may say they never entered

139

it, so as to be known to us."[2] Nevertheless, John and Henry Sheares were found guilty of high treason and hanged.

The testimony of a turncoat, Thomas Reynolds, led to the conviction of three more of the state prisoners: John McCann, Michael William Byrne, and Oliver Bond. McCann was executed, and Byrne and Bond were scheduled to follow in rapid succession. At that point, however, negotiations between the government and the state prisoners were initiated. O'Connor says that the renowned liberal lawyer John Philpot Curran visited him in prison and told him that "some of the ruling party in Ireland" were "sick of the quantity of the blood that was flowing, among those several of the General Officers."[3]

The "ruling party in Ireland" was accountable—in the final analysis—not to the Irish Protestant zealots but to the Pitt ministry in England. The new lord lieutenant and military commander-in-chief of Ireland, Lord Cornwallis, was sufficiently politically astute to understand that gratuitous brutality against the now disarmed and defenseless populace and their imprisoned leaders would only breed a new generation of rebels, which would perpetually undermine Britain's governance of Ireland.

THE KILMAINHAM PACT

Realizing that Cornwallis saw it to be in England's interest to stop the bloodshed in Ireland, some of the United Irish leaders offered him a compromise: They would make a full confession of their revolutionary activities if the government would spare the lives of Byrne and Bond and allow the other state prisoners, themselves included, to go into voluntary exile. Their proposal was accepted, though not in time to save Byrne. The agreement, later altered in significant ways, became known informally as the "Kilmainham pact." Cornwallis subsequently submitted a comprehensive report on the affair to the British secretary of state, the Duke of Portland, entitled "A Narrative of such verbal and written Communications as have passed between Government and the State Prisoners."[4]

The idea of the negotiations reportedly began with a liberal aristocrat, Lord Charlemont. He sent a lawyer, Francis Dobbs, to sound out the prisoners, many of whom were receptive to the proposal. On 24 July 1798 Dobbs presented Castlereagh with a paper signed by seventy of the state prisoners—O'Connor was not among them—and Castlereagh transmitted it to Cornwallis that same evening. The next morning Cornwallis discussed it with high-ranking members of the Irish government who unanimously opposed the prisoners' proposition. The main reasons they gave for their opposition were

> *that several of the most notorious traitors, particularly the O'Connors*
> *and [William] Sampson, had not signed . . . and that their offer of*
> *giving information did not, to them, appear in point of advantage to*
> *counterbalance the discontent which would be occasioned by saving*
> *two of the most leading traitors from the punishment due to their*
> *crimes.*

"Their reasoning," however, "did not altogether satisfy the Lord-Lieutenant."[5] (Although the narrative quoted here was an official representation of Cornwallis's views, it referred to him in the third person as "the Lord-Lieutenant" and "his Excellency.")

Byrne's execution was scheduled for 26 July and Bond's for the following day. In order to pressure O'Connor and the other holdouts into joining the compact, Cornwallis allowed Byrne's hanging to proceed. It was a successful ploy. The morning after Byrne was executed, Dobbs again called on Castlereagh and "intimated to him that Arthur O'Connor, Sampson, Hampden Evans, and several others, who had declined signing the paper, were now desirous of soliciting the mercy of the Crown, in common with the other prisoners."[6]

Cornwallis reassembled the Irish government leaders to tell them of the new circumstances, but this time he "strongly expressed his disposition" to delay Bond's execution in order to facilitate an agreement with the prisoners.[7] He also now had the support of the chancellor, John Fitzgibbon, who had been absent from the previous meeting. Although Fitzgibbon's biographer describes him as "the most arrogant and obdurate champion of the Protestant oligarchy," he was more astute than his colleagues, who were "cruder, less intelligent reactionaries." Fitzgibbon "had no pity for the state prisoners" and "held them all in the utmost contempt," but his "habit of ingratiating himself with the lord-lieutenant" ensured his backing for Cornwallis's policy.[8] The official narrative simply says that the Irish politicians' opinion "perfectly coincided with that of his Excellency" because "the offer of O'Connor to disclose his treasons, appeared to them to make it highly expedient to entertain the proposition so submitted."[9]

Cornwallis's motives were not difficult to discern. He wanted to present an undeniable case to the Irish and English public—and above all to the Foxite oppositionists—that the Irish state had indeed been the target of a widespread international revolutionary conspiracy. That could be accomplished by prosecutions only if credible convictions could be won against O'Connor and other state prisoners. The only solid evidence against them, however, was based on information provided by confidential spies and informers—especially Samuel Turner and Leonard McNally—who could not testify in open court because the government did not want to reveal their identities. Cornwallis and his allies therefore felt that "the confessions of the State Prisoners, particularly of M'Nevin and [Arthur] O'Connor" were "the only effectual means of opening the eyes of both countries, without disclosing intelligence which could by no means be made public."[10] They considered Roger O'Connor's continued refusal to cooperate to be of minor consequence.

Undersecretary Cooke at Dublin Castle stated another reason for the decision: "It was to be feared that many Executions would raise Criminals into martyrs." But the most potent consideration was that if

> all the Capital Traitors, Emmet, O'Connor, McNevin etc. were to come forward, confess themselves conspirators and traitors and engaged for above two years in a correspondence with France . . . what an overthrow would such a confession be to all the Lord Moiras, Mr. Foxes, Duke of Bedfords, Judge Bullers, Maidstone Juries etc.[11]

The Pitt ministry was especially anxious to compromise the Foxites with O'Connor's testimony. William Wickham wrote to Castlereagh:

> It will certainly not escape your Lordship that the nature and extent of Mr. O'Connor's connection in this country should, if possible, be accurately known. It is difficult to believe that some few of his friends here should not have known the real object of one, if not both, his journeys, and it would be a great satisfaction to the Government here to have that line very distinctly drawn.[12]

It was not mere personal gratification that Pitt and Cornwallis were seeking in their desire to triumph over Fox and his friends. It was, to the contrary, completely a matter of *realpolitik*. They were planning a radical revision of British policy toward Ireland, and hoped to silence their parliamentary opponents by embarrassing them. Their success was manifested by the passage and implementation of the Act of Union in January 1801, which tightened England's grasp on Ireland ever further by ending even the formality of legislative independence.

WHY O'CONNOR SIGNED

In an open letter published early in 1799 O'Connor explained that he did not sign the original appeal for negotiations because it asked only for the reprieve of the state prisoners, and with "the massacre of my unarmed countrymen still raging, I did not think that any object, which was not general, could warrant me, in whom such confidence was placed by so many millions of my countrymen, to enter into any such compact." Furthermore, he feared "the possibility of its being attributed to a desire to save my own life." In any event, it seemed to him that "to save the lives of Bond and Byrne, enough had signed" to induce the ministers to acquiesce. "But," he added, "in this I was deceived"—Byrne was hanged despite the other prisoners' offer. The pending execution of Oliver Bond was particularly disturbing to O'Connor, because Bond was "a beloved friend, whom I myself had brought into the undertaking."[13]

"Thus environed with horrors," O'Connor wrote, "it was intimated to me" that the ministers had made his participation in the compact "a sine qua non." He decided that he would enter into negotiations as a step toward "putting a stop to the indiscriminate massacre of a disarmed people." He consented to meet with Castlereagh but, he added, "I expressly stipulated, that some men upon whose honor I could rely, should accompany me—Emmet and McNevin were accordingly joined with me, upon the part of the state prisoners."[14] The meeting was held on Sunday, 29 July; in addition to Castlereagh the government was represented by Edward Cooke and the Chancellor, Lord Clare.

O'Connor sensed that Cornwallis was very anxious to gain his cooperation. Therefore, in spite of being a prisoner facing a death sentence he found himself in a momentary position of strength with regard to the negotiations, and he pressed his advantage. His concern, he later wrote, "was to make the terms as wide as I could. I could not consent to give any information whatever, unless I was assured that no more blood should be shed for any thing that had passed in the Union."[15]

O'Connor, Emmet, and MacNeven made it clear that in the course of their confessions "they should not be required to implicate persons by name."[16] They also insisted that this and all other terms of the agreement into which they were entering be put into writing. That evening the following statement of the terms of the compact, signed by more than seventy of the state prisoners (this time including O'Connor), was delivered to Castlereagh:

> *That the undersigned state prisoners, in the three prisons of Newgate, Kilmainham, and Bridewell engage to give every information in their power, of the whole of the internal transactions of the United Irishmen, and that each of the prisoners should give detailed information of every transaction, that has passed between the United Irishmen and foreign states; but that the prisoners are not, by naming or describing, to implicate any person whatever, and that they are ready to emigrate to such country*

as shall be agreed on between them and government . . . if on their so doing they are to be freed from prosecution, and also Mr. Oliver Bond be permitted to take the benefit of this proposal. The state prisoners also hope that the benefit of this proposal may be extended to such persons in custody, or not in custody, as may choose to benefit by it.[17]

Cornwallis's narrative reveals that O'Connor was correct in perceiving himself to be in a strong negotiating position. The lord lieutenant decided to accept these conditions without quibbling over the wording because he believed that "O'Connor and Emmett, particularly the former, were most reluctant to accede" to the agreement "and would willingly have availed themselves of any pretence which might justify them to their own party in refusing" to sign it. He did not want to take a chance on "losing the now substantial advantage of having the treasons of the distinguished members of the Union proved by their own confession."[18]

THE "CONFESSION"

"Pursuant to this agreement," O'Connor wrote, "Emmet, McNevin and I drew up a memoir containing thirty-six pages, giving an account of the origin, principles, conduct, and views of the Union."[19] It was not, however, a contrite confession that they signed and delivered to Castlereagh on 4 August, but a defiant manifesto justifying the aims and deeds of the United Irishmen.[20] (See Appendix One for the full text.) Two days later Cooke came to their prison and, O'Connor says, although "acknowledging that the memoir was a perfect performance of our agreement," he deemed it unacceptable. He told them "that Lord Cornwallis had read it, but, as it was a vindication of the Union, and a condemnation of the ministers, the government, and legislature of Ireland, he could not receive it, and therefore he wished we would alter it." O'Connor replied that "we would not change one letter, it was all true, and it was the truth we stood pledged to deliver."[21]

Both parties to the Kilmainham pact struggled to shape the public perception of the state prisoners' "confession." The government wanted it to be seen as an abject surrender on the part of the United Irish leaders, while the latter portrayed themselves as prisoners of war forced to make concessions but violating no principles of honor.

Cooke said that the government would publish an abridged version of the statement and did not want the rest to be made public, but the prisoners refused to relinquish their right of "publishing the memoir entire."[22] A compromise was reached whereby O'Connor, Emmet, and MacNeven agreed to be examined before committees of the Irish parliament; the government could then ask them any questions it desired and publish the transcripts of their replies.

Cornwallis's narrative acknowledged that after the three had appeared before committees of the house of lords and the house of commons, "it was the unanimous opinion of both Committees that . . . they had fairly adhered to the spirit of their engagement."[23] Nevertheless, the government published only highly selective excerpts of their answers. O'Connor's testimony was contained in a page and a half of the official government version, but when the prisoners (after their release) published their own version it ran to twenty-nine pages.[24] Although the latter was not an official verbatim transcript, O'Connor explained that after the two sessions (on 9 and 16 August) he put his testimony in writing "the instant I came back to my prison."[25] (See Appendix Two.)

Meanwhile, the United Irish leaders utilized all means at their disposal to counter the government's portrayal of their admissions. On 27 August an "advertisement" signed by O'Connor, Emmet, and MacNeven appeared in two newspapers, the *Hibernian Journal* and *Saunders' News Letter*, condemning the official account of their examinations before the parliamentary committees.[26] The newspapers had also managed to obtain the full text of the state prisoners' original statement that the government tried to suppress, but O'Connor, Emmet, and MacNeven explicitly denied having leaked it to the newspapers.[27]

The timing of the protest was especially troubling to the government because just five days earlier, on 22 August, the French invasion force led by General Humbert had appeared in the west of Ireland and threatened to reignite the Rebellion. Alexander Marsden, Cornwallis's secretary, wrote on 29 August: "The aim of the prisoners evidently was to encourage a revolt now that news had arrived of the landing of the French in Killala Bay." Marsden held separate meetings in prison with O'Connor, Emmet, and MacNeven, all three of whom denied any such intention. Their motive, they all told Marsden, was simply "to do away with the misrepresentations of their Examinations which had appeared in the Newspapers." Marsden reported, however, that when asked to be more specific, "O'Connor could not recollect any particular misrepresentation in the Newspapers." O'Connor's complaint had to do with errors of omission, not commission: "*All* that he had said, had not been given, but nothing he had said [with one exception] had been misstated."[28]

The manner in which Cornwallis and Castlereagh wanted the world to perceive the prisoners' concessions was made clear when a newspaper, the *Courier*, revealed how the Kilmainham pact was presented to the Irish parliament. The United Irish leaders were said to have admitted to "flagrant and enormous guilt, expressed contrition, and humbly implored mercy."[29] Samuel Neilson immediately wrote to the *Courier*, protesting that "none of us, so far as I know, did either acknowledge a crime, retract an opinion, or implore pardon—our object was to stop an effusion of blood."[30] O'Connor later published an open letter to Castlereagh in which he thundered: "I challenge you to produce a syllable that has come from me" that could be construed as "a confession of a consciousness of guilt, an expression of contrition, or any imploring of mercy."[31]

Angered by the repudiations, Cornwallis threatened to retaliate by voiding the Kilmainham pact and resuming the executions.[32] O'Connor believed this to be a bluff, and he was apparently correct. The prisoners were, however, put in solitary confinement and closely watched for the next three months to prevent them from smuggling more messages to newspapers from their prisons.

These measures did not stop the appearance in January 1799 of O'Connor's powerful open letter to Castlereagh, a forty-eight-page pamphlet that circulated widely, to the government's chagrin. Martha McTier commented that "AO's letter to C[astlereagh] steals quickly round to all parties."[33] If O'Connor's main concern had been for his personal safety or comfort, he certainly would not have published it, but his purpose was to reassure rank-and-file United Irishmen throughout the country that their leaders had not capitulated and betrayed their cause. He also wanted to publicly refute the accusation that his admissions contradicted what Fox and his colleagues had said under oath at the Maidstone Trial.

THE FOXITES' EMBARRASSMENT

On the surface, O'Connor's admission that he had negotiated a French invasion of Ireland made it seem that Fox, Sheridan, and the other oppositionists who had testified on his behalf had either been woefully naïve or deliberately complicit in treason. Pitt and his allies mercilessly hammered them with these charges. A widely circulated pamphlet counterposed quotations from the Foxites' encomiums on O'Connor's loyalty to quotations from O'Connor's disclosures to the parliamentary committee.[34] But O'Connor insisted that "nothing ever has, or ever can, consistent with truth, come from me, which can impeach the credit of the great and good men in question." In the first place, he pointed out, the government had seen fit to publish only about one percent of the information he had presented in accord with the Kilmainham pact. If the other ninety-nine percent contained falsehoods, he demanded,

why have I not been exposed by their being published? If they
contain . . . a syllable that impeaches the credit of the opposition
of England, is it credible that they would not have been published?
Give them every line to the world, and if they contain dereliction
of my principles, breach of my engagements, treason to my cause or
my country, or perfidy to my friends, let me be overwhelmed by the
infamy attendant on instant exposure.[35]

Whether people considered O'Connor to be a traitor or not depended upon whether they believed England had a right to dominion over Ireland. Irish patriots, of course, did not consider it treasonable to try to break the connection with England by any means necessary, but British jingoes did. "The charge against me at Maidstone," O'Connor pointed out, "was wholly confined to England; Ireland or its politics were not mentioned in the indictment."[36] Because he had never solicited a French invasion of England, neither he nor his supporters had violated the truth in anything they had said during the trial. Furthermore, the idea that he would have told the Foxites— "those men, who on a change of ministry must form the administration of England"—about his negotiations with Hoche and the French Directory "is too absurd to be mentioned by the most malignant calumniator, or to be credited by the most deludable dupe."[37]

As for his revolutionary views concerning Ireland, they were no secret to anyone in the world, because he had published them repeatedly under his own name:

I refer you to the whole of my second address to the electors of the
County of Antrim, in which I have openly asserted the right of forming
an alliance with France, and if this not be sufficient, I refer you to the
State of Ireland I published, in which I have justified resistance, and
calling in foreign assistance.[38]

Sheridan used some of the same arguments to defend himself on the floor of the house of commons. He had not said anything at O'Connor's trial concerning rebellion in Ireland "because it had nothing to do with the particular charge at Maidstone." He might disagree with O'Connor "respecting the remedy that was to be applied to the situation of Ireland; but upon that point he was not called upon to say any thing." And finally, "Mr. O'Connor never had made him his confidant" concerning his dealings with France.[39]

Although some of the Foxites seem to have been embarrassed by O'Connor's revelations, none were seriously inconvenienced. Many later shunned him in the belief that he had betrayed them, but Fox and Sheridan apparently continued to think fondly of him.

THE TRANSFER TO FORT GEORGE

O'Connor's *Letter to Lord Castlereagh* bitterly protested the government's failure to live up to the promises of the Kilmainham pact. The state prisoners expected to be sent into exile as soon as they had fulfilled their side of the bargain by testifying before the parliamentary committees, but after they had done so they were told that they would not be released until the war with France had ended.[40] Some consideration had initially been given to allowing them to emigrate to the United States, but the American ambassador, Rufus King, squelched that possibility. "I certainly do not think that they will be a desirable acquisition to any Nation," King wrote to the Duke of Portland, "but in none would they be likely to prove more mischievous than in mine."[41] His lobbying effort succeeded; it was reported to Castlereagh that "the Americans absolutely refuse to admit O'Connor and the rest of the Irish traitors into their territories."[42] The United Irish leaders therefore remained behind bars.[43]

Stung by O'Connor's vehement public protest, the government decided to put a stop to such remonstrations by isolating the most "uncontrite" prisoners and making their communications with the outside world as difficult as possible. Accordingly, on 18 March 1799 Arthur and Roger O'Connor and fourteen others were told to pack their belongings and prepare for immediate departure.[44] They were not told where they were being taken, but at six o'clock the next morning they were put aboard a ship leaving Ireland. On 25 March four more prisoners were picked up at Belfast, and on 9 April they all arrived at their destination: Fort George, Scotland, on the south coast of Moray Firth, fifteen miles northeast of Inverness.[45] One of the Belfast men, William Steel Dickson, later published a detailed narrative of their journey and their confinement. Upon arrival,

> twenty rooms, each between sixteen and eighteen feet square, were allotted us by ballot, sixteen of which were laid with brick over the boarded floor. On taking possession, we found them clean, dry, airy, well plaistered and ceiled, with windows sufficiently large, well glazed, and secured, on the outside, with iron bars. In each room was a neat four-posted bed.

In addition to good curtains, sheets, and blankets, each room had "a rush bottomed chair, and small oaken table; a bottle and basin, a commode, fire-irons, coal-box, candlestick, snuffers and extinguisher; all entirely new and good in their kind." The twenty prisoners had four servants assigned to them: "two to make our beds, keep our rooms clean, and do other chamber and personal services; and the other two, to keep our knives, forks, spoons, &c. as they ought to be, bring our provisions from the inn, and attend us at table."[46] O'Connor had no idea how long he would be held there, but in fact Fort George would be his home for the next three years and three months, until the Peace of Amiens in March 1802 brought the war between Britain and France to a temporary end.

At first, Dickson reports, "our confinement was not only almost uninterrupted and solitary, but such as nearly precluded conversation, even during the few hours that our doors were unlocked."[47] The gregarious O'Connor was afflicted by loneliness, alleviated only by having Roger there with him, at least for the first year and a half. He was not entirely cut off from external contact. Jerry Leary frequently sent him news and packages from London and he corresponded with a few of his friends. The most faithful of them, Lady Lucy, preserved some of his letters together with drafts of her replies; their correspondence suggests that the two most salient characteristics of O'Connor's prison experience were boredom and cold. "This place," he complained, "is dullness itself."[48]

"This Siberian climate has kept me in a constant state of suffering," he told her.[49] "All is covered in snow and coldness in Lat[itude] 58," even in the springtime.[50] "What an element for a hot house plant like me."[51] It was even harder on his brother: "R[oger] is very poorly, this cold region agrees but ill with him."[52] Eventually Roger became so sick that he appeared close to death; not wanting to make a martyr of him, on Christmas day 1800 the government transferred him to Newgate Jail in London and the following month released him.[53] After Lucy had seen Roger in England, Arthur wrote her:

> *You see what ravages this northern climate has made upon poor R. He will require the coming summer in a congenial clime to set him up and some repose in the midst of his family. To me the loss of his society is irreparable but the reflection that it was absolutely necessary for the prolonging his life more than counterbalances any inconvenience I felt.*[54]

As for his own health, he attempted to preserve it by daily ice-water baths. The man in charge at Fort George, Mr. Stewart, was a humane prison administrator who tried to make his inmates' stay as tolerable as possible. A letter from Stewart to the government offices in London reports:

It is the intention of Mr. Arthur O'Connor, and some others, to ask permission to bathe in the sea during the summer. I request to have Your Lordship's directions on that head. Should permission be given, I do not apprehend any danger of escape or any attempt that way, as the sea comes up to the foot of the Ramparts.[55]

Permission was granted. O'Connor availed himself of the privilege, and not only in the summertime. In a February letter he wrote: "I bathe every day be it frost or snow. I do so to kick myself from being too tender which is one of the worst consequences of close confinement."[56]

But alas, the extreme regimen was not completely successful. In May 1801 Arthur wrote to Lucy: "I received your letters some days ago, but was too ill to write. In a few weeks I shall have passed my fifth birthday in prisons. It cannot then be matter of surprise that my health should yield to such powerful opponents." On the other hand, he believed he had been able to adequately preserve his mental health: "I felt the value of this the more, from often witnessing, during my prison life, many victims to despondency, occasioned by seclusion. This inevitably happens to those who have no resource in themselves."[57]

His seclusion was at least partially self-induced: "Were I to tell you how few hours I have been out of this room in which I now write, for nearly two years that I have been in this prison, you would think it strange."[58] According to Dickson, the prison regimen eventually eased considerably: "now, our restraints are nearly done away. We have liberty of all each others apartments, and may amuse ourselves as we please, within the bounds prescribed, from eight in the morning, till nearly nine in the evening."[59] But neither of the O'Connor brothers had much to do with the other United Irish inmates. "There is no one here [Roger] knew in Ireland," he wrote to Lucy; "indeed, I know very few of them myself. How I am a perfect hermit and I fear the habit will be so strong upon me that I shall continue one all my life."[60] He added:

It has so happened that there are none of the persons imprisoned with whom I could form any friendship. The habits of men must have been similar for to found friendships, and mine happen to be very dissimilar from those persons, hence I have continued in the ignorance of them.[61]

Lucy was the only one of O'Connor's aristocratic friends who stayed in contact with him throughout the entire period of his incarceration. "All my correspondents have fallen off," he told her (although he subsequently received a very warm message from Burdett just as he was about to leave

Fort George).[62] In addition to letters, Lucy sent him numerous gifts. "I have many of your presents by me this instant, your little velvet purse, your plaid handkerchief, and your amaranth and your ring," he wrote.[63] "The thousand things you sent me remind me of the donor every hour."[64]

He received her last letter on 15 June 1802. In reply he reported that he was finally being released and transported to Hamburg.[65] In spite of an earlier promise from Lord Pelham that he would be allowed to visit England before going into exile,[66] he had been barred from doing so. "It is no small disappointment to me," he wrote, "that I cannot see you & the rest of my friends, if but for a moment, however liberty is so sweet that it qualifies the bitterest accompaniments."[67]

O'Connor had allegedly been carrying on another kind of correspondence as well. Just a few months after the prisoners arrived at Fort George, Sir James Craufurd wrote from Hamburg to Lord Grenville in the Foreign Office to report that

> [William Putnam] McCabe who is lately arrived here from Scotland was charged with a letter from Arthur O'Conner to the French Directory. This intelligence has come to me from two different persons usually thoroughly informed of the practices of these gentlemen. It seems difficult for O'Conner and his associates to elude the extreme vigilance of which I understand they are watched. The letters which they are allowed to send from their prison are I understand always inspected but I have apprehended that perhaps on the same paper on which is written an ostensible letter they may have written a secret one with one of those chymical preparations the use of which is so well known in secret correspondences.[68]

If O'Connor was indeed corresponding with the French directory while at Fort George, it is a tribute to his skill as a conspirator that he was not caught at it and that no further evidence of it has survived, even in the French archives.

FEUDING WITH EMMET AND MACNEVEN

O'Connor's aloofness from the other state prisoners did not prevent him from being drawn into the petty intrigues that commonly afflict groups of people who are involuntarily confined together. Although he and Thomas Addis Emmet had collaborated well in the Kilmainham pact affair (and O'Connor had publicly described Emmet as a man upon whose honor he

could rely[69]), the earlier bad feelings between them surfaced again at Fort
George and threatened to turn deadly.

In 1800 Emmet publicly broke relations with the O'Connor brothers by
declaring in writing that he "had public and private, personal and political
reasons for not having anything to do with, or to put himself in the way
of owing any obligation to either of the Messrs. O'Connor."[70] In 1801
O'Connor complained to William Tennent of "the underhanded intrigues of
Mr. Emmet at Kilmainham," and described Emmet and his supporters as "a
faction, arrogating to itself exclusively all patriotism," that aims to establish
"the most intolerant & sanguinary tyranny" and to proscribe "every thing
that is truly independent, or honourable."[71] Battle lines had been drawn
and the other prisoners began to choose sides. MacNeven, Neilson, Thomas
Russell, and John Sweetman were among Emmet's supporters. O'Connor
may not have had many partisans; a letter Neilson wrote to his wife claimed
that Tennent, Edward Hudson, John Chambers, and Matthew Dowling were
the only ones on speaking terms with him.[72] By the time they were liberated,
relations had deteriorated to the point that both Emmet and MacNeven
intended to challenge O'Connor to duels.[73]

AN EXCHANGE OF LETTERS WITH MACNEVEN

When the war between Britain and France officially ended in March
1802, preparations began for the state prisoners to be discharged from Fort
George and sent into exile. On 31 May, after they had been informed of
their imminent release, MacNeven wrote a formal letter to O'Connor that
sparked a rapid back-and-forth correspondence between them. Because the
exchange is so revealing of the dynamics of the factionalism that ultimately
destroyed the United Irishmen, it is worth reproducing the letters almost in
full, beginning with MacNeven's initial challenge:[74]

> Sir,
>
> I appraised you the moment I saw you at Kilmainham on the 29th
> of July 1798, that I was acquainted with the contents of your letter
> to Ld. Edward, and would hold you accountable for that part of it,
> which reflected on myself. I did not, however, think it worthy of me,
> during the continuance of our imprisonment, to increase its hardships
> by any further offensive proceeding . . . . But since it is announced to us
> from authority, that this long captivity will be speedily at an end, take
> notice, that the hour of reparation must not be deferred beyond our

enlargement. I will accordingly expect from you an explicit disavowal of the aspersion contained in the aforementioned letter, or else, at the very earliest opportunity, that satisfaction which is customary among men of honour.

What letter was MacNeven referring to? O'Connor, somewhat puzzled by this outburst, responded immediately:

Sir,

After more than five years it is impossible I should be able to call to mind the contents of the several letters I wrote to Lord Edward Fitzgerald, and least of all, can I recollect any of the nature you allude to, but if you will inform me of the contents of the particular letter you refer to, and which you say you appraised me in 1798 you were informed of (which your letter just received is the first and only information I have the most distant recollection of) you may be assured you shall receive, with that frankness that belongs to my character, a full and explicit answer.

The letter in question was none other than the infamous "cypher" letter that had been used as evidence against O'Connor at Maidstone,[75] as MacNeven explained in a second message:

Sir,

The letter I allude to is that one to Ld. Edward which has been since published in the report of your trial. Ld. Edward read the most part of it in my presence, and that of several other persons, who were officially qualified, at that time, to hear the most secret communications about our affairs. With that frankness and generosity of character which belonged to Edward, he did not hesitate to acknowledge that some of the insulting expressions, and part of the injurious imputation contained in that letter, were leveled at me. You must excuse me from condescending to repeat them of myself.

It is unclear precisely what MacNeven found objectionable in the letter from O'Connor to Fitzgerald. Perhaps it was the imputation of dishonesty contained in the passage that said some of "the old Committee Patriots" might be promoting an attempt at "separating the Catholics from the Union," and that it would be "every honest man's business to prevent" that from happening.[76] In any event, O'Connor attempted to mollify MacNeven by assuring him that he was mistaken and that no reference to him had been intended:

> Sir,
>
> Having gone into something like a specification of what you seek to have explained, my having read over the letters published in my trial since I came here, enable me to say with confidence, that there is not one word in them that attaches to you or your character.

MacNeven's second message to O'Connor also contained another complaint:

> I afterward learned, but not from Ld. Edward, that the letter you enclosed to him for me, was of such a nature as not to be fit to be delivered, nor did I receive it, tho' I am not the less offended that there should have been any such. . . .

To that charge O'Connor replied:

> As to the letter Ld. Edward did not deliver to you, its contents were principally about Lewines' having drawn on a friend of mine for a considerable sum of money, which exposed him to the greatest danger. It was written under the idea that you knew of his having drawn, and Edward's reason to me for not delivering you the letter was, that he could assure me that you were wholly ignorant of the transaction. The principal object of the letter was to request that you would reimburse me (as I paid the debt) out of the subscription you were making for Lewines, which Edward told me would not answer.[77] You must excuse me from supposing Ld. Edward capable of saying what no act of mine ever authorized. . . .

> If I had anything to say against your character I should have thought myself bound to have denounced you openly to your face, from the place you held in the Union, but I never heard your character impeached and I am confident I never impeached it. I owe this frank avowal, even more to myself than to you in as much as the dishonor of a calumniator is the greatest I know of.

Not only was MacNeven not placated by O'Connor's reassurances, he thought he detected in them yet another insulting implication.

> *Sir,*
>
> *When I sought for the explanation required by my note of this morning, you cannot surely have believed that I would submit to any affront, and yet, there is a sentence in your last note, which to my apprehension, conveys an indignity. The words are these: "You must excuse me from supposing Lord Edward capable of saying what no act of mine ever authorized." As no man alive revered Ld. Edward more than I did, or more fondly cherishes his memory, you cannot imagine I would charge him with any willful misrepresentation. Your expressions, then, seem to me to reflect on my own veracity, and I request you will assure me you had no such intention.*

At this point O'Connor, clearly losing patience, attempted to end the exchange by simply giving MacNeven all of the assurances he could possibly want.

> *Sir,*
>
> *I hope you do not suppose I will go into a disquisition of words spoken by another person, years since, or that I have the presumption to think I could account for the manner Lord Edward might have mistaken the cypher we wrote in, or that I could explain how you may have mistaken his meaning, without entering into any investigation of how you or he may have mistaken, and without wishing to throw any imputation on the intentions of either. I must beg leave to end this correspondence with assuring you that as I have never given you any cause of quarrel, I am determined to avoid any that may arise out of the mode or manner of an expression and therefore must request that all further correspondence may here cease. . . .*

MacNeven, however, was not quite ready to allow O'Connor to unilaterally withdraw from the fray, and so he persisted:

> *Sir,*
>
> *As I began this correspondence without consulting your wishes, so I will continue it for one more letter, without waiting your permission.*

*I am as little inclined as any man to be captious; but, I trust, equally
removed from suffering the slightest imputation. I neither desire you to
explain how Ld. Edward could have mistaken the cyphers you wrote
in, nor how I might have mistaken his meaning; but I require to be
informed of the substantial purpose of the expressions I have already
quoted from your second note of yesterday, and to be explicitly assured,
they were not intended to convey any impeachment of my veracity.
When you have given this a satisfactory answer, I am certainly very
willing to put an end to all correspondence . . . .*

Had O'Connor not clearly enough avowed that he believed the problem
to be a misunderstanding and that he was not accusing MacNeven of
deliberate duplicity? Apparently not, so he tried once again:

Sir,

*I had hoped that my having been so extremely explicit in my last note
to you would have put an end to all correspondence between you and
me. I don't know how words can convey a more full explanation that I
have no intention to call your veracity into question than is contained
in my last note. In order that you may not have occasion to continue
this correspondence I now repeat the substance of what I have written.
I never heard your character impeached, I never did impeach it, no
part of any of the letters I wrote you were intended to impeach your
veracity.*

Whether MacNeven was at last satisfied or not, he did not pursue the
matter further. In spite of his disclaimer ("I am as little inclined as any man to
be captious"), this exchange makes MacNeven appear unreasonably persistent
in his charges against O'Connor, exemplifying what one author called a
"moral self-righteousness bordering on the insufferable" that characterized
several of the United Irish leaders.[78] O'Connor's responses, by contrast, show
him going to great lengths to appease MacNeven, though not without a
certain amount of testiness. MacNeven's suspicions and accusations would
have been justified, of course, if O'Connor was untruthful about the target of
his insults in the letter to Lord Edward, but that cannot be known.

In the end MacNeven apparently dropped his intention to challenge
O'Connor to a duel, at least for the moment. The following month, however,
Emmet would pick up where his friend left off.

EMMET CONFRONTS O'CONNOR

A series of documents published by Madden—statements of Dowling, Chambers, Sweetman, and John Patten—describe an incident that exacerbated the rift between Emmet and O'Connor. According to Patten's statement, O'Connor told him, among other things, that Emmet "gave information of the letter which O'Connor was writing [the open letter to Castlereagh], through which means government became acquainted with the circumstance."[79] This was a serious allegation, of course; it was equivalent to calling Emmet a government informer, and Patten (Emmet's brother-in-law) repeated to Emmet what O'Connor had said.

On 30 June the liberated state prisoners sailed in the *Ariadne* from Fort George, heading for Hamburg. On 4 July the frigate landed at Cuxhaven, one of Hamburg's harbors. But before the boat reached shore, O'Connor was called aside by Dowling who informed him on Emmet's behalf that Emmet "intended to go direct to Hamburgh, where he would remain for some time." Dowling continued: "After some conversation and my repeating the above intimation, Mr. O'Connor, in answer, requested I would let Mr. Emmet know, that he should take his own time and place for calling on Mr. Emmet."[80] Emmet had challenged O'Connor to a duel and O'Connor had responded by issuing a counterchallenge.

The other prisoners feared that if this affair were allowed to proceed it could seriously discredit the cause of the United Irishmen. Chambers therefore approached Sweetman with a proposal to try to bring about a reconciliation. After considerable deliberation, they

> agreed that Mr. O'Connor should withdraw a challenge which he had sent to Mr. Emmet; that on his doing so, Mr. Emmet should declare he had never done, or intended to do him (Mr. O'Connor) any injury; and that then Mr. O'Connor should declare, that in the conversation he had with Mr. Patten he never intended to impeach his (Mr. Emmet's) moral or political character. These terms I communicated to Mr. O'Connor, and Mr. Sweetman did the like to Mr. Emmet.[81]

According to Chambers, O'Connor "said he not only concurred" in the proposed terms, but was "sincerely desirous of fully composing the feelings of Mr. Emmet." It was agreed that "the parties would meet on the foredeck." At that meeting,

> Mr. O'Connor addressed himself to Mr. Emmet, and having spoken of his never harbouring any rancour in his breast towards him, said

that he withdrew his challenge. Mr. Emmet then said, "You are right in withdrawing your challenge. I never did you any injury; I never intended you any."[82]

But, Emmet added, he had come there expecting O'Connor "to explain a business which took place between him and Mr. Patten." O'Connor replied "that in what he had spoken to Mr. Patten, nothing was more distant from his mind than to disparage him (Mr. Emmet) in the esteem of Mr. Patten." Emmet, unsatisfied, responded, "Mr. O'Connor, that is impossible." O'Connor persisted, declaring "that in anything which had fallen from him in the conversation alluded to, he never had the most distant intention to impeach his (Mr. Emmet's) moral or political character, or to hurt his or Mr. Patten's feelings."[83]

Emmet and O'Connor shook hands. O'Connor then addressed the group, urging them "to remove whatever remaining differences subsisted amongst us, that our enemies might not have the satisfaction to find that the first use we made of our liberty was to exercise acts of hostility against each other." Chambers added that he hoped both Emmet and O'Connor would join him and Sweetman in putting an end to the factionalism among them, but "Mr. Emmet said he must be excused from any interference of that kind, and would confine himself solely to what related to himself." In that case, Chambers said, "We will undertake it ourselves."[84]

Emmet had the final word: "Mr. O'Connor, I am happy that everything of a hostile nature has been done away between you and me; but I desire to be understood as not bound to any renewal of intimacy in consequence of what has taken place." Everyone present then "bowed to each other and parted."[85]

FALSE ACCUSATIONS

There is no suggestion in O'Connor's memoirs that he really considered Emmet to have acted as a government agent. Emmet, however, apparently did believe that O'Connor had done so. In 1915 Emmet's grandson and namesake published a *Memoir of Thomas Addis and Robert Emmet* in which he wrote: "Mr. Emmet had good reason to believe that Mr. Arthur O'Connor had 'made his peace' with the Government after his arrest, and that he was sent to Fort George to act as a spy, and Dr. Macneven held the same opinion."[86]

Unfortunately, this false accusation was picked up and repeated in 1916 by Vincent Fleming O'Reilly, editor of the posthumous edition of Dr. Madden's seminal work on the United Irishmen.[87] In doing so, O'Reilly was contradicting Madden's verdict on O'Connor, which was stated clearly in those same volumes. Although Madden detested O'Connor's radical anticlericalism, he gave this testimony to his integrity:

> *There can be no mistake . . . as to the opinion that must be formed by all who are conversant with the history of the leaders of the Society of United Irishmen—namely, that among them no man was more sincere in his patriotism, more capable of making great sacrifices for his country, or who brought greater abilities to its cause, than Arthur O'Connor.[88]*

To support the charge that O'Connor was betraying his comrades, Emmet's grandson cited

> *the unaccountable fact that Mr. O'Connor was never subjected to the close confinement imposed upon the other State prisoners on their first arrival at Fort George. Both Mr. O'Connor and his wife were allowed to come and go without restraint, as if they were most loyal to the Government, and it has been an unexplained circumstance that his wife and children were allowed to join him immediately after he reached Fort George. In every other instance the Government refused permission for the wife of a prisoner even to reside in the neighborhood of the fortress.[89]*

As evidence, he quotes a letter written by Samuel Neilson on 30 March 1800 that says, "Mrs. O'Connor and her children remain with Mr. O'Connor, and they have all the liberty of *ranging the Fort and neighborhood.*" Six weeks later Neilson wrote: "Mrs. O'Connor and her family are still here, but Mrs. Emmet has hitherto failed in all her applications; there appears to be a MARKED difference."[90]

There is an obvious flaw in this exposé of the special privileges granted to Arthur O'Connor's wife and children: he had no wife and children. Neilson was writing about *Roger* O'Connor, whose family had indeed been allowed to accompany him to Fort George. The argument, moreover, is all the more disingenuous because its author was well aware that Emmet's wife and family were also allowed to stay with him at Fort George from June 1800 until his release in 1802.

Was Roger O'Connor a government informer? There is incriminating archival evidence that on one occasion, in 1797, he offered "to give every information, and to render every service to the King's Government, in his power."[91] There is no evidence, however, that he actually gave any information, and his offer to do so can be understood in the context of his standard *modus operandi* of feigning loyalty while engaging in clandestine revolutionary activity. It is unlikely that Roger spied on his fellow prisoners at Fort George. Emmet and MacNeven were correct in their conjecture that one of their comrades was a government informer—it was Samuel Turner—but apparently Turner was never suspected by those who focused their mistrust on O'Connor.[92]

In his zeal to defend his ancestor's honor against O'Connor, Emmet's grandson committed another significant error worth refuting. He claimed that O'Connor, "in a work called 'Monopoly, the Root of All Evil' . . . charges Mr. Emmet, when at the head of the United Irishmen, with being 'a coward, and a man of bad faith.' "[93] His use of quotation marks implies a direct quotation from O'Connor's *Monopoly*. But in fact, nowhere in that three-volume work does O'Connor even mention Emmet. The confusion may have arisen from Madden's citations of a private letter from O'Connor in which the latter accused Emmet of cowardice.[94] The same charge also appears in O'Connor's unpublished memoirs,[95] but it cannot be assumed that he would have left it in the final version, had those memoirs ever been set into print.

Although their Hamburg duel was averted, the feud between O'Connor and Emmet was far from over. It would continue on French soil, and the irreparable split between the two best-known surviving leaders of the United Irishmen would seriously demoralize the organization and undermine its chances of recovery.

8

Le Général O'Connor

As HE WAS WAITING in Fort George for the *Ariadne* to take him to freedom, O'Connor wrote a final letter to Lucy Fitzgerald, thanking her for being "so kind a friend during the long period of my imprisonment." He informed her that "I have escaped from this Siberia better than I expected. Indeed, I have gained in one particular, for I had but a few hairs & now I have them so thick, I fear my head is getting fat."[1]

Lady Lucy married Sir Thomas Foley that same year, 1802; apparently she and O'Connor never saw each other again although both lived another half century.[2] She retained fond memories of him; in 1831 she wrote a harsh criticism of Thomas Moore's biography of her brother and suggested that the only man who fully understood what had been in Lord Edward's heart was his "twin soul," O'Connor: "It was that person who could have told how Ed. once loved."[3]

O'Connor stepped ashore at Cuxhaven on 4 July 1802—his thirty-ninth birthday. From there he went briefly to Hamburg for a tearful reunion with Pamela Fitzgerald; her daughter many years later recalled, "I once saw Arthur O'Connor at Hamburgh when I was a child & just remember a very handsome man patting my head & *crying* over me."[4] From Hamburg he and John Chambers went to Antwerp and then to Calais, where O'Connor remained for several months before traveling on the continent and eventually settling in Paris.

The first major political act of the liberated political prisoners was to issue their own account of the Kilmainham pact "confessions." In spite of the hostility of Emmet and MacNeven toward O'Connor, the three of them collaborated to produce a pamphlet that was published in London. It included the full text of the original written statement that had been rejected by Cornwallis together with complete transcripts of their interrogations before the secret committees of the Irish houses of parliament.[5] By showing them defiantly and proudly defending the aims and actions of the United Irish Society, the pamphlet counteracted the ill effects of the highly expurgated version widely propagated by the British government.

FROM CALAIS TO PARIS

In July an Irishwoman, Melesina St. George, saw O'Connor in Calais and described him in her diary:

> *My eyes presented me with Arthur O'Connor and a group of his associates. His features are regular and his person good. At the moment I saw him, he had a dark and scowling but sensible expression. He wore a green handkerchief as a neckcloth and a tricoloured cockade.[6]*

While in Calais O'Connor had an opportunity to renew old friendships with Fox and other oppositionist Whigs who were taking advantage of the Peace of Amiens to visit France for the first time in many years. Most of them, angered by the Kilmainham revelations, pointedly avoided O'Connor, refusing to attend social functions to which he had been invited. George Tierney denounced him, prompting O'Connor to consider challenging Tierney to a duel, but nothing came of it. Fox, however, demonstrated his continuing friendship for the rebel in exile, as did Lord and Lady Oxford, who invited him to accompany them on a voyage to Italy.[7]

According to J. B. Trotter, Fox's secretary, the first meeting between Fox and O'Connor after the latter's release from prison came about by accident:

> *An incident occurred at Calais, which . . . excited much remark, and roused a good deal of censure at the time . . . . It happened that Mr. Arthur O'Connor had arrived at the inn at which we stopped very shortly before. He waited on Mr. Fox, was received by him with that urbanity and openness which distinguished him, and was invited to dinner by him, which invitation he accepted of. I had never seen this gentleman before. It is well known that, after a long confinement at Fort George, he, and some other Irish gentlemen, had agreed with the Irish government to expatriate themselves for life. Mr. O'Connor was now on his way to Paris accordingly; when chance brought him*

to Killiac's inn, at the same time with Mr. Fox. His manners were
extremely pleasing . . . . Mr. Fox found no difficulty in receiving this
gentleman, (whom he had known before he was so deeply implicated
in Irish politics,) with a friendly and consoling welcome.[8]

Trotter's reminiscences suggest that O'Connor had lost none of his
personal charm, but was less than completely forthcoming in his dinner
conversation with Fox:

Mr. O'Connor dined with us; and I, for one, was much pleased with
his deportment and appearance, though I could not become, in a
manner, a convert to his arguments, to prove that his party had not
attempted, or desired, to rouse the physical strength of his country to
effect a change in Ireland. We all went to the theatre in the evening
. . . . We afterwards saw Mr. O'Connor (who remained some time at
Calais after us,) two or three times at Paris.

Trotter regretted that "prejudice in some, and malignity in others" had
magnified this innocent encounter "into a most improper communication
with a traitorous or rebellious subject."[9]

Criticism of Fox intensified following a dinner in Paris given by Thérèse
Cabarrus, the famous beauty known as *Notre Dame de Thermidor.*[10] At that
party Fox warmly greeted O'Connor and soon "it was all about Paris that Mr.
Fox had brought him in his hand, & introduced him as his particular friend."[11]
Thomas Erskine, one of those most incensed at O'Connor, denounced Fox
for continuing to consort with him. Fox's defenders, however, condemned
as "an abominable lie" the allegation that Fox was responsible for the Irish
rebel's presence at the dinner party. Instead they blamed Lady Oxford, who
they said "was there with her strange *cavaliere servente*, Arthur O'Connor."[12]
In any event, it was obvious to all that Fox had no intention of shunning the
unfortunate exile.

During his stay in Calais, O'Connor had dined several times at the home
of a high-ranking customs official named Mergaud, apparently unaware
that the latter was reporting on the activities "du fameux Irlandais, Arthur
O'Conor" to the Ministry of Justice in Paris. Mergaud found it suspicious
that before the Foxites arrived O'Connor lived alone and strangely isolated
from other English-speaking people in Calais. When O'Connor later asked
him for permission to ship two small boxes, one for himself and one for the
Oxfords, Mergaud contacted his superiors in Paris to ask whether he should
secretly open them and inspect the contents.[13] Although he later complained
that he found the conduct of O'Connor and Lady Oxford "bien impudente,"[14]

Mergaud's reports seem not to have damaged O'Connor's reputation in the eyes of Bonaparte's government.

EMMET VS. O'CONNOR: VYING FOR BONAPARTE'S FAVOR

In November 1802 O'Connor wrote to Talleyrand, the minister of foreign affairs, recalling his 1796 negotiations with General Hoche and asking to be considered once again as the official representative of the United Irish to the French government. After establishing himself in Paris in February 1803 O'Connor wrote again—this time to the minister of justice—stating the same request. Meanwhile, Thomas Addis Emmet had also arrived in Paris in February and he, too, was claiming to be the sole diplomatic agent of the United Irishmen. The conflicting claims were not immediately resolved by the French authorities, but Reinhard's reports of the 1796 negotiations gave O'Connor an advantage.[15] O'Connor further strengthened his credentials by writing an analysis of current British affairs.[16] "Bonaparte asked me to write this work," he claimed; "I gave it into his own hands and he had it printed in the government press."[17] A comment by Drennan attests that it circulated in England and Ireland:

> Arthur O'Connor has published a book to show the stability of the French government and the immediately impending fall of Britain from the state of her finances. It is noticed by the Edinburgh Reviewers, who say O'Connor is an Englishman, and then are exceedingly severe on the apostate of his country. They are themselves in the pay of Ministry.[18]

Emmet claimed that he had been officially appointed as ambassador to the French government by the executive committee of the United Irishmen. O'Connor countered by denying that any such executive committee existed in the wake of the crushing defeat of 1798. Emmet retorted that O'Connor's denial only proved he was so out of touch with the organization that he was ignorant of its highest leadership body. But when pressed by Bonaparte's ministers to provide evidence of the executive committee's existence, Emmet declined, for security reasons, to do so.[19] The French government understandably remained skeptical of Emmet's alleged credentials.

In retrospect it is evident that both Emmet and O'Connor were partially justified in their mutually exclusive claims. The attempted insurrection led by Emmet's brother Robert in July 1803—known to history as "Emmet's

Rebellion"—demonstrated that some sort of executive committee had indeed existed in 1802 and 1803. On the other hand, O'Connor could credibly deny that it was truly representative of the United Irish Society. He later described Emmet's Rebellion as "an act of madness" and claimed that Bonaparte had personally expressed to him "his highest contempt for all those engaged in it." O'Connor depicted its organizers as a narrow faction that originated at Fort George and regrouped in Paris in 1803. "The person in Paris, who in this party had the most influence, was [Thomas] Russell," he said, "and the project devised by him and [Robert] Emmet gave the finishing blow to the United Irish confederacy."[20] Although Emmet's Rebellion has long been romanticized because of the heroic courage and martyrdom of Robert Emmet and his comrades, O'Connor's unsentimental assessment of its tragic outcome and apparent futility was not wholly inaccurate.

O'Connor said that he had been kept informed of the plans for the 1803 uprising by two sources. One was his former codefendant at Maidstone, John Allen, who "was constantly with Robert Emmet," and who gave O'Connor "a most minute account" of his activities. The other source was French government officials, who passed on to O'Connor everything Thomas Addis Emmet was telling them.[21]

Miles Byrne, a United Irish veteran who also spent many years in French exile, described in his memoirs the consequences of the split between O'Connor and Emmet, two men "whom my country men at home looked upon as their most strenuous agents with the French Government." The division "between two of the principal Irish leaders produced at this important moment the worst effect, as it showed clearly to the French Government that already the Irish refugees could not agree amongst themselves abroad; consequently it might be still worse when in their own country." Furthermore, it was profoundly demoralizing to the ranks of the United Irishmen themselves: "Many of us exiles felt grieved at the bad result which this protracted misunderstanding would create; every day I could hear something on the subject discussed at the London coffee-house in the Rue Jacob."[22]

The Peace of Amiens was short-lived; by May 1803 England and France were once again at war. Even before hostilities had officially resumed, Bonaparte had begun to weigh the strategic value of an alliance with the Irish rebels in the context of his plans to invade Ireland or England. Accordingly, he ordered his ministers to try to reconcile Emmet and O'Connor, and if that proved impossible, to decide which of them would prove most useful in accomplishing France's military objectives.

Both O'Connor and Emmet came under intense pressure to put aside their differences for the sake of Ireland—from their own comrades, from French officials, and even from Bonaparte himself. When pressed to state his precise objections to working with his rival, Emmet refused, saying he would only state specific charges in the future, before a tribunal of a liberated Ireland. The clear implication was that Emmet believed O'Connor had in some way betrayed the Irish freedom struggle. Although Emmet was undoubtedly sincere in that belief—all who knew him testify that he was a thoroughly honest man—he never, to the end of his life, offered any evidence to support his implied accusation against O'Connor. It is safe to conclude that Emmet was mistaken; there is no hint in the Irish, English, or French archives that casts doubt upon O'Connor's loyalty to the Irish cause.

Emmet kept a diary of his activities in Paris. Its entry for 10 August 1803 reports that a United Irish exile named Thomas Corbet, one of O'Connor's partisans, called on him. Speaking of the insurrection led by Robert Emmet, Corbet told him that "it was the duty of every Irishman to give it support. For that purpose many of them wished O'Connor and me to forget our animosities and concert and act together, and that O'Connor was perfectly willing." But Emmet would have none of it: "I instantly answered that if my objections to Mr. O'Connor were only personal, I should be ashamed to refuse an offer of reconciliation at such a time." However, he continued, "my objections were *moral and political*. That I conceived him a bad man and a very dangerous character for my country, and should ever reproach myself if on any occasion I lent him the credit of my name."[23]

On 13 August Emmet was introduced to D. J. Garat, a prominent associate of Admiral Truguet, the minister in charge of naval operations for the prospective invasion of Ireland. "Garat," Emmet wrote in his journal, "is personally acquainted with O'Connor, and has been speaking to him, and he mentioned the absolute necessity of my acting with O'Connor... On my saying 'never,' he got into a great passion." The next day Garat again tried to persuade Emmet to collaborate with O'Connor, "an individual whose name was known thro' Europe and whose suffering might entitle him to some credit," but Emmet once again rebuffed Garat's efforts.[24] Meanwhile, Truguet and O'Connor had already formed a close working relationship. A knowledgeable spy reported to the British government that in late 1803 "the Irish expedition was then being planned by O'Connor and Truguet."[25]

Emmet's diary entry for 14 September reads:

> On my way home met Corbet, who . . . proposed an accommodation
> with O'Connor that we might co-operate . . . . I rejected every
> accommodation on the same grounds as before, political and not
> personal. He urged that if we were reconciled O'Connor would sacrifice
> a great deal of his opinions to meet mine and give a joint advice to

Government. I answered that I knew Mr. O'Connor too well . . . that
nothing would be gained on that head.[26]

On 18 September Emmet unexpectedly met O'Connor face-to-face in the Rue de Rivoli. They had both just learned of the definitive failure of Robert Emmet's uprising. Emmet's journal describes their chance encounter: "While I was out Mr. O'Connor and I met plump at the turn of a street, to my surprise he instantly saluted me and enquired very tenderly after my family. I answered him as coldly as I could with politeness." O'Connor, however, "was not to be rebuffed. He said he had long wished for this opportunity of speaking to me on a subject which had probably been mentioned to me by Mr. Corbet."[27]

O'Connor proposed that the two of them establish a basis of collaboration by exchanging information, to make sure that the French government was not playing each of them off against the other. "I listened with the utmost patience and silence to this discourse," Emmet wrote; "I suspected he was laying the foundation of some future impeachment. I therefore answered him that I did not think myself at liberty to disclose the communications that had been made to me."[28]

Ever suspicious of O'Connor's motives, Emmet noted that they had stood and talked in front of the Palais Royal for about three-quarters of an hour. He believed their conversation "had been studiously protracted in hopes of its being perceived by some one to whom we and our differences were both known." Finally, O'Connor asked Emmet "to think on it, and give him a definite answer, which he had a reason for wishing me to give before Tuesday at twelve. I said I would, and very politely concluded this extraordinary interview." On Tuesday, 20 September, Emmet sent O'Connor the same negative answer he had earlier given Corbet. Thus ended O'Connor's attempt at personal diplomacy with Emmet.[29]

Although adjudicating historical disputes of this sort is never a simple matter, a reading of Emmet's Parisian journal makes it difficult to avoid the conclusion that he must ultimately bear the onus of the debilitating split in the United Irish leadership. While O'Connor seemed ever willing to collaborate with him to attain their common goal, Emmet stubbornly resisted having anything to do with O'Connor. Whether O'Connor's offers of cooperation were sincere or, as Emmet insisted, merely tactical, Emmet's repeated refusals diminished his own credibility in the estimation of the French government.

Perhaps the most significant political difference separating Emmet and O'Connor was their attitude toward the military assistance both were seeking. Emmet was highly distrustful of Bonaparte's motives, and he did not hide his distrust from the French officials. Alexandre Berthier, the minister of war, informed Bonaparte that Emmet and his friends "are afraid of introducing the French into the country in case they interfere in the establishment of an Irish government," whereas O'Connor "had complete trust in the French."[30] Emmet made it clear that he wanted only a relatively small French force to invade Ireland and expel the British, because he feared that a large French force would simply conquer Ireland and convert it from a British to a French colony. O'Connor, by contrast, asked for as large an invading force as the French were willing to send; he wanted to defeat the British by any means necessary and would worry later about negative consequences, if any. Given their respective attitudes, it is not surprising that the French officials found O'Connor easier to deal with than Emmet.

In early 1804 Bonaparte intervened directly in a final effort to try to bring unity to the divided Irish movement. On 18 January his intermediary, General Alexandre Dalton, gave Emmet a message that "expresses the First Consul's wish for the formation of a Committee" to provide leadership to the Irish exiles in their quest to liberate their country. Furthermore, Dalton told him, "it was the First Consul's wish that Mr. O'Connor and I should be of that Committee." Emmet commented in his diary: "This proposal has embarrassed me more than I can well express." Realizing that "I could be of no further use to Ireland if he [Bonaparte] took offence at my refusal," he agreed to join the committee, on condition that it would not be dominated by O'Connor's supporters. O'Connor, meanwhile, "offers to go into the Committee heart and hand."[31]

By 7 February Emmet had concluded that O'Connor's influence in the proposed committee would be too great: "I had seen enough to convince me that no Committee was necessary and that no proper one would be formed." Bonaparte was not pleased by Emmet's recalcitrance. On 17 February General Dalton told Emmet "that the First Consul had taken him aside and talked to him a great deal about me, that he expressed great anxiety that Mr. O'Connor and I should be brought together and to act together." Emmet began to explain why he rejected the proposed committee, but Dalton said "it was not a committee the Consul alluded to, but that *we two* should act together without any committee. I instantly replied that was what I would never do."[32]

Meanwhile, Bonaparte had already begun to organize the Irish exiles into a military force to liberate their homeland. On 31 August 1803 he decreed the formation of an Irish legion in the service of France. Miles Byrne, a veteran of that corps, described it in his memoirs:

The officers were all to be Irishmen, or Irishmen's sons born in France. The pay was to be the same as that given to officers and soldiers of the line of the French army. No rank was to be given higher than captain till they should land with the expedition in Ireland. There were two exceptions. Captain Blackwell, whose long services and campaigns with the French armies entitled him to promotion, received his commission as chef de battalion [lieutenant colonel] to the Irish legion. The second was Arthur O'Connor. . . . He received his commission as general-of-division [lieutenant general] in the service of France, dated the 24th of February, 1804, with orders to repair to Brest to make part of General-in-Chief Augereau's staff.[33]

On 3 March Emmet wrote in his diary:

What vexes me . . . and astonishes me above measure, is that O'Connor is appointed a General of Division, and is to set off in fifteen days for Brest! He says that he has the First Consul's promise that when they land in Ireland, Augereau will yield the command to him, is that possible? . . . O'Connor is going on rapidly to the object I know he aims at, being First Consul in Ireland, but I hope my countrymen will have spirit and virtue to prevent him.[34]

The final entry in Emmet's journal, dated 10 March 1804, complained about his relations with the French government: "I am treated very cavalierly, for no communication or message direct or indirect has been made to me." O'Connor, then by far the highest ranking United Irishman in the Irish legion, had clearly won the contest for Bonaparte's favor. "I shall therefore," Emmet concluded, "avoid doing anything and keep myself in the background unless Government chooses to show me some little civility and to convince me that they wish for the continuance of my communications."[35] After half a year passed with no further encouragement, in October Thomas Addis Emmet left for the United States and never returned to France.

In spite of O'Connor's triumph, however, neither his dream (to be Ireland's liberator) nor Emmet's nightmare (that O'Connor would become Bonaparte's puppet dictator) were realized. For the decade to come O'Connor would figure prominently in Bonaparte's repeated plans to wrest Ireland from British domination, but none ever came to fruition.

GENERAL O'CONNOR VS. GENERAL MACSHEEHY

The first of those plans called for an invasion force of 12,000 troops to sail for Ireland on 20 January 1804. The naval operations had been formulated by Truguet in close collaboration with O'Connor.[36] The overall commander was General Augereau, but the Irish legion encamped at Brest was under the immediate command of Adjutant General Bernard MacSheehy, the man whom Hoche had sent on a mission to Ireland in 1796. He was a talented Irish expatriate who had been working his way upward to a position of importance in the French army since 1793.

MacSheehy had earlier backed O'Connor's claims against Thomas Addis Emmet,[37] but with O'Connor himself now holding the rank of general and serving on Augereau's staff, MacSheehy began to view O'Connor as a potential rival. The expedition did not sail in January 1804 as originally planned; the Irish legion was relocated in February, first to Quimper and then to Carhaix where it remained until August. When O'Connor arrived at Carhaix in July, he came into immediate conflict with MacSheehy, who resented O'Connor's usurpation of his authority.

The struggle between MacSheehy and O'Connor reproduced within the Irish legion the factional divisions that had previously existed among the United Irishmen, and in even more virulent form. MacSheehy aligned himself with those who had been supporters of Thomas Addis Emmet, while those officers with grievances against MacSheehy gravitated toward General O'Connor.

Before O'Connor's arrival the contending factions clashed over an incident that occurred on 4 June 1804 at a ceremony organized to celebrate Bonaparte's ascension to the imperial throne as Napoleon I. The soldiers of the Irish legion were called upon to raise their hands and swear an oath of loyalty to the new emperor and the new French constitution under which he ruled. One of Emmet's partisans, John Swiney, publicly expressed misgivings but went ahead and took the oath.[38] That evening, however, some of O'Connor's supporters, including Thomas Corbet, refused to certify that the oath had been taken unanimously. Swiney angrily confronted Corbet and their loud argument rapidly escalated into a violent altercation between the two factions. MacSheehy broke up the fight, but in the aftermath he supported Swiney against Corbet.

Augereau sent O'Connor to Carhaix to investigate the incident. O'Connor overruled MacSheehy's recommendations to expel Corbet from the legion and to exonerate Swiney. On 24 June O'Connor wrote to Augereau:

> *I greatly regret having to inform you, my dear general, that on my arrival I found the Irish legion in the greatest confusion, divided into two parties, with Adjutant-Commandant MacSheehy at the head of one, and the other complaining that the interest and well-being of the corps had been sacrificed to the spirit of intrigue and factionalism.*[39]

Miles Byrne, whose memoirs are even-handed with regard to the conflict between Emmet and O'Connor, agreed with O'Connor's assessment of MacSheehy. "Unfortunately for the Irish officers," he wrote, MacSheehy "proved himself quite unfit to remain at their head. He was capricious, passionate and vindictive; consequently, not impartial as a chief should be."[40]

O'Connor placed the blame for "these miserable intrigues" on MacSheehy and recommended to Augereau that he be "assigned to other functions."[41] Augereau concurred; on 18 September MacSheehy was relieved of his command and prohibited from having any further contact with the Irish legion.[42] Having vanquished his rivals, O'Connor was from that point unchallenged in his dominance of Irish exile politics in France. Bonaparte's generals and admirals consulted him on invasion plans and usually heeded his recommendations. A tragic echo of the factional conflict occurred, however, when Swiney challenged Corbet to a duel. They fought on 20 September and Corbet was killed.

Earlier, in July, after O'Connor had completed his official inquiry into the turmoil in the legion, he was preparing to return to Augereau's headquarters at Brest when, Miles Byrne reports, "the corps of Irish officers, in their splendid full uniform," called on him. "It was the first and only time that the Irish officers of the Legion paid a visit *en corps* to General O'Connor. As they were not under his orders in any manner, it was not required."[43] O'Connor made a speech to them in English.

MacNeven was among the Irish officers present on that occasion. According to Byrne, "Captain MacNeven thought there were allusions to himself" contained in O'Connor's speech. He subsequently resigned from the Irish legion and "wrote a challenge to General Arthur O'Connor, then at Brest, in which he mentioned that he would remain a month at Bordeaux before sailing for America, inviting him to fix a rendezvous."[44] O'Connor's response, if any, is unknown, but no duel took place. Like his colleague Thomas Addis Emmet, MacNeven left France forever and spent the rest of his life in New York.

BONAPARTE'S PLANS FOR IRELAND

At about the same time as MacSheehy's tenure with the Irish legion ended, Bonaparte began to make new plans for an invasion of Ireland in the coming winter. On 6 September 1804 he wrote to Admiral Ganteaume, asking whether he could be ready in two months to transport 16,000 men and 500 horses to Ireland. "See the Irish general, O'Connor," he continued, "and talk with him about the places you might be able to land."[45] Accordingly, a week later Ganteaume reported to the minister of the navy that he had "had occasion to consult with General O'Connor on the possibility of an expedition to Ireland and on the means of assuring its success." With regard to the north of Ireland, he said, "General O'Connor claims that he would have 50,000 men at his disposition very rapidly if we were to land in that area." The stormy seas would prevent a winter landing there, however, so Ganteaume proposed Galway Bay as the primary target.[46] O'Connor's recommendations encouraged Bonaparte to tell his minister of war: "The expedition to Ireland is definite. We have the means to send 18,000 men from Brest. General Marmont, for his part, is ready with 25,000 men" at Texel.[47]

Bonaparte's renewed attention to Ireland did not last long, however. Less than two weeks into October, fearing that enemy spies had gained knowledge of his plans, the emperor once again cancelled the preparations for the expedition. Before they could be relaunched, a major shift in the axis of the war with England occurred. In July and August of 1805 England gained Russia and Austria as coalition partners. The troops under General Augereau's command, including the Irish legion, were marched toward the Rhine to join the Grand Army, leaving O'Connor an "officier général sans destination."[48] The devastating defeat of the French fleet at Trafalgar in October 1805 made plans to invade Ireland all the more remote.

With the focus of French military activity on the continent rather than the British Isles, O'Connor's usefulness to the high command was greatly diminished and he found himself increasingly ignored. In mid-September 1805 he asked for, and subsequently received, permission to live in Paris while awaiting further assignment.[49] He would not be required to relinquish his rank or his military salary, but would in effect be on reserve status—officially, a *général disponible*. As Miles Byrne described it, "General O'Connor was allowed the full appointments of a general of division, though not in command."[50]

There is an undated, unsigned summary of O'Connor's military service in his dossier in the French military archives at the Château de Vincennes in Paris. After mentioning his negotiations with Hoche in 1796 it says: "He remained *Général en Chef* [of the Irish insurgent army] in all the campaigns of 1797, 1798, 1799, 1800 & 1801. During all these years France made unfruitful efforts to render aid to Ireland."[51] Then came his appointment as lieutenant general in the French army and eighteen months of active duty under Augereau at Brest in 1804–1805. After that, however, O'Connor would for the rest of his life be an inactive military officer with no assignment or duties.

The official documents, however, do not shed much light on the circumstances that led O'Connor to leave Augereau for inactive status in Paris. Many years later another veteran of the Irish legion, one Andrew O'Reilly, claimed in his memoirs that O'Connor "quitted the coast, whither he had been summoned to embark, and returned to Paris" filled with disgust and disillusionment at Bonaparte's failure to pursue the plans to invade Ireland. "For this act of disobedience," O'Reilly says, O'Connor

> *was never brought to trial, nor even rebuked, and thenceforward he declined presenting himself at the levées of the First Consul, or Emperor. Believing that he had sinned passed forgiveness, and that his elevation to the rank of general would be annulled in consequence, he refrained from drawing his appointments for some months. One day, however, he was agreeably surprised by a communication from the Ministry of War, that it would be convenient if he were to take up his overdue pay, and this he did to the day of his death, nearly fifty years afterwards, without having been again called into service, however. General O'Connor was the only superior officer in France who had not been decorated with the cross of the Legion of Honour, so offensive to Napoleon was his stern republicanism.[52]*

O'CONNOR, THE EMPEROR, AND THE *IDÉOLOGUES*

O'Reilly's gossipy account cannot be taken at face value, but it serves to illuminate the complexity of O'Connor's political attitude toward Emperor Napoleon I. O'Connor was a high-ranking officer in the Napoleonic army and his hopes for liberating Ireland were vested in the emperor, but when he arrived in Paris he gravitated, much as he had earlier in England, to the salons of a dissident elite. In London it was oppositionist Whigs whose company he had kept; in Paris, in the fashionable suburb of Auteuil, he befriended adherents of a liberal democratic school of thought known as the *Idéologues*.

He frequented the houses of Madame de Condorcet and Madame Helvetius, where he socialized with prominent intellectuals and politicians, including Garat, Sieyès, Cabanis, Volney, Destutt de Tracy, Benjamin Constant, M. J. Chénier, and the physicist Ampére.[53] Benjamin Constant recorded his impression of O'Connor in his personal diary:

> 8 January 1805. . . . *Met Gallois and O'Connor at dinner. . . . O'Connor is a man of acute mind* [un esprit fin]. *There is a subtlety in his sense of humor that is ordinarily lacking in foreigners, even to the point that he has the French defect of poking fun at his own opinions. He seems more a man of ambition than a friend of liberty, but he is nonetheless a friend of liberty because that is the refuge of ambitious men whose ambitions have been thwarted.*[54]

Most of the men and women O'Connor met at the elite salons were political moderates who opposed restoration of the Bourbon monarchy, but they had become increasingly hostile toward Bonaparte as his regime had become ever more imperial, dictatorial, and undemocratic. In his later years, after Bonaparte was long out of power, O'Connor let it be known that he believed he had been denied appointment to military commands after 1805 because he had earned the emperor's displeasure for consorting with the *Idéologues*. That is possibly true, but the fact that O'Connor maintained his rank and his full salary throughout the Napoleonic era suggests that he was not perceived by Bonaparte as a foe.

Furthermore, the emperor continued to consult with O'Connor from time to time on the subject of invading Ireland. In July 1811 he instructed his minister of war, the duc de Feltre (formerly General Henri Clarke, with whom Tone had negotiated), to confer with O'Connor because he planned to launch an expedition to Ireland in the month of October.[55] Apparently this order was not carried out, because in September O'Connor wrote a long letter directly to the emperor saying that he had been attempting to communicate with him through his ministers, but had not received answers. "The present moment is critical for Ireland," O'Connor declared.

> *It would be presumptuous on my part to belabor the advantages that could be gained from making contact with Ireland. The expense would be minimal and the results could be of the greatest importance. If Your Majesty sees the situation from the same point of view that I have presented here, I will always be prepared to carry out any orders that you care to give me.*[56]

The emperor immediately wrote to the duc de Feltre: "I have read with interest this letter from General O'Connor that I am sending along to you. It seems to me very important that this contact with Ireland be established . . . because I am about to send 30,000 men and 6,000 horses."[57] Bonaparte continued planning this expedition to Ireland into the following year, but once again it came to naught.

THE O'REILLY AFFAIR

O'Connor's name figures prominently in an account recorded in the British government's archives of a shadowy plot to overthrow Bonaparte.[58] On 4 February 1806 a man with a United Irish background, one Richard O'Reilly, appeared at the ministry offices in London claiming that he had just arrived from France and was carrying a secret message to Prime Minister Pitt from General Arthur O'Connor. Pitt, however, had died two weeks earlier; the new prime minister, Grenville, had formed a coalition cabinet called the Ministry of All Talents because it comprised the leading Foxites and Pittites. Instead of Pitt, then, O'Reilly found himself telling his story to O'Connor's old friend Charles James Fox.

O'Reilly said he was the emissary of O'Connor, who represented "a strong and well organized political party in Paris" that desired the overthrow of Emperor Napoleon I and sought British financial support to accomplish it.[59] According to O'Reilly, the conspirators aimed at replacing the imperial regime with a government headed by generals O'Connor and Moreau. Moreau was at that time in exile in America, having previously been involved in a royalist plot to dethrone Bonaparte. As part of the deal, O'Reilly said, O'Connor pledged to cease supporting French military efforts to separate Ireland from England.

Fox never mentioned this episode to anyone, possibly out of embarrassment over his previous personal connections with O'Connor. The British intelligence services, however, apparently treated O'Reilly's proposition seriously, although nothing more ever came of it. There can be no doubt that O'Reilly had been in contact with O'Connor; he had letters O'Connor had asked him to carry to his friend and business agent in London, Hugh Bell.[60] Furthermore, he is almost surely the "Mr. O'Realy" that O'Connor described as "a man of the highest sense of honour" in a later letter.[61]

But whether O'Connor had any involvement in a plot such as O'Reilly described is another matter. There are numerous reasons to think it improbable. Aside from O'Reilly's claims, there is no evidence that any such conspiracy existed. No matter how much O'Connor may have distrusted or disliked the emperor, it is difficult to imagine him conspiring with *ancien régime* elements to overthrow Bonaparte's rule. That O'Connor would approach Pitt, toward whom he expressed a lifelong burning hatred, seems doubly doubtful. That he would throw Ireland's independence into the bargain goes against the grain of the rest of his life's work. And finally, it is highly unlikely that a seasoned conspirator of O'Connor's caliber would expose himself to such large risks with so little prospect of success.

While the validity of O'Reilly's story cannot be absolutely ruled out, it is more likely that he was acting as a French agent and his "plot" was disinformation designed to divert attention from covert operations in Ireland. If it was simply an elaborate cover story it was successful. O'Reilly was subsequently captured in Ireland in circumstances that made him legally liable to be hanged, but after suspicious Irish police officials checked his story with their counterparts in London he was released.[62]

O'CONNOR AND THE "HUNDRED DAYS"

In April 1814, in the wake of military defeat, Bonaparte was overthrown, stripped of power, and exiled to the island of Elba. The victors restored the Bourbon monarchy with Louis XVIII as king. A groundswell of support for the deposed emperor, however, especially among soldiers fiercely loyal to him, recalled him to France in March 1815, and at their head he fought his way back into power. His spectacular political resurrection lasted only a hundred days; after his defeat at Waterloo he was imprisoned on the faraway island of St. Helena, never to return, and Louis XVIII reclaimed the throne.

Following Bonaparte's initial fall from power, General O'Connor wrote to the minister of war offering his services to the new regime.[63] His request generated an inquiry into his status that concluded with the recommendation that he be retired on half pay,[64] but before it was implemented Bonaparte reappeared on the scene with a vengeance. O'Connor must have feared that his letter would be compromising, so he wrote three more,[65] this time praising Bonaparte and damning the Bourbons. He had reason to regret those letters as well when Bonaparte was deposed for the second time.

O'Connor's first letter was simply an attempt to protect himself from the purge that would be expected to follow a radical change of government. The three to Bonaparte, on the other hand, may have been motivated by more than a concern for self-preservation. Despite O'Connor's distaste for the monarchical trappings of Napoleon's imperial regime, he undoubtedly considered it preferable to the Bourbon restoration. With Bonaparte in power there could still be some hope, however small, of a French-assisted liberation of Ireland; with the anglophilic Bourbons there would be none. O'Connor's offer to serve Bonaparte against the royalists was thus in accord with his republican ideals.

O'Connor's letters to Bonaparte during the Hundred Days did indeed cause him serious difficulties. Excerpts from them ("We have just avoided the horrible abyss of counterrevolution into which the Allies and the Bourbons tried to throw us"[66]) circulated among the king's ministers. A report to the king stated that O'Connor, by his "conduct during the usurpation," had "declared himself the personal enemy of Your Majesty."[67] O'Connor's days in France appeared to be numbered. An official order expelling him from the army and requiring him "to leave our realm with the shortest delay possible" was drawn up but not executed; it remains, unsigned, in his personnel dossier in the French military archives.[68]

O'Connor evidently had protectors in high places, and it would seem that the minister of war, the duc de Feltre, was among them. Feltre, having survived the transition from serving Bonaparte to serving the restored monarch, was himself in a delicate position, so his defense of O'Connor could only be conducted in the most subtle and indirect manner. His written report to the king stated that O'Connor deserved to be cashiered and banished from France, but behind the scenes he apparently succeeded in negotiating a far less drastic punishment.

Feltre wrote an official letter to O'Connor harshly admonishing him for writing "improper things against the royal family in order to obtain Bonaparte's favor," but added that the king, in his benevolence, had decided not only to allow him to remain in France but to grant him a pension, assuming, of course, that "in the future your conduct gives his Majesty no cause for complaint."[69] O'Connor was thus compelled to retire as of 19 June 1816 and his pension was fixed at six thousand francs per year.

It is worth noting that O'Connor, in spite of his own tenuous position, aggressively wielded his influence with the duc de Feltre not only on his own behalf but also on behalf of other victimized United Irish exiles. After Bonaparte's final defeat, the Irish legion was disbanded and many of its officers were treated with hostility. John Allen was arrested at Paris and ordered to leave French territory without delay. According to Miles Byrne's memoirs,

> Lieutenant-General Arthur O'Connor waited on the Duke of Feltre and insisted that Commandant Allen should be brought to trial, saying, "It was too bad to see him worse treated here than he had been when tried and acquitted with him at Maidstone." The Duke . . . seeing that General O'Connor took up the matter so warmly . . . consented to have Allen set at liberty, and allowed him to retire to Tours on half pay.[70]

After having narrowly avoided expulsion from the country himself, O'Connor solidified his legal position by applying for French citizenship. His petition for naturalization was accepted and he officially became a citizen of France on 10 April 1818.[71]

O'Connor continued to act as an advocate for the interests of former members of the Irish legion. In January 1828 he approached Miles Byrne with a request for help in lobbying the government "respecting the pay of the Irish officers not employed." O'Connor asked Byrne to introduce him to an aide to the minister of education, the Abbé de Frayssinous, and Byrne complied.[72] The aide was Laurence de Lewens, son of the deceased United Irish leader Edward Lewins. Although relations between O'Connor and Edward Lewins had often been somewhat contentious,[73] Byrne says that O'Connor "seemed much struck with young Lewens' talents and great kindness." O'Connor and Byrne called on him at his home on a Sunday morning. Byrne describes the encounter:

> Mr. de Lewens wished the conversation to be in French, as he could the more readily explain to the minister the object of General O'Connor's demand, which was simply this: At the formation of the Irish legion, Alexandre Berthier, minister of war, afterwards Prince Berthier, gave a document in writing to General O'Connor, assuring him that the Irish officers, whether actively employed or not, should always receive their full pay, as they would have no home to retire to, like the native officers, after the disbanding of their regiments.[74]

Lewens transmitted O'Connor's concerns to the Abbé de Frayssinous and arranged a meeting, which took place two days later. The minister, Byrne reports,

> kindly took upon himself to bring the business before the Government, and to use all his influence to have General O'Connor's demand taken into consideration; adding, "General, I know well the sacrifices you have made in your own country, endeavouring to have the Catholics there emancipated, and it will afford me great pleasure now, if I can in any way serve you or your countrymen."[75]

In spite of the cordiality of the meeting, nothing came of it. "We had every reason," Byrne lamented, "to expect a favourable issue to our demand, from the kind interest the Abbé de Frayssinous, the Bishop of Hermopolis, took in the matter; but unfortunately he resigned and quit the ministry before General O'Connor got any answer to his demand."[76]

That he had asked Byrne for an introduction to an aide to a minister illustrates how far removed O'Connor had become, by 1828, from the upper circles of political influence and power. That is also evidenced by the lack of success of his continued efforts to seek redress of his own personal grievances. He considered his forced retirement a violation of the sacred promises that successive French governments had made to him and he repeatedly requested reinstatement to active status,[77] but to no avail.[78] Nonetheless, as a retired general O'Connor would continue to enjoy the social status conferred by high military rank, and at his death in 1852 his widow, Eliza Condorcet O'Connor, would be granted the right to continue receiving his military pension.

9

Husband, Father, Scientific Farmer

U PON RETURNING TO PARIS in 1805 after his tour of duty with General Augereau at Brest, O'Connor was drawn to the intellectual and social milieu of the capital's salons. One in particular attracted him—Madame de Condorcet's on rue Verte. Sophie de Condorcet was as able an intellectual as her late husband. As translator of the works of Adam Smith into French, she was considered a leading authority on O'Connor's favorite subject. The widow of the martyred *philosophe* welcomed the personable Irish general; their shared interests and his conversational skills made him a favored guest.

He befriended many important people at her salon, including her brother, General Emmanuel Grouchy, who had commanded the 1796 attempted landing at Bantry Bay in Hoche's absence. One of the leaders of the *Idéologues*, Cabanis, was the husband of Sophie de Condorcet's sister Charlotte. It was probably there also that he began a lifelong friendship with a revolutionary savant whose writings had been inspirational for the United Irishmen: Constantine François Volney, author of *The Ruins of Empire*.[1]

But the person O'Connor met at Madame de Condorcet's who most influenced the course of his life was her young daughter Alexandrine Louise Sophie de Caritat de Condorcet—Eliza for short—who became his wife. Miles Byrne's memoirs provide a contemporary view of their marriage that is essentially accurate:

General Arthur O'Connor . . . married the daughter and only child of the celebrated and unfortunate Condorcet; this union was his great ambition, and indeed it proved a happy one. Mademoiselle Condorcet had the advantage of being brought up by her high-minded and accomplished mother the Marquise de Condorcet, whose courage and fortitude during the cruel terror and persecution of 1793 acquired for her the greatest consideration from the true patriots of every country; she knew well how to appreciate the sacrifices and sufferings, and imprisonments which Arthur O'Connor had undergone, endeavouring to obtain the freedom of his native country; and her brother, General Grouchy, highly approved of his niece's marriage with his friend General O'Connor. They were considered a very handsome pair; Mademoiselle Condorcet was a fine, sprightly, animated young girl, scarcely twenty; General O'Connor nearly forty, with very distinguished manners.[2]

Byrne understated the difference in their ages: In 1807 when they were married O'Connor was forty-four and Eliza seventeen. The disparity was not very much greater than that of her parents, however; the marquis de Condorcet had been forty-three when he married the twenty-two-year-old Sophie de Grouchy. The two age differentials combined to make O'Connor and his mother-in-law almost exactly the same age.[3]

Byrne was correct in suggesting that O'Connor was extremely pleased to be marrying into the Condorcet family. Although Eliza had been only three years old at the time of her father's death in March 1794, she was closely associated with him in the public mind because of one of his last essays, "Advice from an Outlaw to His Daughter," which he had written to her while in hiding from the Robespierrian authorities.[4] Late in life, Eliza would lament that "as the wife and the daughter of outlaws, misfortune and sadness have not been unknown to me."[5]

In 1807 the Irish outlaw who had just become Eliza's new husband proudly added her prestigious surname to his own; from that time forward his signature would read "General Arthur Condorcet O'Connor."[6] In his subsequent writings, he frequently listed Condorcet among his intellectual heroes, and made a point of referring to him as "my father-in-law." Furthermore, he devoted several years of hard work and scholarship to editing and publishing, in collaboration with one of France's premier scientists, François Arago, the complete works of Condorcet in twelve volumes.[7] It should be noted that Eliza herself apparently played the primary role in initiating that project. She had been promoting it and collecting material for it from at least 1824, whereas its actual execution by O'Connor and Arago did not occur until the 1840s.[8]

By all appearances the marriage was, as Byrne supposed, a happy one, and there is no evidence to the contrary.[9] Like Eliza's parents, she and Arthur formed an "enlightened" companionship in which the female partner neither was, nor was treated as, an intellectual inferior. The family correspondence reveals relationships of considerable intelligence, tenderness, and sensitivity.[10] The great sadness of the Condorcet O'Connor family, however, was that all three of the children, all sons, predeceased their parents. The first son, Arthur, died in 1829 at the age of twenty. The second, Daniel, was forty-one at his death in 1851, just a year before his father's.[11] The youngest, George (born when O'Connor was sixty), died in 1834 at the age of twelve. The family line was continued by Daniel O'Connor's children, but in the fourth generation there were no male offspring, so it ceased to bear the names Condorcet or O'Connor.

The family correspondence also provides ample evidence of the high value the Condorcet O'Connors placed on the education of their sons. The boys' letters to their mother, father, and grandmother are filled with reports of what they had been studying, which evidently is what they thought their elders wanted to hear. Eleven-year-old Arthur, for example, wrote to "Maman Condorcet" in Paris: "I have finished the second volume of Boileau's book on the art of poetry and have begun the sixth of Ovid's *Metamorphoses*. The German is going rather well. I have already almost finished the third volume of Gibbons, as well as Hume's history of England."[12] Furthermore, the older boys took some responsibility for the education of their little brother. Arthur informed his father: "I make George do every day his English lesson and he spells allso *(sic)* with me. He knows a great many English words and I think he will have soon learnt it."[13]

They wrote to Papa in English, to Mamma in either French or English, and to Maman Condorcet in French. On the occasion of one of Maman's birthdays, Daniel demonstrated his erudition by writing her a letter in three versions: English, French, and Latin. Arthur likewise wrote a substantial birthday greeting to his mother in English, Latin, and Greek.[14] Both boys' penmanship was impeccable.

In preserving the family correspondence, a selection principle no doubt operated to filter out material that might have reflected badly on its members. Nonetheless, a few letters have survived that reveal some tensions between the parents and their children. One, for example—a letter of contrition written by young Arthur, then twelve years old, to "My dearest Papa"—says:

I am very sorry to have given you so much pain. I will make all my efforts in future never to be headstrong any more; for I see that obstinacy is very bad and unreasonnable (sic), and so I have resolved to break myself entirely of it. Mr. Drot has had since your departure no subject of complaining of my temper. . . . Adieu, my dear Papa, I embrace you with all my heart. I will try to make amends for my past conduct.[15]

Another letter—from Eliza to her son Daniel in 1844—expresses strong resentment over a perceived slight on the part of Daniel's wife, Ernestine. Eliza felt her daughter-in-law was deliberately avoiding bringing their newborn child to see her.[16] These relatively insignificant squabbles represent the only discordant notes in the record of a generally harmonious domestic life that began in 1807 and lasted until the General's death in 1852.

LE BIGNON

On 7 February 1807 O'Connor wrote in a letter to his brother Daniel Conner: "Nothing delays my marriage but the finding a farm where we may reside."[17] Cabanis had told him of an estate with a château that was for sale; it was about seventy miles southeast of Paris in a "little commune of four hundred and fifty souls" named Le Bignon.[18] O'Connor reckoned that the property, which had previously belonged to the celebrated Mirabeau, was not beyond his means, but he did not have the cash at hand to make the purchase. The problem was that his personal fortune was still based on landed property in Ireland to which he did not have direct access.

O'Connor's property had earlier been placed under the management of his brother Roger, but Roger had not been a faithful agent, so Arthur asked Daniel to assume the fiduciary duties. In the long run, Arthur wanted Daniel to liquidate all of his holdings in Ireland and forward the proceeds to him.

Desperate to buy the estate at Le Bignon, Arthur turned to a friend and United Irish comrade, William Putnam McCabe, to borrow, on the security of his Irish property, the money necessary to close the deal. He wrote to McCabe:

Since I saw you I have found the most advantageous and eligible estate that I could have wished. . . . If this estate that offers slips through my hands for want of £4000 it will be a constant source of regret to me all my life, for it is the place of all others where I could be happy. There is a rapid stream that tumbles down through the whole property with every other advantage we could wish. Don't let me lose it if you can. The person who sells wants ready money.[19]

McCabe made him a loan, and O'Connor wrote to Daniel to ask him to repay McCabe:

A real true friend who seeing the cruel situation I was reduced to has lent me £4750. As I am ignorant of what sums you may have been able to collect for me I leave it to you to do all you can to satisfy my friend in the manner most agreeable to his wishes. . . . The £4000 is to pay an interest of 5 per cent until you can pay it; the rest you will pay him with my rents. As he will not meet any one that can give him better advice for the plan that he should adopt I request you will be of all the use you can not only on the subject of his money matters but on any other, all which his kindness to me merits.[20]

O'Connor was thus able to purchase the estate at Le Bignon and he and Eliza were married on 4 July 1807, his forty-fourth birthday.[21] They lived there to the end of their lives and the château du Bignon is occupied by their descendants to this day. The force of O'Connor's personality still lingers there in the stern gaze and heroic pose of Hugh Douglas Hamilton's enormous full-length portrait, which dominates the château's library.[22]

SCIENTIFIC AGRICULTURE AT LE BIGNON

In his letter to McCabe, O'Connor said he expected the value of his new French estate to double in six years.[23] He planned to introduce to France the knowledge of scientific agronomy he had learned in England and practiced in Ireland. Late in life he described his success in doing so. "When I purchased the domain of Bignon, about the beginning of the century," he wrote, "and cultivated all the arable lands myself, there was not a single acre in the whole country" that was planted according to rational principles. What he observed was

one year wheat, and the year after oats or barley, and so on, alternating without any intermission of ameliorating crops: all kinds of artificial grasses were utterly unknown, not even a potatoe crop was to be seen. By this miserable system there was no fodder; consequently the cattle were few, and there was no manure. In a state of such wretched husbandry, the produce scarcely paid the expense of cultivation, and in bad years the cultivator-proprietor did not get back his outlay.[24]

O'Connor says that when he introduced his system at Le Bignon his neighbors were impressed with its success and began to emulate it:

When they saw the lands I cultivated covered with lucerne, clover, sainfoin, vetches, turnips, potatoes, beet-root, etc., and the quantity of good food these afforded me, the numerous cattle their produce enabled me to feed, the quantity of manure they supplied, and that my corn crops yielded fourfold more than theirs, this ameliorating system of artificial grasses soon began to extend itself.[25]

By 1846, he says, "all the country" was "covered far and near, with the most luxuriant crops of lucerne, clover, sainfoin, potatoes, etc." and the farmers were prospering accordingly:

Small proprietors who, in the old system, had but wherewith to feed one cow, and that only during the summer months, have now wherewith to keep four or five the whole year round; and the larger farmers who, under the old system, had but fifty or sixty half starved sheep and three or four stunted cows, have now well fed flocks of two and three hundred sheep and fifteen or twenty cows. By the immense augmentation of manure, the lands which yielded but six or seven dozen of sheaves per acre, now bear twenty, twenty-five and even thirty dozen of sheaves per acre; and the oats that were scarcely a few inches above the ground are now three feet high.[26]

The productivity of the land had quadrupled, he claimed, and its value had increased proportionately. "On my arrival at Bignon," he wrote,

it was thought a novelty that some prime acres had been sold at one hundred francs. Since the adoption of the alternating system, the prices of land have been continually augmenting, so that now, in 1846, the worst land, fit only for planting wood, sells for 300 francs the acre, and wheat land sells as high as eight and nine hundred francs, and some at even a thousand.[27]

On 26 November 1830 O'Connor's neighbors showed their appreciation for the agricultural expertise he had shared with them by electing him to serve a term as mayor of the little commune of Le Bignon. According to local tradition, O'Connor gained a reputation as a generous man, but with a somewhat "difficult character"; as mayor his relations with some of the village's inhabitants were "often stormy."[28]

The estate at Le Bignon, when O'Connor bought it in 1807, consisted of "a little less than a thousand acres." By 1846, he had "purchased lands in the neighborhood that have nearly doubled the domain."²⁹ With a steadily growing estate and with land values rising, it would seem that the Condorcet O'Connors must have enjoyed a comfortable financial position all along. That was not the case. In 1819 O'Connor wrote in a letter:

> *All my wife's property, for I have no property in France, has been seized for my debt, even to my own, my wife's, and my children's clothes and all published to be sold by public auction, and under the care of a guardian named by the court. All the woods seized to be cut down and sold and all the tenants' rents under sequestration and the whole of my family since a whole year driven from home, and tho' the friendship of Philip Courtnay has enabled me by lending me a considerable sum to come home, to get in my harvest within a few days, yet the whole of my wife's property at this instant remains under seizure sequestration.³⁰*

MONEY TROUBLES

O'Connor's personal financial crisis derived from the fact that in the eyes of the British authorities he was an exiled traitor with no property rights in Ireland. He had taken steps early in 1798 to protect his patrimony from confiscation by transferring the legal title to his lands to Sir Francis Burdett. On 13 February 1798 he wrote to his brother Roger:

> *I have sold all my property to Burdett, yet it may still go on in my name, and the rents are to be transmitted to Hugh Bell, No. 40 Charterhouse Square. Sweeny said he would undertake to receive the rents and after paying all the charges transmit the remainder. . . . I beg of you to lose no time in putting my affairs on the best footing. If you can sell the estate of Cork, Burdett will sign the deed of sale as he has a deed from me.³¹*

In August 1802 Arthur officially gave Roger "the fullest power, to receive my income, to set my lands, and to sell the whole of my fortune." Almost immediately, Roger proved unworthy of Arthur's trust. As early as 1803 reports began to reach Arthur in France that Roger was selling off parts of his property, and "that he had bought a considerable estate for himself." Arthur at first refused to believe that Roger was cheating him, but the fact that Roger had discontinued communicating with him aroused his suspicions. In 1806 he asked a "Mr. O'Realy" (probably the previously mentioned Richard O'Reilly), who had known Roger well when both had been state prisoners, to go to Ireland to investigate. On returning, "Mr. O'Realy assured me the reports were but too true."[32]

Arthur then asked "an intimate friend" of Roger's, George Evans, to have Roger "submit the account of his agency, and all accounts between him and me, to the arbitration of some common friend or friends." Evans tried to fulfil the request, but was frustrated by Roger's stalling tactics. In May 1807 Evans wrote to Arthur:

> *The six weeks asked for by Roger, and granted by me, have been nearly spun out to three months, with assurances from time to time that this delay would not be much longer. One day he must be in England; another day he must be in Dublin, on what he would call his own business; the beginning of this week, I understand he sets out for Cork . . . .*[33]

Evans marveled at "how fertile he is in expedients" and concluded, "The fact is I much doubt if any thing can be done with him, but through the hard and cruel path of law." Arthur concurred; at the beginning of 1808, he said, "I was necessitated, as my only resource, to have recourse to the laws, and file a bill against him, and to force him to account."[34] The wheels of law, however, turned very slowly, and Roger was still evading arbitration in 1815 when Arthur asked his wife to travel to Ireland to personally intervene in the proceedings. Eliza was still only twenty-five years old, but Arthur had no doubts about her ability to represent their interests.

Eliza's permit to visit Ireland was limited, and she was obliged to leave before the matter could be brought to completion. In spite of her competence, she was no match for Roger's craftiness. Before her departure from Ireland Roger agreed to "a final and conclusive meeting at Cork" with the arbitrators, but as soon as she was gone, he sent a letter saying he was too busy to attend. At that point, Arthur says, all attempts at compromise through arbitration ended. "The wretch," Arthur wrote, "has forfeited every title to the name of brother or friend."[35] Finally, Arthur's agents had Roger arrested and jailed.

In 1819 Arthur received a long letter from Sir Francis Burdett, accusing him of a disgraceful breach of fraternal loyalty for having Roger imprisoned. Arthur was infuriated. "The last letter I received from you," he replied, "was written 17 years ago and . . . was filled with the warmest professions of affection, esteem and friendship for the man you called, *the chosen friend of your heart*." After that long interval, "without *the smallest difference ever happening between us, or the smallest cause of difference* you have at length broken silence by a letter" abounding in "injurious imputations." What disturbed Arthur most was that Burdett had "not waited to hear one word from the opposite party" before championing Roger's cause. The rest of

Arthur's twenty-seven page response to Burdett is a carefully documented recitation of the facts of how Roger had "enriched himself by despoiling an exiled brother that had placed the most unlimited confidence in him."[36]

Arthur disclaimed responsibility for having Roger put behind bars. One of Arthur's lawyers in Ireland, whom he had never met, had advanced money to Arthur based on Roger's promises to make certain payments. When Roger defaulted on those promises the lawyer had him arrested. Arthur could have saved Roger from being jailed, he said, only by paying Roger's debt himself, but that was "out of all question."[37]

Roger's imprisonment was brief and eventually Arthur recovered part of what remained of his patrimony. Meanwhile, however, the effects of Roger's embezzlement had been ruinous. When Arthur first began to realize that Roger was not to be trusted he turned to his brother Daniel to take over management of his business affairs in Ireland. Daniel was at a disadvantage, however, because the deeds and other legal documents defining Arthur's holdings were all in Roger's possession. Nonetheless—and in spite of his disgust at Arthur's having been "unfaithful to his King & Country"—Daniel agreed to act as his agent.[38] "Though I have not seen the unfortunate man for more than twenty years," Daniel wrote to McCabe; "though no mortal can look on his conduct in so black a light as I have ever done, compassion for a wretched exile prompted me to grant his request and prevent his late trustee from reducing him to beggary."[39]

WILLIAM PUTNAM McCABE'S LOAN

When McCabe loaned O'Connor £4,750 in 1807 for the purchase of the estate at Le Bignon, O'Connor instructed him to arrange with Daniel for repayment, "for if you do not, it will distress us both beyond measure." Through no fault of their own, or of Daniel's, the transaction could hardly have caused them more distress; it ultimately destroyed their friendship. McCabe was supposed to have Daniel make regular payments of £200 to Hugh Bell in London, who would in turn pass them on to McCabe, "so that," O'Connor told him, "you may not have to call on me here for one *sous* of it."[40]

O'Connor had acted in good faith.[41] In a letter of 17 March 1807 he told Daniel that "you are in receipt of all my property," and that Roger had been definitively removed as trustee.[42] "Assuredly," Arthur then wrote to McCabe, "with Daniel's fortune & all mine in his hands he cannot find the smallest difficulty" in repaying the loan. He had just received assurances from George Evans, he added, that "Roger's account with me is likely to be settled by arbitration."[43] That supposition proved to be unduly optimistic; as we have seen, Roger managed to confound the arbitrators and paralyze Arthur's financial affairs for more than another decade. Daniel, understandably, refused to repay McCabe out of his own pocket and he was blocked by Roger from access to Arthur's resources. In 1809 McCabe, fearing that he had been done out of his life's savings, took legal action—in both Ireland and France—against Arthur to recover his money.[44]

The acrimonious affair dragged on for almost two decades. In his 1819 letter to Burdett, O'Connor bewailed "the state of misery [Roger] has brought me, my wife, and children to, by withdrawing so large a portion of my fortune, which by preventing me from being able to pay my debts has exposed me to the most expensive and cruel pursuit on the part of an inexorable creditor [McCabe]."[45]

In 1819 the French courts ordered General O'Connor to reimburse McCabe 135,000 francs, but that partial repayment did not end the litigation. McCabe died in 1821, but his daughter, Elizabeth Nesbitt, carried on in his stead. In 1827 Mrs. Nesbitt was finally awarded the balance of the debt, but the delayed triumph came too late to alleviate the suffering the affair had caused poor McCabe.[46]

O'Connor came close to bankruptcy, but he survived the financial crisis caused by Roger's embezzlement and McCabe's litigation. He managed to retain control of the estate at Le Bignon, which produced a substantial income, and he probably eventually received some fraction of the value of his Irish lands (though when and how much is unknown). Sophie de Condorcet died in 1822 and bequeathed her estate to her daughter; although she had not been wealthy, the inheritance must have helped ease the Condorcet O'Connors' financial crisis. Taking the general's military pension into consideration as well, it is evident that by 1830 he and Eliza were no longer in danger of facing an impoverished old age.

THE EVENTS OF 1830

Bonaparte's final defeat at Waterloo in 1815 marked the collapse of O'Connor's dream of a triumphant return to Ireland at the head of a liberating army. For the next fifteen years France and Europe were mired in the reactionary era of the Bourbons, Metternich, and the Holy Alliance. In 1830, however, Europe was once again aflame with revolution, awakening new hopes.

In France the July Revolution ended the rule of the Bourbons once and for all and brought a new regime to power. The prominence of Lafayette in the revolutionary events led many, including O'Connor, to eagerly anticipate a renewed triumph of republicanism in France. But alas, whatever illusions

O'Connor held with regard to Lafayette quickly dissipated, as Andrew O'Reilly's memoirs make clear:

> *Among those whom I knew in the crowd at the Hôtel de Ville on the 30th of July, 1830, was General Arthur O'Connor (the Arthur O'Connor). He was coming down the steps from it when I met him, and wore an air of unutterable chagrin and disgust. "Well, General," said I, "how are matters going on within?"*

> *"To utter ruin," said he. "I came hither to ascertain what we were to derive from the victory just achieved by the people, and was struck to the heart by the adulation heaped upon honest old 'Fayette,' and his intoxication from its fumes. . . . It made me sick, and I have withdrawn from the pack of intriguants and dupes."* And fearful boding shook him as he spoke.[47]

O'Connor's subsequent meeting with the new monarch reinforced his negative assessment of the new regime's political direction. O'Reilly's narrative continues:

> *A few days afterwards I met General O'Connor again, and asked him whether he had been present at the investiture of Louis Philippe at the Hôtel de Ville.*

> *"No," replied he; "but, resolved upon ascertaining whether my misgivings were justified, I presented myself at the Palais Royal next day and saw 'Orleans.' Fully prepared to permit no evasion and also to withstand cajolery, I was nevertheless worsted in 'the keen encounter of our wits,' but had all my fears confirmed. We separated, notwithstanding, on civil terms; he professing liberalism, which I accepted at its true value. It would seem that on his side he was impatient to indulge in self-gratulation at his supposed victory over me, for while I was taking leave of him, he could not suppress a look which spoke clearly (to use an Irish homely figure), 'I have thrown dust into that fellow's eyes;' but he had not."[48]*

O'Connor, his republican hopes disappointed, published a 74-page pamphlet in April 1831 in the form of an open letter to Lafayette. He charged the new regime with betraying the principles for which the July Revolution had been fought. Addressing his 'ever dear and ancient friend' Lafayette, he wrote:

> From the day the Duke of Orleans made the solemn engagements with you, acting for the nation, at the Hotel de Ville on the 30th of July, I have anxiously watched every act of the Government to enable me to discover in what interest it was directed. It is with grief I am forced to declare, that not an act has been done that was not indicative . . . that the old system of the Restoration was to be servilely followed, and that the men of the last thirty years' despotism, prodigality and corruption were to be the instruments of the new dynasty, as they have been of Bonaparte and of the Restoration.[49]

Although frustrated in his broader political aims, O'Connor had initially hoped that the change of government might at least provide an opportunity to revive his military career. On 8 September 1830 he addressed a letter to the minister of war requesting that his retirement be voided and that he be placed on active duty.[50] Although he was sixty-seven years old, his military records listed him as sixty-three; O'Connor had earlier falsely reported his birthyear as 1767, apparently to enhance his chances of being reactivated.[51] The supporting letters he solicited could hardly have been more impressive: Lafayette, Lamarque,[52] and former naval minister Truguet all submitted strong testimonials on O'Connor's behalf.[53] However, the publication of his pamphlet undoubtedly eliminated all possibility of reinstatement. Toward the end of 1831 he received a curt notice from a functionary in the war ministry saying, "I regret that various considerations prevent my being able to give your request a favorable answer."[54]

REVISITING IRELAND

When the political excitement of the early 1830s subsided O'Connor refocused his attention on his private affairs. His Irish property had still not been finally disposed of and he believed that task could only be satisfactorily accomplished by himself. With his former friend Charles Grey in office as Britain's prime minister, he petitioned the British government to allow him a brief visit to Ireland for business purposes, and permission was granted. On 9 May 1834 a local newspaper in Cork reported: "Arthur O'Connor: Yesterday, this Gentleman arrived in our City accompanied by Mrs. O'Connor, and his eldest son [Daniel]."[55] Later in 1834, however, a change of ministry led to the revocation of his travel visa and he was forced to leave Ireland in December.

O'Connor received a surprisingly warm welcome from some members of Ireland's elite; he was invited to dine with Viscount Morpeth, who was soon to become Chief Secretary.[56] He also paid visits to the two aristocratic friends with whom he had traveled to France in 1784, Standish O'Grady and John Waller, and even had a cordial encounter with his future *bête noire*, Daniel O'Connell.[57]

During his brief stay in his homeland O'Connor called on his nephew, Feargus, one of Roger's sons. Roger had just died and O'Connor hoped that Feargus would return the deeds to the property Roger had embezzled from him. Feargus O'Connor had by that time become a celebrated radical politician in his own right. He was a member of parliament, to which he was elected as an advocate of the repeal of the union with Britain. He would later gain renown as the leader of the Chartist movement in England, hailed by Karl Marx and Friedrich Engels as the first example in history of a class-conscious workers' organization. The great irony of Feargus's career as a revolutionary is that he might never have achieved his fame had he not inherited a great deal of property that enabled him to win his parliamentary seat—property unexpectedly left to him by his ultrareactionary uncle Robert Conner, who in 1797 had attempted to have his father hanged for sedition.[58]

O'Connor's encounter with his nephew ended in frustration. Eight years later he had occasion to comment on it:

> In 1834, I went to Ireland, where I demanded of Feargus to give me my title deeds I had confided to his father. He gave me his word of honor he had them not, but that he knew they were in the possession of the servant maid that was with his father at his death. To her, he gave me a letter enjoining her to give me all my deeds. On delivering his letter the servant assured me she had given them all to Feargus and offered to give her oath on it. On reporting this to Feargus he broke out in asseverations that the servant was a perjured liar and that she never gave him any deeds of any sort, but having heard from a lawyer to whom Feargus showed the deeds that it was he that possessed them, during four years I repeatedly demanded my title deeds and always received the same assertions that he never had them; but when they were put up for sale, at length I received a letter from him acknowledging he had my title deeds and that if I would specify which of them I wanted, he would give them to me. I did so, but have since not gotten deeds or answers.[59]

In 1834 the memory of Arthur O'Connor's role as a principal leader of the United Irishmen remained strong in Ireland, especially in Cork. Feargus, who held his parliamentary seat as a representative of that county, proudly and loudly laid claim to his uncle's legacy as an Irish patriot. Indeed, his first publication, in 1822, was entitled *The State of Ireland*, the same as Arthur O'Connor's 1798 pamphlet, and he named the newspaper he established in England the *Northern Star* in the erroneous belief that his uncle had founded the original journal of that name. In the revolutionary year of 1848 he wrote in the *Northern Star* the ludicrous boast that "his exiled uncle Arthur was about to become president of the new French Republic."[60]

But Arthur O'Connor, whose radicalism had been considerably diminished by age, did not reciprocate his nephew's admiration, and was in fact embarrassed by it. On 1 December 1834, during O'Connor's visit to Cork, Feargus addressed a mass rally in that city in which he vociferously protested the revocation of his uncle's travel visa by the Duke of Wellington. His denunciation of "the tyranny of the Duke practised against my relative, and your friend—and Ireland's friend—Arthur O'Connor," was greeted with "loud cheers," according to a newspaper account. "In the autumn of his life," Feargus continued, "now in his seventy-second year, he is once more ordered from his native land." The blustery orator vowed to "raise such a hillabellew about their ears as will make the tyrant ruffians draw their half short-horns again into their snail shells." Then, the newspaper reports, "Mr. O'Connor sat down amid rapturous and long continued applause."[61]

The same issue of the newspaper, however, carried a rebuttal signed by Arthur Condorcet O'Connor sharply dissociating himself from his nephew's speech. "I have received *no* letter from the Duke of Wellington," he declared.

> *Having come to this country upon a solemn pledge, asked, and freely given, to abstain from any interference with public affairs or questions . . . I shall as rightly, for the few days I have to remain, as I have hitherto done, adhere to my word; and I have only to regret that any circumstance should have drawn me from the privacy in which I desired to remain.*[62]

Elsewhere O'Connor expressed strong opposition to his nephew's political views, which he considered to be the opposite of his own: "never were principles more antipode than his or mine."[63] With regard to Ireland, he faulted Feargus for adopting the outlook of Daniel O'Connell who, far from attempting to unite Catholics and Protestants in common struggle, was in O'Connor's opinion mobilizing Catholics against Protestants. Moreover, he later deplored the Chartists' class-struggle ideology that pitted the working class against the capitalist class, and he had little interest in his nephew's leadership of that movement. "I am thoroughly convinced," he wrote in 1842,

> *that if any thing can save England from a violent revolution, it is the uniting the middling and the productive working classes. . . . I have seen with infinite sorrow and with indignation that there is a set of profligate, ignorant, ambitious men, who are labouring to . . . dissuade the productive working classes from uniting with the middling class. In my mind it is not possible to conceive greater wickedness than this.*[64]

As for "the man who has set himself up as the leader of this disunion," he declared, "I need not tell you I mean Feargus O'Connor."[65]

In 1846, some of Feargus's political opponents inside and outside the Chartist movement attempted to embarrass him by enlisting Arthur O'Connor in their cause. Joseph Sturge, a prominent middle-class radical, and Thomas Cooper, a Chartist who had formerly been one of Feargus's lieutenants but had broken with him, both wrote to the octogenarian at Le Bignon urging him to send them testimonials accusing Feargus of dishonesty. Sturge informed him they had discovered in Feargus's possession some of the deeds Roger had stolen from him.[66] In July 1846 Cooper told O'Connor that a Chartist convention was to be held at Leeds on the 29th of that month, and that an exposé of his nephew "from your own hand" could help to "prevent him from committing further injury to the Democratic cause."[67] O'Connor's response was sympathetic, but apparently not of great value to them. At the Leeds convention Feargus's followers expelled Cooper, and both he and Sturge thereafter abandoned the arena of working-class politics altogether.

O'CONNOR *VS.* O'CONNELL

Feargus's earlier political associations were especially abhorrent to his uncle Arthur. When Feargus entered parliament in 1832 he was a follower of Daniel O'Connell, the Irish public figure toward whom Arthur O'Connor later directed his most bitter invective. To O'Connor, Daniel O'Connell was not "the Liberator" but "the Calumniator." "There is not a greater example of national ingratitude," O'Connor wrote, "than that which the after generation have shown to the United Irish, to whose noble sacrifices they owe their freedom. This has been greatly owing to the vile calumnies O'Connell has been constantly propagating against the United Irish."[68]

In fact, O'Connell had frequently denounced the United Irishmen— and Arthur O'Connor in particular—as violent republicans, calling them, for instance, "weak and wicked men who considered sanguinary violence as part of their resources for ameliorating our institutions."[69] The desire to respond to O'Connell served as a primary motive for the literary efforts of O'Connor's old age. "It is a sacred duty," he wrote to Madden in 1842, "for me to vindicate the generous generation of United Irishmen from the calumnies of their ungrateful detractors."[70] In reply to O'Connell's charge of fomenting violence, O'Connor declared:

> *He accuses us of drawing the sword. Ireland had lain for a century and more under the imputation of low cowardly slaves, who had not the spirit to vindicate her rights. It was imperatively essential we should show our oppressors we had the spirit to reclaim our rights; this we did, and by so doing we have convinced England it was impossible to longer withhold Catholic emancipation and reform.*[71]

Although his memoirs remain unpublished, O'Connor devoted a considerable amount of space in a published work, *Monopoly, the Root of All Evil*, to blasting O'Connell.[72] He depicted "O'Connell and his Jesuit priests" as "devouring locusts" whose every act "goes directly to keeping the Irish papists in the most beastly ignorance, superstition, filth, and sloth." Their motive, he charged, was to maintain the Catholic population as "beastly instruments of their wealth and power."[73] Madden, who found O'Connor's religious views extremely offensive, characterized his polemic as "that rabid hostility against the great Catholic leader, which he has indulged in the expression of so unscrupulously and so unsparingly."[74]

Monopoly was by far O'Connor's largest published work (not counting the collected writings of Condorcet that he coedited with Arago). The value of its three hefty volumes is largely in the eye of the beholder. To Madden it was a "farrago of polemical twaddle,"[75] while another historian described it as "brilliant," and O'Connor's "greatest work."[76] Frank MacDermot, author of an important article on O'Connor, agreed with Madden that it was "a boring mixture of economics, politics and anti-clerical rant."[77] *Monopoly* is, to be sure, an uneven work; a balanced assessment might recognize flashes of brilliance amidst a great deal of twaddle. O'Connor devoted hundreds of *Monopoly*'s pages to an exposition of those ideas that Madden characterized as anti-Catholic ("the foulest slanders, most violent abuse, and reckless outrages on the religion of the great mass of people in Ireland,"[78]) but which MacDermot described more accurately as anticlerical.

A few years earlier O'Connor and some of his cothinkers had launched an anticlerical periodical, the *Journal de la liberté religieuse*.[79] Although this monthly publication, which appeared from May 1843 through February 1844, promised to "wage war, blow for blow, against the intolerant priesthood," its general tenor was not provocative; to the contrary, its tone was moderate and sober.[80] Its primary concern was to defend the separation of church and state by resisting the encroachment of religious influence on governmental affairs, especially in the arena of public education. It was to be an organ of opposition to "a system of concessions that undermine all the guarantees conquered by fifty years of revolutions."[81] The publication's mission, it declared in its prospectus, "is to protect the plurality of beliefs from intolerance and domination, and from the attacks of the Jesuit or Ultramontane party."[82] Although the quality of its editorial content was impressive, the *Journal de la liberté religieuse* lasted less than a year, and *Monopoly* would become the primary vehicle of O'Connor's religious views. Without the moderating influence of his colleagues, he expressed himself in *Monopoly* in more extreme and less reasonable terms.

THE LAST YEARS

The healthy Voltairean skepticism of the youthful Arthur O'Connor had ossified in the octogenarian's mind into an obsessive abhorrence of organized religion. Madden was justified in characterizing O'Connor's fears of a "grand Jesuit conspiracy against the liberties of every European people" as "the poor old general's *cheval de bataille*, which he mounted ever and anon." However, Madden did not believe that O'Connor was senile. In fact, he had seen and talked with the eighty-five-year-old O'Connor in Paris in 1847 and had found him "in the possession of his faculties."[83]

O'Connor did not greet the tumultuous political upheavals of 1848 with revolutionary enthusiasm. As Feargus O'Connor was fantasizing about his uncle becoming president of a French Republic, the proprietor of Le Bignon was fretting about the possibility that anarchists and communists— he used the terms interchangeably—might be voted into power. In a May 1849 letter to the chief administrator of the Loiret, O'Connor expressed his uneasiness about the more democratic electoral system that had been introduced the previous year:

> *This letter is for your eyes only. You know that I have always been a republican. . . . The establishment of the Republic therefore represented the realization of my life's fondest desires. But in order for universal suffrage to function properly for everybody, and especially for the uneducated masses, I have always thought that it should be of the two-stage kind. . . . I have therefore viewed direct universal suffrage with an intense fear of the civil unrest that it could incite. I have dreaded*

the civil war—or to put it more accurately, the jacquerie—*that is now threatening us.*[84]

When the new system was first introduced, he explained, "all the peasants came to consult me and the other educated landowners to find out who they should vote for." But that was the previous year:

> *This year it's not at all the same. The anarchists are going all over the countryside, signing up everyone they can; they promise you mountains and miracles if you vote for them. They'll swear to do anything, no matter how impossible, and people believe them. Their systematic denigration of those whom they call "the rich" is now being carried out indiscriminately.*

Nevertheless, he saw a glimmer of hope, at least in the immediate local state of affairs: "Since a large number of the inhabitants of this area are landowners, the communists don't have a very good chance."[85] With the passage of time the perceived threat to property diminished, and so did O'Connor's worries.

The memoirs that O'Connor had been writing for at least the last twenty years of his life steadily grew in volume but never progressed beyond the roughest of preliminary drafts. A family friend reported that Eliza had secretly asked him to try to dissuade her husband from working on the project, perhaps because arousing memories of past animosities put the irascible old general in a bad mood.[86] After his death, however, she wrote to Madden:

> *General O'Connor had begun writing his memoirs, but the state of his health did not allow him to finish them. Our excellent friend Mr. Isambert has been and is still very busy gathering from the archives of the different ministries all the documents, public as well as secret, relative to General O'Connor & Irish affairs, as he intends writing an account of the life of my dear late husband as soon as we have all the necessary documents.*[87]

Arthur O'Connor died on 25 April 1852, a few months short of his eighty-ninth birthday. Isambert, a high-ranking judge and royal counselor who served as the Condorcet O'Connors' legal advisor, was the main speaker at the funeral, but his intention to write his friend's biography was never realized.

Isambert had been one of O'Connor's principal collaborators on the *Journal de la liberté religieuse*. He represented O'Connor's posthumous legal interests by successfully petitioning the war ministry to continue paying the deceased general's pension to his widow. He also defended O'Connor's estate against a claim of an Irishman, a Mr. William Conner, who maintained he was the late general's natural son. Because the man could produce no documentary evidence to support his claim, it was disposed of with little difficulty. In the course of a letter on the subject, Isambert declared: "I have lived above twenty-five years on terms of intimacy with the General . . . . Never did he speak to me upon a matter of so much importance in his life as that of a son whom he had left in his native land, worthy of his name and of his assistance."[88]

It is quite possible, however, that the claimant was telling the truth, and that O'Connor's failure to acknowledge paternity was unjust. As previously noted, Lady Lucy Fitzgerald's diary reported the presence of an illegitimate son of O'Connor's at Lord Edward's house in 1797.[89] Furthermore, an account of Conner family genealogy mentions a "William Conner, Esq, late of Inch, near Athy, in the Queen's County, author of 'The true Political Economy of Ireland', etc," and identifies him as "the son of the celebrated Arthur Condorcet O'Connor."[90] The titles of this William Conner's published pamphlets indicate that he aspired to be a radical publicist in emulation of the man he believed to be his father.[91] Nonetheless, his claim was officially ignored by the French authorities.

In his oration at O'Connor's funeral, Isambert began by calling attention to the fact that "you see no ministers of religion around this tomb." He noted that because only a small number of mourners were present to pay their last respects, "it would appear that he died surrounded by few friends." (We can surmise that the cantankerousness O'Connor had exhibited in his last years had alienated many of his neighbors.) "You are perhaps unaware," Isambert continued, "that an entire people of seven to eight million would have come to render him their final homage, had he not chosen to abandon his parents' hearth in order to win civil and religious liberty for his fellow citizens." It was "for the Catholics of Ireland," he concluded, that "this good, great, and generous man made all his sacrifices."[92]

Eliza Condorcet O'Connor died seven years later, in 1859. Her testament directed that she be buried "without any religious ceremony" alongside "my dear husband and my dear children Arthur, Daniel and George" in the family vault at Le Bignon.[93] And there they remain to this day.

10

Conclusions and Reflections

G.D.H. COLE ONCE WROTE, in a sketch of the life of the English revolutionary Ernest Jones, that he "was, by all ordinary standards, an unsuccessful man."[1] The same could be said of Arthur O'Connor. He was educated to become a lawyer but never practiced law. He was a parliamentarian whose career was cut short by his inability to tolerate the corruption it entailed. He was a central leader of an Irish revolution that failed to take power. He was Bonaparte's anointed king-in-waiting whose coronation never came to pass. And for half a century he was a general who never saw battle.

Nonetheless, like Ernest Jones, Arthur O'Connor led a remarkable life of considerable historical significance. He did not succeed in his primary objective of liberating Ireland from British domination. However, the movement he helped to create and lead—the United Irishmen of 1798— had a powerful impact on his own era and left an important legacy of revolutionary precedent for subsequent generations of Irish republicans and nationalists. Although O'Connor was not among the original founders of the United Irish Society, he was the foremost engineer of its transformation from a small reformist propaganda group into a powerful underground revolutionary army.

Historians' speculations concerning "what might have been" are always open to challenge, but few would deny that the Rebellion of 1798 might have succeeded in ending British rule in Ireland had O'Connor, Fitzgerald, and other authoritative leaders been on the scene to coordinate the actions of the rebel armies. The British victory was predicated on the decapitation of the United Irish movement.

Among O'Connor's most important specific contributions was his attempt in 1796 to enlist France's military support for an Irish revolution. He was neither the first nor the last representative of the United Irishmen to engage in such diplomacy with the French government, but he was certainly the most effective. Before he and Fitzgerald appeared on the scene, the negotiations had stalled on the French insistence that the Irish rebels rise in advance of the arrival of French troops. It was O'Connor's firm refusal to accept that condition that broke the diplomatic stalemate and brought about General Hoche's offensive in late 1796, the largest and most serious of the French military expeditions to Ireland.

O'Connor brought a number of positive attributes to the Irish revolutionary struggle. His social status as a landowning gentleman with an aristocratic pedigree gave him a major advantage in assuming a position of leadership. He was a charismatic orator, an accomplished writer, an able political organizer, and a diligent student of military strategy and tactics. As the most philosophically inclined of the United Irish leaders and arguably the most intellectually gifted, O'Connor became the movement's leading theoretician. He utilized the most advanced socioeconomic views of the time (the "economical science" of Adam Smith) in an effort to develop a systematic theory of how a social transformation could be accomplished in Ireland. His 1798 work *The State of Ireland* was the most fully developed expression of his revolutionary ideology.

O'Connor's influence was magnified considerably by his association with Lord Edward Fitzgerald, who affectionately called O'Connor his "twin soul." As a member of Ireland's premier aristocratic family, Lord Edward's social standing far eclipsed O'Connor's, but in their joint political activities Fitzgerald looked to his more talented friend for guidance. They nevertheless perceived their relationship to be one of equals because its primary bond was their common devotion to Irish patriotism. After Lord Edward's death and O'Connor's banishment from Ireland, however, the nature of their relationship was frequently misrepresented as one in which O'Connor was responsible for drawing a naïve Lord Edward into the revolutionary activities that ultimately cost him his life.[2] That this accusation is unfair—to Fitzgerald as well as to O'Connor—is established by evidence that Fitzgerald actively solicited French military support for the Irish freedom struggle in 1792, the year before he and O'Connor first met. A report in the French diplomatic archives states:

Toward the end of 1792, an Irishman of considerable import (whose name is written in the margin) came to Paris with the sole purpose of seeing [Thomas] Paine and telling him that if 40,000 Volunteers (who normally only assemble for a single day) were given wherewithal to support them for three months, a revolution would be inevitable.[3]

The name of the *Irlandais considérable* in the margin was written in code; historian Lionel Woodward deciphered it and identified it as Lord Edward's.[4] If Fitzgerald went to France seeking armed assistance before he knew O'Connor, he obviously could not have been "led astray" by the latter.[5]

CHARACTER ISSUES: COWARDICE? OPPORTUNISM?

With regard to O'Connor's character, historians and other commentators have frequently based their judgments on the testimony of those who for personal or political reasons disliked him. Also, as one of the few leading United Irishmen to survive the failed Rebellion he naturally became a target of blame for the defeat. Lord Edward's daughter, for example, reflected unfounded suspicions that O'Connor had through cowardice or avarice betrayed his comrades: "I knew he [O'Connor] was suspected by most '98 men from his having *unaccountable* money with which he bought property in France, where he settled when he was let out of prison."[6] The source of O'Connor's money has been adequately explained in the preceding chapters, but can the fact of his survival nevertheless be attributed to serious flaws in his character?

The Kilmainham pact saved O'Connor's life and extended it by more than half a century, but his participation in it cannot be imputed to cowardice. Archival evidence makes it clear that the driving force behind the pact was not the United Irish prisoners' fears for their lives but political machinations of the Pitt ministry and its agent in Ireland, Cornwallis.[7] It is also worth noting that O'Connor's factional foes Emmet and MacNeven, who have usually been portrayed by historians as brave patriots, joined in formulating and signing the Kilmainham pact. Generally speaking, O'Connor's persistence in revolutionary activity in face of continuous threats against his life does not support the conclusion that he lacked physical courage.

The charges of opportunism—a term often used vaguely and inconsistently—cannot be discussed without settling on a specific meaning. By my definition, an opportunist is a person who alters his or her self-professed principles to suit the immediate needs of narrow self-interest. A classic historical example of an opportunist in this sense is Talleyrand, who advanced his career by serving a variety of regimes founded on thoroughly incompatible political principles. Once O'Connor reached adulthood and broke definitively with his aristocratic uncle, he maintained a remarkable consistency in his principles. His actions were generally guided by those principles, in contrast to the opportunistic practice of making up *sui generis* "principles" to fit any desired course of action.

Far from obsequiously bending his knee to power as Talleyrand did, O'Connor seemed always to go out of his way to seek out oppositionists to side with. In Ireland he scuttled a promising political career to throw in his lot with revolutionaries engaged in a dangerous conspiracy. In England he was drawn to a group of reformers who at the time represented a small minority of the ruling circles. In France he jeopardized his relations with Bonaparte by gravitating toward the *Idéologues*. It could be argued that O'Connor opportunistically took up the revolutionary cause because he felt he could ride it to power,[8] but that was a high-risk option at best, and taking risks does not fit the profile of an opportunist. Genuine opportunists only flock to a revolutionary banner after the revolution succeeds in coming to power. There were minor episodes in O'Connor's later life that might be interpreted as instances of opportunism, but the overall pattern was quite the opposite.

It has also been suggested that O'Connor's famous speech on Catholic emancipation was opportunistic because he was not really interested in Catholic emancipation per se and simply entered the debate on that subject in order to make a revolutionary proclamation. But in that speech he threw down the gauntlet to the established powers in Ireland and England and intentionally wrecked his parliamentary career. It was widely recognized at the time that he had taken a courageous (some said foolhardy) stand, something no genuine political opportunist would ever have dreamed of doing. That Catholic emancipation was not the speech's primary concern was not a matter of hypocrisy on his part; he was genuinely committed to Catholic emancipation but believed it could only be achieved by revolutionary means. O'Connor's life-long aversion to "popery" and priestcraft did not prevent him from abhorring the oppression of Irish Catholics.

O'CONNOR *VS.* EMMET

In the final analysis, the quintessential element of O'Connor's character was that he was a *revolutionary* in a sense that his factional opponent Thomas Addis Emmet was not. Both men possessed physical courage in equal measure, but O'Connor exhibited a far greater degree of *political* courage than the ever-hesitant Emmet. O'Connor believed that the common people of Ireland, if properly armed and organized, were capable of fighting for their liberation and winning, and he therefore pressed for revolutionary action that Emmet resisted. When O'Connor many years later referred to Emmet as a coward, Emmet's defenders understandably took umbrage, believing that their friend's physical courage had been impugned. What O'Connor had alluded to, however, was a lack of political courage on Emmet's part that he believed stymied the revolutionary movement at critical junctures.

The dispute between O'Connor and Emmet that split the United Irishmen into warring factions and ultimately destroyed the organization was therefore not merely an ego-driven personality clash. On the surface, it would seem that the onus for the split must be placed on Emmet and his supporters, who were utterly intransigent, while O'Connor apparently sought compromise. O'Connor, however, was no less stubborn than Emmet; his olive-branch offerings may have simply been political maneuvers. The underlying problem was political irreconcilability of the most fundamental kind: O'Connor was a revolutionary and Emmet was a reformist. Their conflict was an Irish analogue—all proportions guarded—of the historic clashes between Jacobins and Girondins, or Bolsheviks and Mensheviks.

If the Rebellion had triumphed with French military assistance, would Bonaparte then have attempted to rule Ireland in Britain's stead—with O'Connor as his puppet dictator—as Emmet feared? Bonaparte's record in other territories that he "liberated" was not one that democrats were likely to applaud. O'Connor, however, argued that once the Irish populace had been mobilized, organized, and armed to win their independence, no external army could then take it away from them again. Whether he was right or wrong in that belief cannot be known with certainty, but it is a reasonable proposition and his sincerity in holding it seems beyond question. Emmet's denunciations of O'Connor as an opportunistic demagogue or worse were unwarranted; the words and deeds of O'Connor's long life demonstrate that he was a sincere and principled Irish republican.

Although O'Connor was a republican revolutionary, he was not a social revolutionary. He was a warrior for political equality, but not an advocate of social or economic equality. He was not what the seventeenth century would have called a "leveller" or what the nineteenth and twentieth centuries would have recognized as a communist. In his eyes, Lafayette was a hero of the French Revolution and Marat was a scoundrel. O'Connor believed that everyone should enjoy an equal legal opportunity to make their fortune as best they could, but that natural differences in ability would mean that some people would deservedly become rich while others would not. The apparently counterrevolutionary opinions he expressed regarding communists during the revolutionary events of 1848 were therefore not inconsistent with his lifelong outlook. Although O'Connor did not aspire for the meek to inherit the earth, he belonged to the class of eighteenth-century revolutionaries that Bernadette Devlin McAliskey extolled as "intelligent leaders who . . . risk their lives and livelihoods in the attempt to remove the barriers to a better future for their own people and their kind."[9]

Some earlier commentators, echoing the charges of Daniel O'Connell, have laid the blame for the horrors of the Rebellion and its aftermath at the feet of O'Connor and the other leaders of the United Irishmen. As recently as 1966, for example, Frank MacDermot concluded that Arthur O'Connor's career was of historical interest because he was "a key figure in the great conspiracy" that "deluged Ireland in blood" and "provoked the catastrophe of the union."[10] Because few if any Rebellion scholars today subscribe to this view,[11] arguing against it may seem like breaking down an open door. Nonetheless, I feel it necessary to explicitly reject it as not only erroneous but morally upside down. It condemns the defensive violence of an oppressed people and excuses the cruel and unjust violence of their oppressors. The struggles and sacrifices of Arthur O'Connor, Lord Edward Fitzgerald, Wolfe Tone, the Emmet brothers, and their entire generation of Irish freedom fighters deserve not denigration but appreciation—and unconditional moral approbation.

Let us then give the last word to Arthur O'Connor himself. In a letter written in 1842 the old warrior summed up how he felt about his life's travails and accomplishments. We need not accept at face value his claim to have transcended resentment over the persecutions he endured, but we can at least take notice of how he wanted to be remembered:

> *The example of my life may be encouraging for the persevering friends of Union. I have now arrived on the verge of my 80th year. The far greater part has been passed in prisons, in prosecutions and in exile, yet I do assure you that while all idea of suffering is completely effaced from my mind, the reflection that I have contributed to the Union and liberties of the people, puts my happiness beyond the reach of any human power to affect it.*[12]

NOTES TO CHAPTER ONE

1. Arthur O'Connor, "Memoirs," O'Connor Papers, CBF, f. 5, pp. 243-244. O'Connor's manuscript has been arranged into five sections, labeled folios 1 through 5. Because the page numbers overlap, the folio numbers are necessary to specify the location of a specific quotation.

2. For an analysis of the effects of the weather on the Bantry Bay expedition of 1796, see John Tyrrell, "The Weather and Political Destiny," in John A. Murphy, ed., *The French Are in the Bay: The Expedition to Bantry Bay 1796* (Cork and Dublin, 1997).

3. Jane Hayter Hames, *Arthur O'Connor, United Irishman* (Cork, 2001), p. ix. (See Appendix Three for a review of this biography.)

4. Tone's journal, 9–18 February 1797. Bartlett, *Life of Theobald Wolfe Tone* (Dublin, 1998), p. 732.

5. David A. Wilson, *United Irishmen, United States: Immigrant Radicals in the Early Republic* (Ithaca, New York, 1998), p. 26.

6. John Binns, *The Recollections of the Life of John Binns* (Philadelphia, 1854), pp. 84–85.

7. Drennan to Sam McTier, 27 January 1794, *The Drennan-McTier Letters, 1794–1801*, Jean Agnew and Maria Luddy, eds. (Dublin, 1999), II, p. 8.

8. *Drennan-McTier Letters*, 3 volumes.

9. Drennan to Martha McTier, 24 April 1798, *Drennan-McTier Letters*, II, p. 395.

10. Drennan to Martha McTier, November 1796, *Drennan-McTier Letters*, II, p. 276.

11. Drennan to Martha McTier, 1 August 1797, *Drennan-McTier Letters*, II, p. 331.

12. Martha McTier to Drennan, [February 1797], *Drennan-McTier Letters*, II, p. 298.

13. Martha McTier to Drennan, 1 January 1798, *Drennan-McTier Letters*, II, p. 357.

14. Martha McTier to Drennan, 6 January 1798, *Drennan-McTier Letters*, II, p. 359.

15. Martha McTier to Drennan, 21 November 1802, *Drennan-McTier Letters*, III, pp. 83–84.

16. Martha McTier to Drennan, 13 January 1797, *Drennan-McTier Letters*, II, p. 285.

17. Drennan to Martha McTier, 14 January 1797, *Drennan-McTier Letters*, II, p. 288.

18. R. R. Madden, *Lives and Times of the United Irishmen* (New York, 1916), IV, p. 23.

19. John A. Murphy, "Introduction," in *The French Are in the Bay*, p. 8.

20. See, for example, E. Guillon, *La France et l'Irlande pendant la Révolution* (Paris, 1888), p. 192. For a recent example, see Thomas Bartlett, Kevin Dawson, and Dáire Keogh, *Rebellion: A Television History of 1798* (Dublin, 1998), p. 52.

21. Édouard Desbrière, *Projets et Tentatives de Débarquement aux Iles Britanniques: 1793–1805* (Paris, 1900), I, pp. 105–106 (translated by the author).

22. O'Connor, "Memoirs," f. 5, p. 215.

23. Ibid. f. 3, p. 160.

24. Ibid. f. 5, p. 134a.

25. Desbrière, *Projets et Tentatives*, I, 107–110. See especially footnote 2, page 110.

26. Compare O'Connor's analysis as presented in chapter 4 below with the account of Tone's negotiations with the Directory in Marianne Elliott, *Wolfe Tone: Prophet of Irish Independence* (New Haven, 1989), pp. 281–299.

27. Nancy J. Curtin, *The United Irishmen: Popular Politics in Ulster and Dublin, 1791–1798* (Oxford, 1998), pp. 92, 61.

28. Ibid. pp. 31, 98, 287. See also Nancy J. Curtin, "The Transformation of the

Society of United Irishmen into a Mass-based Revolutionary Organisation, 1794–6," *Irish Historical Studies*, XXIV, no. 96 (November 1985), pp. 463–492.

29. Although O'Connor and Fitzgerald did not formally join until 1796, they were *de facto* participants in the United Irishmen in 1795. See chapter 4.

30. Elliott, *Wolfe Tone*, p. 301.

31. Lady Lucy Fitzgerald, quoted in Brian Fitzgerald, *Emily, Duchess of Leinster, 1731-1814: A Study of Her Life and Times* (London, 1949), p. 225. Also see Gerald Campbell, *Edward and Pamela Fitzgerald* (London, 1904), pp. 13–16.

32. Frank MacDermot, "Arthur O'Connor," *Irish Historical Studies*, XV (1966), p. 51.

33. *Notes and Queries*, First series, V, p. 579 (June 19, 1852). The author of these words is identified only as "J. R. (of Cork)." Dr. Fintan Lane has suggested to me that perhaps "J. R." was a radical lawyer named John Reynolds.

34. Rebellion scholar Richard Aylmer wrote, in a personal communication to the author, "I see O'Connor's 'Memoirs' to be a very important rebellion text. . . . it might be just about the only text available from an intimate, leading participant that doesn't lie or prevaricate. That is not to say that he didn't omit or slant things in his own way."

35. O'Connor, "Memoirs," f. 3, p. 210.

NOTES TO CHAPTER TWO

1. The coincidence of names may lead the reader to wonder whether I share a genealogical relationship with my subject. Ironically, my forebears traversed the opposite surname path: Their family name was O'Connor and my great-great-grandfather Henry changed his last name to Conner (and his religious identification from Catholic to Protestant) when he emigrated from County Armagh to the United States in 1848. There is no identifiable connection between the Conners of Cork and the O'Connors of Armagh, so it would seem that Arthur O'Connor and I are not related.

2. W. J. Fitzpatrick, *Ireland Before the Union* (London and Dublin, 1867), p. 223.

3. NAI 620/32/2, Robert Longfield Conner to Thomas Pelham, 1 August 1797. See also Sean O'Coindealbhain, "The United Irishmen in Cork County," *Journal of the Cork Historical & Archaeological Society*, Vol. LIII, no. 178 (July–December 1948), p. 124.

4. NLI Ms. 15,481, O'Neill Daunt to W. J. Fitzgerald, 14 September 1868.

5. Sir Bernard Burke, *A Second Series of Vicissitudes of Families* (London, 1860), p. 30. Burke's source of information on the Conner family was W. J. O'Neill Daunt. See Daunt, *A Life Spent for Ireland* (London, 1896), p. 160.

6. Hames, *Arthur O'Connor*, p. 34.

7. From information provided by O'Connor to Madden, in Madden, *United Irishmen* (1916), IV, pp. 8–9. See also James Livesey's introduction to O'Connor's *The State of Ireland* (Dublin, 1998), p. 4.

8. Burke, *Second Series of Vicissitudes of Families*, p. 32.

9. Sir Bernard Burke, *Burke's Irish Family Records* (London, 1976), p. 734.

10. Ian d'Alton, *Protestant Society and Politics in Cork, 1812–44* (Cork, 1980), p. 21.

11. Burke, *Second Series of Vicissitudes of Families*, p. 38.

12. O'Connor, "Memoirs," f. 5, p. 286.

13. O'Connor to Madden, in Madden, *United Irishmen* (1916), IV, p. 12.

14. O'Connor, "Memoirs," f. 3, p. 225.

15. Ibid. p. 286.

16. Sheridan to his wife, 22 May 1798, *The Letters of Richard Brinsley Sheridan*, Cecil Price, ed. (Oxford, 1966), II, p. 92.

17. *Walker's Hibernian Magazine*, March 1798. Quoted in Burke, *Second Series of Vicissitudes of Families*, p. 35.

18. Arthur O'Connor, *Arthur O'Connor's Letter to Lord Castlereagh*, 4 January 1799, p. 44.

19. O'Connor to Sir Francis Burdett, 24 July 1819, O'Connor papers, CBF.

20. Madden, *United Irishmen* (1916), VIII, pp. 135–152. See also, M. W. Patterson, *Sir Francis Burdett and His Times (1770–1844)*, Vol. II, ch. XVII.

21. Roger O'Connor, *Chronicles of Eri* (London, 1822).

22. TCD 873/754, Neil Conner to Madden, 27 October 1852.

23. O'Connor, "Memoirs," f. 3, p. 26.

24. For a sympathetic account of the claim to royal ancestry, see Hames, *Arthur O'Connor*, chapter 2.

25. O'Connor's papers at Le Bignon include a genealogical list of 52 generations of O'Connors, from Sean Conchubhar (early seventeenth century) to Ciar [Kerry] (first century).

26. Burke, *Second Series of Vicissitudes of Families*, p. 30.

27. Madden, *United Irishmen* (1916), IV, p. 5. Madden credits the information to "the eminent and accurate Irish historical antiquarian, John Cornelius O'Callaghan, Esq."

28. Donald Read and Eric Glasgow, *Feargus O'Connor: Irishman and Chartist* (London, 1961), p. 9.

29. O'Connor to Madden, in Madden, *United Irishmen* (1916), IV, pp. 9–10. See also TCD 873/744.

30. Madden, R. R. *Lives and Times of the United Irishmen, Second Series* (London, 1843), II, p. 523.

31. O'Connor, "Memoirs," f. 3, p. 14.

32. Ibid. pp. 17, 19–20.

33. Rosemary Ffolliott identifies him as "Apollos Morris of Clonkeen in the parish of Kilmacabree, sometime Major 27th Foot Inniskelling Regiment" (*The Pooles of Mayfield and Other Irish Families* [Dublin, 1958], p. 62).

34. O'Connor, "Memoirs," f. 3, pp. 21–22.

35. Ibid. p. 22.

36. Ibid. p. 23.

37. Ibid. p. 31.

38. Ibid. pp. 31–32.

39. Ibid. pp. 32–33.

40. Ibid. p. 98.

41. Ibid. p. 101.

42. *L'Eclaireur du Gatinais*, 12 December 1993. Miles Byrnes, on the other hand, reports that in 1828 O'Connor "spoke English and French equally well." Miles Byrne, *Memoirs of Miles Byrne* (Dublin, 1907), II, p. 184.

43. O'Connor, "Memoirs," f. 3, p. 98.

44. Ibid. p. 102.

45. Ibid. p. 112.

46. Ibid. p. 116.

47. Ibid. p. 145.

48. Ibid. pp. 39–40.

49. Ibid. p. 41.

50. Madden, *United Irishmen* (1916), IV, p. 6.

51. O'Connor, "Memoirs," f. 3, p. 26.

52. Madden *United Irishmen* (1916), IV, p. 6.

53. O'Connor, "Memoirs," f. 3, p. 26.

54. Ibid. p. 152.

55. Ibid. p. 154.

56. Ibid. pp. 154–155.

57. Ibid. p. 155.

58. Ibid. p. 159.

59. Ibid. p. 159.

NOTES TO CHAPTER THREE

1. O'Connor, "Memoirs," f. 3, p. 37.

2. Ibid. p. 36.

3. On the Shannons and political patronage, see d'Alton, *Protestant Society and Politics in Cork, passim.*

4. O'Connor, "Memoirs," f. 3, p. 36. Lord Shannon was Richard Boyle, second earl of Shannon (1728–1807); Lord Kingsborough was Edward King, Earl of Kingston (1726–1797).

5. Ibid. p. 37.

6. Ibid. p. 38.

7. Ibid. p. 201.

8. Ibid. p. 201.

9. Ibid. p. 202.

10. Ibid. p. 203.

11. Ibid. p. 204.

12. Ibid. p. 206.

13. Ibid. p. 206.

14. Ibid. p. 207.

15. Ibid. p. 207.

16. Ibid. p. 208.

17. Ibid. p. 209.

18. Ibid. p. 209.

19. Ibid. pp. 211–212. This is confirmed by "The Minute Book of the Catholic Association," entry for 17 December 1791, *Archivium Hibernicum*, IX (1942), pp. 140-1.

20. Ibid. p. 210.

21. Ibid. p. 212.

22. On agrarian agitation at the time, see M. R. Beames, "Peasant Movements: Ireland, 1785–95" in *Journal of Peasant Studies*, II, no. 4 (July 1975), pp. 502–506.

23. O'Connor, "Memoirs," f. 3, p. 214.

24. Ibid. p. 215.

25. Ibid. p. 215.

26. Ibid. p. 217.

27. Wolfe Tone concurred in this assessment; in his memoirs he wrote of "an old friend of mine, Sir Laurence Parsons, whom I look upon as one of the *very few* honest men in the Irish House of Commons." Bartlett, *Life of Theobald Wolfe Tone*, p. 30 (emphasis in original).

28. O'Connor, "Memoirs," f. 3, p. 218. O'Connor had evidently forgotten, or considered not worth mentioning, his one rather insignificant parliamentary intervention in 1791. *Parliamentary Register, Ireland*, 1791, pp. 350–352 (19 March 1791).

29. O'Connor, "Memoirs," f. 3, p. 219.

30. Ibid. p. 219.

31. Ibid. p. 220.

32. Ibid. p. 221.

33. Ibid. pp. 221–222. O'Connor's account in his memoirs is an accurate synopsis of his speech as it is recorded in *Parliamentary Register, Ireland*, 1792, pp. 99–101 (8 February 1792). The speaker who followed him was his friend, Sir Laurence Parsons.

34. O'Connor, "Memoirs," f. 3, p. 222.

35. Ibid. p. 223.

36. Ibid. p. 223.

37. Ibid. p. 224.

38. Ibid. p. 226.

39. Ibid. p. 226.

40. Ibid. p. 227.

41. Ibid. p. 228.

42. Ibid. p. 228.

43. Arthur O'Connor, *Address from Mr. O'Connor to the Free Electors of the County of Antrim* (Dublin, 1797). Also see NAI 620/15/3/20.

44. O'Connor, "Memoirs," f. 3, p. 231.

45. Ibid. pp. 231–232.

46. Ibid. p. 232.

47. Ibid. p. 232. The officer in question was Théobald-Hyacinthe Dillon, not to be confused with General Arthur Dillon, who was guillotined in 1794.

48. Ibid. pp. 233–234.

49. O'Connor, "Memoirs," f. 4, p. 99.

50. Ibid. pp. 99–101.

51. Ibid. pp. 102–103.

52. Ibid. p. 103.

53. Ibid. p. 105.

54. Ibid. p. 106.

55. O'Connor, "Memoirs," f. 5, p. 187.

56. NAI 620/15/3/3, Fox to O'Connor, 28 March 1796.

57. O'Connor, "Memoirs," f. 3, p. 134.

58. Arthur Condorcet O'Connor, *Monopoly, the Cause of All Evil* (London, 1848), III, p. 585.

59. William Fitzmaurice Petty. He was prime minister from July 1782 through April 1783.

60. O'Connor, "Memoirs," f. 4, p. 94.

61. Ibid. p. 95.

62. Ibid. pp. 95–96.

63. Ibid. p. 96.

64. Ibid. p. 97.

65. O'Connor, "Memoirs," f. 5, p. 315.

66. O'Connor, *Monopoly*, I, p. 275.

67. O'Connor, "Memoirs," f. 4, pp. 110–112.

68. Ibid. p. 126.

69. Ibid. p. 126.

70. Ibid. p. 131.

71. Ibid. p. 127.

72. On O'Connor's relationship with Knox and the concern it caused in some quarters, see W. E. H. Lecky, *A History of Ireland in the Eighteenth Century* (London, 1892), IV, pp. 234–236. See also Knox's 1795–6 letters to O'Connor, NAI 620/15/3/2 and NAI 620/15/3/8.

73. O'Connor, "Memoirs," f. 4, p. 128.

74. A Stoic [Arthur O'Connor], *The Measures of Ministry to Prevent a Revolution Are the Certain Means of Bringing It On* (London, 1794), p. 23.

75. O'Connor, "Memoirs," f. 5, pp. 194–195.

76. Ibid. p. 195.

77. Ibid. p. 195.

78. Ibid. p. 196.

79. Ibid. p. 196.

80. Ibid. p. 196.

81. Ibid. p. 197.

82. O'Connor, "Memoirs," f. 3, p. 141.

83. Burke to Earl Fitzwilliam, 15 May 1795, and Burke to Thomas Hussey, 18 May 1795, *The Correspondence of Edmund Burke*, R. B. McDowell, ed. (Cambridge, 1969), VIII, pp. 242, 245.

84. O'Connor, "Memoirs," f. 3, pp. 141–142.

85. Ibid. p. 142.

86. Ibid. pp. 134–135.

87. O'Connor, "Memoirs," f. 5, p. 198.

88. O'Connor, "Memoirs," f. 3, p. 143. Chatham is the elder William Pitt (1708–1778). Among the others referred to by Burke are Isaac Barré (1726–1802) and (probably) James Townsend (1737–1787).

89. Ibid. p. 144.

90. Ibid. p. 137.

91. Ibid. p. 138.

92. Ibid. p. 140.

93. Ibid. p. 138.

94. Ibid. p. 138.

95. O'Connor, "Memoirs," f. 5, p. 197.

96. Ibid. p. 198.

97. Ibid. p. 291.

98. Ibid. p. 292.

99. Ibid. p. 293.

100. Fintan O'Toole, *A Traitor's Kiss: The Life of Richard Brinsley Sheridan* (New York, 1998), p. 322.

101. *The Trial of James O'Coigly, . . . Arthur O'Connor, esq., John Binns, John Allen, and Jeremiah Leary . . . at Maidstone in Kent* (London, 1798) [hereafter, "Maidstone Trial Transcript"], p. 413.

102. Ibid. p. 413.

103. O'Connor, "Memoirs," f. 5, p. 197.

104. Ibid. p. 192.

105. Ibid. p. 294.

106. O'Connor, "Memoirs," f. 5, p. 188 and f. 3, p. 135.

107. O'Connor, "Memoirs," f. 5, pp. 191, 193.

108. Maidstone Trial Transcript, pp. 408–409.

109. *Private Correspondence of Granville Leveson Gower* (London, 1916), I, p. 360.

110. Stella Tillyard, *Citizen Lord: The Life of Edward Fitzgerald, Irish Revolutionary* (New York, 1999), p. 167.

111. Campbell, *Edward and Pamela Fitzgerald*, p. 15.

112. Tillyard, *Citizen Lord*, p. 167.

113. NAI 620/15/3/31, Richard Longfield to Edward Cooke, 7 November 1798.

114. Quoted in E. H. Stuart Jones, *An Invasion that Failed: The French Expedition to Ireland* (Oxford, 1950), p. 168.

115. Madden, *United Irishmen* (1916), IV, p. 24.

116. Tone's journal, July 23, 1796, Bartlett, *Life of Theobald Wolfe Tone*, p. 590.

117. NAI 620/15/3/2, Knox to O'Connor, 11 May 1795.

118. Fitzgerald, *Emily, Duchess of Leinster*, p. 224.

119. *Parliamentary Register, Ireland, 1795*, pp. 286-302. Quotations are from a published version: *Speech of Arthur O'Connor, Esquire, delivered in the House of Commons of Ireland on Monday, May 4, 1795, upon the important question of Catholic Emancipation* (London, 1795), p. 20.

120. Ibid. p. 24.

121. Ibid. p. 7.

122. Ibid. p. 8.

123. Ibid. p. 9.

124. Ibid. p. 19.

125. Ibid. pp. 20–21 (emphasis in original).

126. Ibid. p. 17.

NOTES TO CHAPTER FOUR

1. O'Connor, "Memoirs," f. 5, p. 186.

2. Ibid. p. 185.

3. Ibid. pp. 185–186.

4. Ibid. p. 214.

5. Ibid. pp. 213–214.

6. O'Connor's opposition to primogeniture was an implicit acknowledgement of the need for eventual land reform, but he was thoroughly opposed to the program of immediate land reform encapsulated in the revolutionary slogan "Land to the Tiller."

7. Madden, *United Irishmen* (1916), IV, pp. 213, 225.

8. O'Connor, "Memoirs," f. 5, p. 186.

9. Madden, *United Irishmen* (1916), IV, p. 10.

10. "In the contemporary commonplace, a gentleman's word was his bond. . . . To require any further surety was to express doubt that he was indeed a gentleman." Steven Shapin, *A Social History of Truth* (Chicago, 1994), p. 65.

11. Madden, *United Irishmen* (1916), IV, p. 226 (citing Thomas Moore, *The Life and Death of Lord Edward Fitzgerald*, London, 1831).

12. NAI 620/15/3/7, O'Connor to Fox, 24 December 1796.

13. O'Connor, "Memoirs," f. 5, p. 205.

14. Ibid. pp. 203-204.

15. Ibid. p. 204.

16. Madden, *United Irishmen* (1916), IV, p. 12.

17. Marianne Elliott, *Partners in Revolution: The United Irishmen and France* (New Haven and London, 1982), p. 35.

18. Some accounts have erroneously placed O'Connor at this prorevolutionary celebration. See, for example, Georges Escande, *Hoche en Irlande 1795–1798* (Paris, 1888), p. 66.

19. O'Connor, "Memoirs," f. 5, p. 234.

20. Returns submitted to the United Irish Society National Committee, 26 February 1798. See Appendix XVII to *Report from the Committee of Secrecy of the House of Commons in Ireland* (London, 1798), p. 143.

21. O'Connor, "Memoirs," f. 5, pp. 205–206. O'Connor testified to the Secret Committee of the House of Lords (see Appendix Two), that "I left this country [Ireland] in February, 1796."

22. O'Connor, "Memoirs," f. 5, p. 206.

23. Ibid. p. 206.

24. O'Connor, *Monopoly*, III, p. 553.

25. O'Connor, "Memoirs," f. 2, p. 1.

26. O'Connor, "Memoirs," f. 5, p. 207.

27. Ibid. p. 208.

28. For the importance of Hamburg to United Irish diplomacy, see Paul Weber, *On the Road to Rebellion: The United Irishmen and Hamburg, 1796–1803* (Dublin, 1997).

29. Ibid. p. 53.

30. The comtesse de Genlis was a prominent literary figure and educational reformer.

31. O'Connor, "Memoirs," f. 5, p. 208. See Reinhard's report to Delacroix on this meeting, 29 floréal an 4 (18 May 1796), AAE, Corr. Pol. Angl., v. 589, f. 111; also see Lecky, *History of Ireland*, III, pp. 501–3.

32. O'Connor, "Memoirs," f. 5, p. 208.

33. Ibid. p. 209.

34. Reinhard to Delacroix, 18 prairial an 4 (6 June 1796), AAE, Corr. Pol. Angl., v. 589, f. 125 (translated by the author).

35. Unfounded suspicions regarding Reinhard seem to have originated with William James MacNeven in his *Pieces of Irish History*, published in 1807. MacNeven, referring to a document that identified an informer as "R," jumped to the false conclusion that it referred to Reinhard. "R" in fact stood

for "Richardson," a pseudonym used by the disloyal United Irishman Samuel Turner. See W. J. Fitzpatrick, *Secret Service Under Pitt* (London and New York, 1892), pp. 66–67.

36. Weber, *On the Road to Rebellion*, p. 48.

37. Paul Barras, *Mémoires de Barras, Membre du Directoire* (Paris, 1895), II, p. 156 (translated by the author). Entry dated 3 messidor an 4 (21 June 1796).

38. O'Connor, "Memoirs," f. 5, pp. 209–210.

39. Tone's journal, 28 June 1796. Bartlett, *Life of Theobald Wolfe Tone*, p. 568.

40. Barthélemy to Delacroix, 2 messidor an 4 (20 June 1796), AAE, Corr. Pol. Angl., v. 589, f. 133 (translated by the author). See also, Guillon, *La France et l'Irlande*, p. 167.

41. François Barthélemy, *Mémoires de Barthélemy* (Paris, 1914), p. 155 (translated by the author).

42. O'Connor, "Memoirs," f. 5, p. 210.

43. Barthélemy to Delacroix, 18 messidor an 4 (6 July 1796), AAE, Corr. Pol. Ang., v. 589, f. 141; reproduced in Guillon, *La France et l'Irlande*, p. 168.

44. O'Connor, "Memoirs," f. 5, p. 211. SHAT B11 no. 1, Barthélemy to the Directory, 12 thermidor an 4 (30 July 1796).

45. Delacroix to Barthélemy, 4 messidor an 4 (22 June 1796), AAE, Corr. Pol. Angl., v. 589, f. 135 (translated by the author; emphasis added).

46. O'Connor, "Memoirs," f. 5, p. 211.

47. Delacroix to Reinhard, 12 prairial an 4 (31 May 1796), AAE, Corr. Pol. Angl., v. 589, f. 116.

48. Barthélemy to Delacroix, 18 messidor an 4 (6 July 1796), AAE, Corr. Pol. Ang., v. 589, f. 141 (translated by the author); reproduced in Guillon, *La France et l'Irlande*, p. 169.

49. Ibid.

50. O'Connor and Fitzgerald to the Directory, 18 messidor an 4 (6 July 1796), AAE, Corr. Pol. Ang., v. 589, f. 194 (translated by the author; emphasis

added); reproduced in Guillon, *La France et l'Irlande*, pp. 170–171. The key sentence reads: "Après tout ce que nous avons déjà dit, il parait peut être superflu d'ajouter qu'il y a deux points sur lesquels nous avons des instructions positives de ne pas départir; savoir: 1º, de ne rien intreprendre sans avoir fait un arrangement complet du projet, et 2º, que l'arrivée des secours français soit le signal pour l'éclat de l'insurrection."

51. See the Directory to Barthélemy, 4 thermidor an 4 (22 July 1796); reproduced in A. Debidour, ed., *Recueil des Actes du Directoire Exécutif* (Paris, 1913), III, p. 167.

52. The Directory to Hoche, 1 and 2 thermidor an 4 (19 and 20 July 1796); reproduced in Debidour, *Recueil des Actes*, III, pp. 140–144 and 150–151.

53. Edward Fitzgerald to the Duchess of Leinster, 29 July 1796; reproduced in Campbell, *Edward and Pamela Fitzgerald*, pp. 107–108.

54. Tillyard, *Citizen Lord*, p. 198.

55. The Directory to Barthélemy, 4 thermidor an 4 (22 July 1796); reproduced in Debidour, *Recueil des Actes*, III, p. 167.

56. SHAT B11 no. 1, Barthélemy to the Directory, 12 thermidor an 4 (30 July 1796; translated by the author).

57. O'Connor, "Memoirs," f. 5, pp. 211–212.

58. Tone's journal, 23 July 1796. Bartlett, *Life of Theobald Wolfe Tone*, p. 590.

59. O'Connor, "Memoirs," f. 5, p. 212.

60. For a positive appreciation of Duckett, see Weber, *On the Road to Rebellion*, pp. 43, 123. Also, see Duckett's letters to the Directory in Guillon, *La France et l'Irlande*, pp. 159–165.

61. O'Connor, "Memoirs," f. 5, p. 212.

62. Ibid. p. 212.

63. Albert Sorel, "Les vues de Hoche: La Vendée, l'Irlande et le Rhin." *Revue de Paris*, July/August 1895, p. 242.

64. O'Connor, "Memoirs," f. 5, p. 228.

65. Ibid. p. 228.

66. See Carnot's "Instructions pour l'établissement d'une chouannerie en Angleterre," cited by Guillon, *La France et l'Irlande*, p. 85. See also, the Directory to Hoche, 29 germinal an 4 (18 April 1796), in Debidour, *Recueil des actes*, II, p. 176.

67. O'Connor, "Memoirs," f. 5, p. 228 bis.

68. Ibid. p. 228 bis.

69. Ibid. p. 228/3.

70. Ibid. p. 228/4.

71. Ibid. p. 228/5.

72. Ibid. p. 228/5.

73. Ibid. p. 228/6.

74. Ibid. pp. 229–230.

75. Ibid. p. 230.

76. Ibid. p. 230.

77. Ibid. p. 231.

78. Ibid. p. 232.

79. Ibid. pp. 233–235.

80. Ibid. p. 236.

81. Ibid. p. 237.

82. Ibid. pp. 237–238.

83. Ibid. p. 238.

84. Ibid. pp. 238–239.

85. Ibid. p. 241. See also O'Connor, *Monopoly*, III, pp. 554–555.

86. O'Connor, "Memoirs," f. 5, p. 242.

87. Ibid. p. 242.

88. Ibid. p. 243.

89. Ibid, pp. 245–246.

90. Hoche to Clarke, 12 fructidor an 4 (29 August 1796), AN AF III, 186b, doss. 859 (translated by the author). Quoted in Escande, *Hoche en Irlande*, pp. 151–152. See also, Desbrière, *Projets et Tentatives*, I, p. 139, footnote 3. For security reasons (the message was written in code) Hoche did not name the person he was describing and took for granted that Clarke would know he had been meeting with O'Connor. Escande erroneously believed Hoche was referring to Fitzgerald, and Desbrière erroneously believed he was referring to Tone.

91. O'Connor, "Memoirs," f. 5, p. 245.

92. The Directory to Hoche, 1 messidor an 4 (19 June 1796); see Desbrière, *Projets et Tentatives*, I, pp. 107–109 (translated by the author).

93. Hoche to Clarke, 12 fructidor an 4 (29 August 1796), AN AF III, 186b, doss. 859; O'Connor to the Directory, 18 messidor an 4 (6 July 1796), AAE, Corr. Pol. Ang., v. 589, f. 194; reproduced in Guillon, *La France et l'Irlande*, pp. 171 (translated by the author).

94. Tone's journal, Bartlett, *Life of Theobald Wolfe Tone*, 13 April 1796, p. 534.

95. Ibid., 2 May 1796, p. 542 (emphasis in original).

96. Ibid., 22 May 1796, p. 551.

97. Ibid., 23 June 1796, p. 563.

98. Hoche to the Directory, 21 prairial an 4 (9 June 1796); reproduced in Guillon, *La France et l'Irlande*, p. 90 (translated by the author).

99. The Directory to Hoche, 1 messidor an 4 (19 June 1796); see Desbrière, *Projets et Tentatives*, I, pp. 107–109 (translated by the author).

100. The Directory to Hoche, 1 thermidor an 4 (19 July 1796); reproduced in Debidour, *Recueil des Actes*, III, pp. 140–144 (translated by the author).

101. The Directory to Hoche, 2 thermidor an 4 (20 July 1796); reproduced in Debidour, *Recueil des Actes*, III, pp. 150–151.

102. Guillon, *La France et l'Irlande*, p. 192 (translated by the author).

103. William B. Kennedy, "French Projects for the Invasion of Ireland,

1796–1798," unpublished Ph.D. dissertation, University of Georgia, 1966, p. 82.

104. The Directory to the Minister of Foreign Affairs, 8 prairial an 4 (27 May 1796); reproduced in Debidour, *Recueil des actes*, II, pp. 489–491 (translated by Kennedy, "French Projects for the Invasion of Ireland," p. 61).

105. O'Connor, "Memoirs," f. 5, p. 246.

106. Ibid. p. 247. The professor at Lausanne was probably Sir Charles Blagden, the Duchess's mentor in mineralogy.

107. Ibid. pp. 247–248.

108. See chapter 6 below.

109. O'Connor, "Memoirs," f. 5, p. 249.

110. Ibid. p. 249.

111. Ibid., p. 249. Elsewhere in his memoirs O'Connor refers to him as "my beloved Jackson" (p. 341).

112. Ibid. p. 250.

113. Drennan to Sam McTier, 28 January 1793, *Drennan-McTier Letters*, I, p. 472. See also the similar statement in Drennan to Sam McTier, I, p. 474.

114. O'Connor, "Memoirs," f. 5, p. 250.

115. Elliott, *Partners in Revolution*, p. 108.

116. PRO P.C. 1/44/155: "Communication of T. Conway of Cork—watchmaker," April 13, 1799. Emphasis in original.

117. Ibid.

118. Ibid.

119. O'Connor, "Memoirs," f. 5, p. 262.

120. Fitzgerald, *Emily, Duchess of Leinster*, p. 225.

121. Campbell, *Edward and Pamela Fitzgerald*, p. 103.

122. Fitzgerald, *Emily, Duchess of Leinster*, p. 230. See Lucy's diary in

Campbell, *Edward and Pamela Fitzgerald*, p. 111.

123. Campbell, *Edward and Pamela Fitzgerald*, p. 112.

124. The Earl of Ilchester, ed., *The Journal of Elizabeth Lady Holland* (London, 1908), I, pp. 235–236.

125. NLI Ms. 35,005 (11).

126. Amanda Foreman, *Georgiana, Duchess of Devonshire* (New York: 1998), jacket copy.

127. Dorothy Stuart, *Dearest Bess: the Life and Times of Lady Elizabeth Foster, afterwards Duchess of Devonshire, from her unpublished journals and correspondence* (London, 1955), p. 81.

128. Drennan to Martha McTier, 1 August 1797, *Drennan-McTier Letters*, II, p. 331.

129. Unpublished entries in Lucy Fitzgerald's diary, 19 and 21 March 1797, cited by MacDermot, "Arthur O'Connor," p. 50. MacDermot reported that the diary was privately owned by the Hon. Charles Sturt *(sic)*. My colleague Richard Aylmer succeeded in contacting the Hon. Charles *Strutt*, but alas, it seems that in the intervening years since MacDermot's visit Lady Lucy's diary was lost. For more on the subject of O'Connor's alleged illegitimate son, see chapter 9 below.

130. It should be noted that O'Connor himself could not have been at Lord Edward's house in March 1797 because he was in prison from February through July of that year. Perhaps the boy was entrusted to Lord Edward's care.

131. Tillyard, *Citizen Lord*, p. 179.

132. O'Connor, "Memoirs," f. 5, pp. 257–258.

133. Quoted in Tillyard, *Citizen Lord*, p. 209.

134. O'Connor, "Memoirs," f. 5, pp. 251–252.

135. Ibid. pp. 253–254.

136. Ibid. p. 254.

137. Campbell, *Edward and Pamela Fitzgerald*, p. 112; diary entry for December 11, 1796.

138. O'Connor, "Memoirs," f. 5, p. 255. The reference is to *Memoirs of the Life and Writings of the late Charles O'Conor of Belanagare, Esq. M.R.I.A.*, by the Rev. Charles O'Conor, D.D. (Dublin, undated).

139. O'Connor, "Memoirs," f. 5, p. 256.

140. Ibid. p. 251.

141. Ibid. p. 256.

142. See Lucy's diary in Campbell, *Edward and Pamela Fitzgerald*, p. 112.

143. O'Connor's wording is ambiguous: he says the messenger was sent *to him*, but does not explicitly say that contact was made. It seems that in fact he and the messenger (MacSheehy, who was in Ireland November 26–29) did not meet on this occasion.

144. O'Connor, "Memoirs," f. 5, p. 259. The other two Catholic leaders were Richard McCormick and Edward Lewins.

145. See Reinhard's report to Delacroix,10 germinal an 5 (30 March 1797), AAE, Corr. Pol. Angl., v. 590, f. 218.

146. C. J. Woods, "The Secret Mission to Ireland of Captain Bernard MacSheehy, an Irishman in French Service, 1796," *Journal of the Cork Historical and Archaeological Society*, vol. LXXVIII, no. 228 (July–December 1973), pp. 93–108. MacSheehy's mission was of no use to Hoche because he returned to Brest four days after Hoche's expeditionary force had sailed.

147. Martha McTier to Drennan, November 1796, *Drennan-McTier Letters*, II, 277.

148. O'Connor, "Memoirs," f. 5, p. 260.

149. Quoted in Fitzgerald, *Emily, Duchess of Leinster*, p. 232.

150. NAI 620/15/3/8, Knox to O'Connor, 26 December 1796.

151. NAI 620/15/3/7, O'Connor to Fox, 24 December 1796.

152. NAI 620/15/3/9, Peter McKenna to O'Connor, 27 December 1796.

153. O'Connor, "Memoirs," f. 5, p. 263. Also see *Drennan-McTier Letters*, p. 282, McTier to Drennan, 2 January 1797.

154. O'Connor, "Memoirs," f. 5, p. 264.

155. Ibid. pp. 265–266.

156. Ibid. p. 266.

157. See Elliott, *Partners in Revolution*, pp. 107–108.

158. Desbrière, *Projets et Tentatives*, I, p. 113, Clarke to the minister of war, 27 and 29 September 1796.

159. O'Connor, "Memoirs," f. 5, p. 261.

160. Thomas Bartlett, "The Invasion That Never Was," in Murphy, *The French Are in the Bay*, pp. 54–55.

161. John Tyrrell, "The Weather and Political Destiny," in Murphy, *The French Are in the Bay*, p. 46.

162. See, for example, Barras, *Mémoires de Barras*, II, p. 302.

163. Hoche to the Directory, 22 frimaire an 5 (12 December 1796); reproduced in Guillon, *La France et l'Irlande*, p. 244 (translated by the author).

164. Hoche to the Minister of War, 18 frimaire an 5 (8 December 1796); reproduced in Guillon, *La France et l'Irlande*, p. 241 (translated by the author).

165. The Directory, in fact, attempted to cancel the expedition but the order arrived after Hoche had sailed. The Directory to Hoche, 27 frimaire an 5 (17 December 1796), in Debidour, *Recueil des Actes*, IV, pp. 477–478.

166. O'Connor, "Memoirs," f. 5, p. 262.

167. See the examples cited in Elliott, *Partners in Revolution*, p. 121.

168. John A. Murphy, "Introduction," *The French Are in the Bay*, p. 7; Lecky, *History of Ireland*, III, p. 540 and IV, p. 3.

NOTES TO CHAPTER FIVE

1. O'Connor, "Memoirs," f. 5, p. 270.

2. *Northern Star*, 23–27 January 1797. NAI 620/15/3/20 contains both manuscript and printed versions.

3. NAI, 620/36/227, 9 February 1797.

4. Martha McTier to Drennan, 2 February 1797, *Drennan-McTier Letters*, II, p. 296.

5. Martha McTier to Drennan, [February 1797], *Drennan-McTier Letters*, II, pp. 298–300.

6. O'Connor, *To the Free Electors of Antrim*.

7. NLI Ms. 35,004, Lady Sarah Napier to Lady Sophia Fitzgerald, 8 February 1797 (emphasis in original). Reproduced in Campbell, *Edward and Pamela Fitzgerald*, pp. 130–132.

8. O'Connor, "Memoirs," f. 5, pp. 269–270.

9. Ibid. pp. 270–271.

10. Martha McTier to Drennan, 30 January 1797, *Drennan-McTier Letters*, II, pp. 294–295.

11. Curtin, *United Irishmen*, p. 210.

12. Elliott, *Partners in Revolution*, pp. 107, 126.

13. For a concise summary of the mutinies, see chapter 5 of Roger Wells, *Insurrection: The British Experience, 1795–1803* (Gloucester, 1983), pp. 79–109.

14. Wells, *Insurrection*, p. 83.

15. Elliott, *Wolfe Tone*, 265. Elliott notes that Tone's estimate "was certainly exaggerated," but "it was a common exaggeration at the time." O'Connor estimated that "half of the sailors on board the English fleet are Irish" (O'Connor and Fitzgerald to the Directory, 18 messidor an 4 [6 July 1796], AAE, Corr. Pol. Ang., v. 589, f. 194 [translated by the author]; reproduced in

Guillon, *La France et l'Irlande*, p. 170).

16. Pelham to the Duke of York, 14 November 1796, cited in Wells, *Insurrection*, p. 82.

17. Tone's journal, 9–18 February 1797. Bartlett, *Life of Theobald Wolfe Tone*, p. 732.

18. Campbell, *Edward and Pamela Fitzgerald*, p. 114.

19. O'Connor, "Memoirs," f. 5, p. 271.

20. Ibid. pp. 271–272.

21. Ibid. p. 272.

22. NLI Ms. 35,005 (12). See also, Campbell, *Edward and Pamela Fitzgerald*, p. 114.

23. O'Connor, "Memoirs," f. 5, p. 272.

24. Campbell, *Edward and Pamela Fitzgerald*, p. 114.

25. NLI, Ms. 35,005 (12). See also, Campbell, *Edward and Pamela Fitzgerald*, p. 115. The letter bore the multiple dates 14, 16, and 17 February 1797.

26. Burdett's speech of 23 March 1797, in *Cobbett's Parliamentary History of England*, XXXIII, pp. 155-157.

27. O'Connor, "Memoirs," f. 5, p. 274.

28. Ibid. p. 271.

29. *The Beauties of the Press* (London, 1800), pp. 478–480.

30. Drennan to Martha McTier, 1 August 1797, *Drennan-McTier Letters*, II, p. 331.

31. O'Connor, "Memoirs," f. 5, p. 275.

32. "Minutes of a Conversation between Mr. Marsden and Dr. McNevin, Arthur O'Connor, and J. *(sic)* A[ddis] Emmet, State Prisoners. 29 August 1798." Reproduced in J. Holland Rose, "Papers relating to the Irish Rebellion," *English Historical Review*, XXV (October 1910), pp. 751-752. Marsden was secretary to Cornwallis, lord lieutenant of Ireland.

33. O'Connor, "Memoirs," f. 5, p. 275.

34. Ibid. p. 277 bis.

35. Ibid. p. 282.

36. *Report from the Committee of Secrecy of the House of Commons in Ireland, as reported by the Right Honourable Lord Viscount Castlereagh, August 21, 1798* (London, 1798).

37. *Faulkner's Dublin Journal*, 2 and 9 January 1798, quoted by Kevin Whelan, "The United Irishmen, the Enlightenment and Popular Culture," in David Dickson, Dáire Keogh, and Kevin Whelan, eds., *The United Irishmen: Republicanism, Radicalism and Rebellion* (Dublin, 1993), p. 278.

38. O'Connor, "Memoirs," f. 5, pp. 276–277. See also O'Connor, *Monopoly*, III, pp. 548–549.

39. Madden, *United Irishmen* (1916), IV, pp. 28–32.

40. Curtin, *United Irishmen*, p. 176.

41. Madden, *United Irishmen* (1916), IV, p. 30.

42. See also Brian Inglis, *The Freedom of the Press in Ireland, 1784-1841* (London, 1954), pp. 100–101.

43. Madden, *United Irishmen* (1916), IV, pp. 31–32.

44. O'Connor, "Memoirs," f. 5, p. 277 bis.

45. Madden, *United Irishmen* (1916), IV, p. 31. Martha McTier commented that if O'Connor "stands forth as the publisher" of *The Press* "the demand will be trebled." McTier to Drennan, 1 January 1798, *Drennan-McTier Letters*, II, p. 357.

46. O'Connor, "Memoirs," f. 5, p. 277 bis.

47. Inglis, *Freedom of the Press in Ireland*, p. 101.

48. Ibid. p. 277/3. This incident, it should be noted, most likely occurred before O'Connor was announced as the legal owner of *The Press*, because O'Connor left Ireland within a few days of that announcement.

49. Madden, *United Irishmen* (1916), IV, p. 32.

50. Lake to Pelham, 13 March 1797; quoted in Wells, *Insurrection*, p. 113.

51. Lecky, *History of Ireland*, IV, p. 265.

52. Curtin, *United Irishmen*, p. 89.

53. O'Connor, "Memoirs," f. 5, p. 274.

54. Ibid. p. 273.

55. Madden, *United Irishmen* (1916), IV, p. 10, and (1843), II, p. 34. See also TCD 873/744.

56. NAI 620/10/121/95, 9 March 1798.

57. Madden, *United Irishmen* (1916), IV, p. 10.

58. Charles Vane, Marquess of Londonderry, ed., *Memoirs and Correspondence of Viscount Castlereagh, Second Marquess of Londonderry* (London, 1848), I, p. 283.

59. NAI 620/36/227, 3 September 1796.

60. NAI 620/10/121/86, 26 December 1797.

61. NAI 620/36/227, 9 January 1798.

62. NAI 620/10/121/87, 29 December 1797.

63. It would not be paradoxical, however, if having lost a vote to call an insurrection without French aid he decided the only remaining course of action was to step up the effort to solicit a French invasion.

64. Tillyard, *Citizen Lord*, p. 235.

65. O'Connor, "Memoirs," f. 5, p. 281. Beresford was "a notorious sadist who delighted in flogging suspected rebels" (Inglis, *Freedom of the Press in Ireland*, pp. 102–103).

66. Was Walter Cox a government informer as some of his contemporaries believed and as numerous historians have alleged? A letter from Cooke to Pelham, 14 December 1797, indicates that Cox gave information about O'Connor and Fitzgerald to the authorities at Dublin Castle (British Library, Pelham papers, Add. MS. 33105, ff. 262–263). O'Connor, however, says in his memoirs that he himself advised Cox "to call upon Secretary Cooke" as a tactical maneuver, and described Cox as "a perfectly honest man, good

Irishman and good patriot" (O'Connor, "Memoirs," f. 5, pp. 278–279). O'Connor also wrote to Madden in 1842: "You seem to imagine Cox was a false Irishman while the Union lasted, whereas I have the most singularly honourable positive proof that he was firm against the greatest temptations offered by government" (Madden, *United Irishmen* [1916], IV, pp. 19–20). Michael Durey's description of Cox as "a spy who did not give away vital secrets nor implicate his close compatriots" seems to me a valid assessment (Durey, *Transatlantic Radicals and the Early American Republic* [Kansas, 1997], p. 120). See also, W. J. Fitzpatrick, *The Sham Squire, and the Informers of 1798* (Dublin, 1869), pp. 258–263.

67. O'Connor, "Memoirs," f. 5, p. 282.

68. Lord Lieutenant Camden to Chief Secretary Pelham, 27 December 1797, *Documents Relating to Ireland, 1795-1804*, Sir John Thomas Gilbert, ed. (Dublin, 1893), p. 119.

69. NAI 620/36/227, 7 January 1798.

70. NAI 620/36/227, 9 January 1798.

71. Drennan to Martha McTier, [February 1798], *Drennan-McTier Letters*, II, p. 358.

NOTES TO CHAPTER SIX

1. O'Connor, *To the Free Electors of Antrim*, p. 15.

2. Martha McTier to Drennan, 13 January 1797, *Drennan-McTier Letters*, II, p. 285.

3. The letter was undated, but it was most likely sent on February 13 or 14. Maidstone Trial Transcript, p. 514.

4. Maidstone Trial Transcript, p. 236. That the pamphlet had already been set in type by mid-February is indicated by O'Connor's further instructions for William Dowdall, whom O'Connor had left in charge of *The Press*: "one of the Copies are for Dowdall, and let him insert as much of it, or all of it, as he likes; he will observe the Errata and Corrections."

5. James Livesey, "Introduction," in O'Connor, *State of Ireland*, p. 10.

6. O'Connor, *State of Ireland*, p. 34.

7. Ibid. p. 56.

8. Ibid. p. 35.

9. Ibid. p. 37.

10. Ibid. pp. 37–38.

11. Ibid. p. 39.

12. Ibid. pp. 40–41.

13. Ibid. p. 48.

14. Ibid. pp. 53–55.

15. Ibid. p. 63.

16. Ibid. p. 69.

17. Ibid. p. 76.

18. Ibid. pp. 116–117.

19. Ibid. p. 121.

20. O'Connor, "Memoirs," f. 5, pp. 283–284.

21. Ibid. p. 284.

22. Ibid. p. 287.

23. Maidstone Trial Transcript, p. 471. Lucy Fitzgerald reported seeing O'Connor in London on 8 January.

24. O'Connor, "Memoirs," f. 5, p. 295.

25. See, for example, Weber, *On the Road to Rebellion*, p. 93, and Dáire Keogh, ed., *A Patriot Priest: The Life of Father James Coigly, 1761–1798* (Cork, 1998), p. 17.

26. Elliott, *Partners in Revolution*, p. 130.

27. O'Connor, "Memoirs," f. 5, p. 315.

28. "Narrative of B. P. Binns," in Madden, *United Irishmen* (1846), I, pp. 415–416.

29. Samuel Turner to Lord Downshire, 19 November 1797; quoted by Fitzpatrick, *Secret Service Under Pitt*, p. 6.

30. Maidstone Trial Transcript, p. 406.

31. O'Connor, "Memoirs," f. 5, p. 296. O'Connor also publicly defended Binns against malicious rumors that he had betrayed the Reverend James O'Coigley during the Maidstone trial. See Wilson, *United Irishmen, United States*, pp. 73–74.

32. John Binns, in his memoirs, denied even having heard of the United Britons, but his denial is not credible (Binns, *Recollections*, p. 143). Benjamin Binns explicitly acknowledged representing the United Britons in 1797 ("Narrative of B. P. Binns," in Madden, *United Irishmen* [1846], I, pp. 405).

33. O'Connor, "Memoirs," f. 5, p. 314.

34. Ibid. p. 297.

35. Madden, *United Irishmen* (1916), IV, p. 17.

36. Clifford D. Conner, *Colonel Despard: The Life and Times of an Anglo-Irish*

Rebel (Conshohocken, Pennsylvania, 2000).

37. PRO TS 11/122/133, no. 9, "Secret information res. Quigley, Despard, etc."

38. PRO TS 11/122/133, no. 13, "Information given yesterday and this day to the Duke of Portland by a person who became acquainted and has ever since kept up his acquaintance with Edw. M. Despard," 13 February 1798. Quoted in full in Conner, *Colonel Despard*, pp. 179–180.

39. Most sources, drawing upon Rowan's own autobiographical writings, place Rowan in America at the time, but at least one researcher believes it possible that Rowan had surreptitiously returned to England for conspiratorial purposes (Richard Aylmer, personal communication).

40. A report by the informer Francis Higgins connects Lord Edward with Despard: "On Saturday night last, a meeting was held at Hamill's, Dominick Street, where Lord Edward FitzGerald attended. He was one of the delegates of the United Irishmen with Lewines, Chambers and others who were recently in London. [They] applied to a Monsieur Le Despaurd *[sic]* (who lives somewhere very near Soho Square) to obtain a certificate or passport for France for Lewines. Le Despaurd, who is a spy or an agent for the French directory, made application but was refused as were three delegates from Belfast." NAI 620/18/14, 27 June 1797.

41. John Binns, *Recollections*, pp. 83–84.

42. O'Connor, "Memoirs," f. 5, p. 299.

43. Keogh, *Patriot Priest: The Life of Father James Coigly*.

44. O'Connor, "Memoirs," f. 5, pp. 299–300.

45. Madden, *United Irishmen* (1846), II, pp. 16–17.

46. O'Connor, "Memoirs," f. 5, pp. 300–301.

47. NAI 620/36/2, "James Wallis" (John Binns) to Hugh Bell, 25 February 1798.

48. O'Connor, "Memoirs," f. 5, p. 301.

49. Ibid. pp. 301–302.

50. Ibid. p. 300.

51. Maidstone Trial Transcript, p. 80.

52. Binns, *Recollections*, p. 88.

53. Vane, *Memoirs and Correspondence of Castlereagh*, I, pp. 237–238, Wickham to Castlereagh, 25 July 1798. On Turner's career as an informer, see Weber, *On the Road to Rebellion*, pp. 66–99 and 178–186. W. J. Fitzpatrick first exposed Turner's treachery in *Secret Service Under Pitt*.

54. Lecky, *History of Ireland*, IV, p. 234.

55. Binns, *Recollections*, pp. 84–86.

56. Ibid. p. 88.

57. Ibid. pp. 88–89.

58. Ibid. p. 89.

59. Ibid. p. 90.

60. Ibid. p. 92.

61. O'Connor, "Memoirs," f. 5, p. 304.

62. Ibid. p. 304.

63. Binns, *Recollections*, p. 101.

64. O'Connor, "Memoirs," f. 5, pp. 305–306.

65. Lord John Russell, ed., *Memorials and Correspondence of Charles James Fox* (London, 1853-1857), III, p. 277, Fox to R. Fitzgerald, 9 March 1798.

66. O'Connor, "Memoirs," f. 5, p. 306.

67. Martha McTier to Drennan, [April 1798], *Drennan-McTier Letters*, II, p. 389.

68. Russell, *Memorials and Correspondence of Charles James Fox*, III, p. 277.

69. Binns, *Recollections*, p. 121.

70. Ibid. p. 122.

71. Ibid. p. 124.

72. Ibid. pp. 124–125.

73. O'Connor, "Memoirs," f. 5, p. 307.

74. Maidstone Trial Transcript, p. 10.

75. O'Toole, *A Traitor's Kiss*, p. 332.

76. Campbell, *Edward and Pamela Fitzgerald*, p. 142.

77. O'Connor, "Memoirs," f. 5, p. 312.

78. Maidstone Trial Transcript, pp. 47–48.

79. NAI 620/18A/11, Wickham to Castlereagh, 23 May 1798.

80. Maidstone Trial Transcript, p. 93.

81. Ibid. pp. 237–238; NAI 620/15/3/36.

82. Maidstone Trial Transcript, p. 236.

83. Ibid. p. 375.

84. Ibid. p. 446.

85. *Memoirs of Miles Byrne*, II, pp. 73–75, 146, 299. See also, Richard Hayes, *Biographical Dictionary of Irishmen in France* (Dublin, 1949), pp. 3–4.

86. Maidstone Trial Transcript, p. 443.

87. Ibid. p. 384.

88. W. J. Fitzpatrick, ed. *The Life, Times, and Cotemporaries* [sic] *of Lord Cloncurry* (Dublin, 1855), p. 603.

89. Maidstone Trial Transcript, p. 231.

90. Ibid. p. 231.

91. Ibid. p. 197.

92. Lord Holland, "History of the Whig Party," in *Frazer's Magazine*, April 1852 (cited in Binns, *Recollections*, p. 136).

93. Binns, *Recollections*, p. 136.

94. John Fenwick, *Observations on the Trial of James Coigly, for High Treason*

(London, 1798), pp. 118–119.

95. Binns, *Recollections*, pp. 92, 138; O'Connor, "Memoirs," f. 5, pp. 304–305.

96. O'Connor, "Memoirs," f. 5, p. 306.

97. Maidstone Trial Transcript, pp. 319, 403–425.

98. Ibid. p. 408.

99. Ibid. p. 425.

100. Ibid. p. 82.

101. Price, *Letters of Sheridan*, II, pp. 92–93, Sheridan to Hecca, 22 May 1798.

102. O'Connor, "Memoirs," f. 5, pp. 319–320.

103. Maidstone Trial Transcript, p. 380. See also, *Chester Chronicle*, 25 May 1798, quoted in *Letters of Sheridan*, II, p. 92, footnote.

104. Drennan to Martha McTier (undated), *Drennan-McTier Letters*, II, p. 395.

105. Price, *Letters of Sheridan*, II, p. 92, Sheridan to Hecca, 22 May 1798.

106. O'Connor, "Memoirs," f. 5, p. 319 (emphasis in original).

107. Ibid. p. 321.

108. Maidstone Trial Transcript, p. 391.

109. O'Connor, "Memoirs," f. 5, pp. 307, 310 (emphasis in original).

110. Ibid. p. 308.

111. Ibid. p. 309.

112. Historical Manuscripts Commission, *Charlemont MSS* (1894), II, p. 317 (HMC Thirteenth Report, Appendix VIII). Moira to Charlemont, 25 March 1798.

113. O'Connor, "Memoirs," f. 5, pp. 307–308.

114. Ibid. p. 309.

115. Curtin, *United Irishmen*, p. 217.

116. Maidstone Trial Transcript, p. 524.

117. Ibid. p. 529.

118. Martha McTier to Drennan, [April 1798], *Drennan-McTier Letters*, II, p. 389.

119. *The Whole Proceedings . . . against the Right Hon. Sackville Earl of Thanet, Robert Fergusson, Esq., and Others, for a Riot and Other Misdemeanours* (London, 1799) [hereafter: "Thanet Trial Transcript"], p. 115.

120. O'Connor, "Memoirs," f. 5, p. 318.

121. Thanet Trial Transcript, p. 18.

122. Ibid. p. 40.

123. Binns, *Recollections*, p. 134.

124. *Journal of Elizabeth Lady Holland*, p. 247.

125. Price, *Letters of Sheridan*, II, p. 94, Sheridan to Hecca, 23 May 1798.

126. O'Toole, *A Traitor's Kiss*, p. 334.

127. "Narrative of B. P. Binns," in Madden, *United Irishmen* [1846], I, p. 417.

128. Binns, *Recollections*, p. 134.

129. O'Connor, "Memoirs," f. 5, p. 323.

130. *Journal of Elizabeth Lady Holland*, p. 184.

131. Price, *Letters of Sheridan*, II, pp. 94–95, Sheridan to Hecca, 23 May 1798.

132. O'Toole, *A Traitor's Kiss*, p. 338.

133. Maidstone Trial Transcript, p. 539.

134. See Conner, *Colonel Despard*, chapter 13.

135. PRO HO 100/76, Wickham to Edward Cooke, 21 April 1798.

136. O'Connor, "Memoirs," f. 5, p. 324.

137. Binns, *Recollections*, p. 130

138. Ibid. p. 131.

139. "Memoir of the Rev. James Coigly," in Madden (1846), II, pp. 28–30. See also *A Patriot Priest: The Life of Father James Coigly*, pp. 45, 54–60. Ironically, one of O'Coigley's brothers, Micheal O'Coigley, was reportedly "a spy in the pay of Dublin Castle" (Wells, *Insurrection*, p. 242).

140. Benjamin Binns to Madden, 30 January 1843, in Madden, *United Irishmen* (1846), I, p. 403.

141. O'Connor, "Memoirs," f. 5, p. 324.

142. Ibid. pp. 323–324.

143. Ibid. p. 340.

144. TCD 873/744 (O'Connor's answers to Madden's questionnaire in 1842).

145. On 23 May Lady Lucy received word from Burdett that O'Connor had been found "not guilty" at Maidstone. Her joy at that news was short-lived, however, because it was followed the same day by news of her brother's arrest and injuries. Campbell, *Edward and Pamela Fitzgerald*, p. 142.

146. O'Connor, "Memoirs," f. 5, p. 341.

147. Ibid. pp. 343–344.

148. On the role of the Catholic clergy in the Rebellion, and perceptions thereof, see Dáire Keogh, "Scoundrels All—Priests and Prelates in '98," in Cathal Póirtéir, ed., *The Great Irish Rebellion of 1798* (Dublin, 1998).

149. O'Connor, "Memoirs," f. 5, p. 344.

150. Ibid. p. 352

151. Ibid. p. 348.

152. Ibid. pp. 349–351.

NOTES TO CHAPTER SEVEN

1. O'Connor, *Letter to Lord Castlereagh*, p. 43.

2. Madden, *United Irishmen* (1916), IV, p. 20. See also TCD 873/742. Were the Sheares brothers United Irishmen? They certainly were prominent spokesmen for the Dublin branch in its early days when it attempted to exist as an open and legal organization. But did they remain leaders in the later underground phase of which O'Connor was writing? Numerous historians, citing Marianne Elliott as their source, have identified the Sheares brothers as members of the reorganized executive committee that was formed following the 12 March 1798 arrests at Oliver Bond's house. Elliott herself, however, is less categorical; she says the executive committee *"seems . . . to have been composed of"* the Sheares brothers and others (Elliott, *Partners in Revolution*, p. 195, my italics). In any event, O'Connor's direct knowledge of the Sheares brothers' involvement (or lack thereof) was limited to the years 1796 and 1797.

3. O'Connor, "Memoirs," f. 5, p. 343.

4. Vane, *Memoirs and Correspondence of Castlereagh*, I, pp. 347–372 (14 September 1798).

5. Ibid. p. 348.

6. Ibid. p. 348.

7. Ibid. p. 349.

8. Ann C. Kavanaugh, *John FitzGibbon, Earl of Clare: Protestant Reaction and English Authority in Late Eighteenth-Century Ireland* (Dublin, 1997), pp. 3, 344, 347.

9. Vane, *Memoirs and Correspondence of Castlereagh*, I, p. 349.

10. Ibid. p. 349.

11. British Museum 33106/48, Cooke to Pelham, 9 August 1798.

12. Vane, *Memoirs and Correspondence of Castlereagh*, I, p. 317, Wickham to Castlereagh, 23 August 1798 (emphasis in original).

13. O'Connor, *Letter to Lord Castlereagh*, pp. 4–5.

14. Ibid. pp. 5–6.

15. Ibid. p. 7.

16. Vane, *Memoirs and Correspondence of Castlereagh*, I, p. 350.

17. O'Connor, *Letter to Lord Castlereagh*, pp. 9–10.

18. Vane, *Memoirs and Correspondence of Castlereagh*, I, p. 351.

19. O'Connor, *Letter to Lord Castlereagh*, p. 10.

20. T. A. Emmet, A. O'Connor, and W. J. MacNeven, *Memoire; or, Detailed Statement of the Origin and Progress of the Irish Union* [London, 1802], pp. 1–25; Vane, *Memoirs and Correspondence of Castlereagh*, I, p. 353–372.

21. O'Connor, *Letter to Lord Castlereagh*, pp. 10–11.

22. Ibid. p. 11.

23. Vane, *Memoirs and Correspondence of Castlereagh*, I, p. 352.

24. *Report from the Committee of Secrecy of the House of Commons in Ireland*, pp. 68–69; Emmet, O'Connor, and MacNeven, *Memoire*, pp. 38–66.

25. O'Connor, *Letter to Lord Castlereagh*, p. 26.

26. Vane, *Memoirs and Correspondence of Castlereagh*, I, p. 352; Madden, *United Irishmen* (1916), V, p. 312.

27. "Minutes of a Conversation between Mr. Marsden and Dr. McNevin, Arthur O'Connor, and J. *(sic)* A[ddis] Emmet, State Prisoners. 29 August 1798," in Rose, "Papers relating to the Irish Rebellion," p. 751.

28. Ibid. pp. 751–752.

29. O'Connor, *Letter to Lord Castlereagh*, p. 15.

30. Ibid. pp. 15–16. Neilson's letter was dated 12 September 1798.

31. Ibid. p. 20.

32. Ibid. p. 17. O'Connor's assertion is corroborated by Pitt's advice to Castlereagh, 1 September 1798, in Vane, *Memoirs and Correspondence of Castlereagh*, I, pp. 329–330.

33. Martha McTier to Drennan, 2 March 1799, *Drennan-McTier Letters*, II, p. 474.

34. *Evidence to Character, or, The Innocent Imposture: Being a Portrait of a Traitor by his Friends and by Himself* (London, [1798]).

35. O'Connor, *Letter to Lord Castlereagh*, pp. 35–36.

36. Ibid. p. 34.

37. Ibid. p. 33.

38. Ibid. p. 32.

39. Richard Brinsley Sheridan, *The Speeches of the Late Right Honourable Richard Brinsley Sheridan* (London, 1816), V, p. 89.

40. O'Connor, *Letter to Lord Castlereagh*, p. 18.

41. Rufus King to the Duke of Portland, 13 September 1798. Charles R. King, ed., *The Life and Correspondence of Rufus King* (New York, 1971), II, p. 640.

42. Elliot to Castlereagh, 24 October 1798, in *Memoirs and Correspondence of Viscount Castlereagh*, I, pp. 403–405.

43. Rufus King's role in blocking the United Irish leaders' release in 1798 damaged his later political career; it contributed to his failure to win election to the New York assembly in 1807 and to his defeat in a race for governor of New York nine years later. See Wilson, *United Irishmen, United States*, pp. 64–68.

44. See Emmet's letter of 18 March 1799, NAI 620/15/2/18.

45. Madden, *United Irishmen* (1916), VI, p. 4.

46. William Steel Dickson, *A Narrative of the Confinement and Exile of William Steel Dickson, D.D.* (Dublin, 1812), p. 128.

47. Ibid. p. 129.

48. NLI Ms. 35,005 (11), 16 August 1801.

49. Ibid. May 1801.

50. Ibid. 10 December 1800; 10 April 1801.

51. Ibid. 10 April 1801.

52. Ibid. 10 December 1800.

53. PRO H.O. 79/10, p. 97, 17 December 1800.

54. NLI Ms. 35,005 (11), 24 February 1802.

55. PRO P.C. 1/3117, part 3, folio 132.

56. NLI Ms. 35,005 (11), February 1802.

57. Ibid. May 1801.

58. Ibid. 24 February 1802.

59. Dickson, *A Narrative of the Confinement*, p. 146.

60. NLI Ms. 35,005 (11), 10 December 1800.

61. Ibid. 24 February 1802.

62. Ibid. 2 March 1802; O'Connor Papers, CBF, O'Connor to Burdett, 24 July 1819.

63. NLI Ms. 35,005 (11), February 1802.

64. Ibid. 24 March 1802.

65. Ibid. 12/15 June 1802.

66. Ibid. 24 March 1802.

67. Ibid. 12/15 June 1802.

68. PRO F.O. 33/19/68, Craufurd to Grenville, 23 August 1799.

69. O'Connor, *Letter to Lord Castlereagh*, p. 6.

70. Quoted by Madden, *United Irishmen* (1916), VI, p. 22.

71. Cited by Wilson, *United Irishmen, United States*, p. 174. I am indebted to David A. Wilson for providing me with the full text of the quotation from O'Connor's letter to Tennent, which is in the Tennent papers at the Public Record Office of Northern Ireland.

72. Neilson to his wife, 4 November 1801, quoted by Madden, *United Irishmen* (1916), IX, p. 32.

73. Madden, *United Irishmen* (1916), VI, p. 25; NAI 620/12/143.

74. The following are major excerpts of letters between MacNeven and O'Connor dated 31 May and 1 June 1802. All of the letters were copied by John Swiney and incorporated into a letter he wrote to William Dowdall dated 4 June 1802 (NAI 620/12/143/1).

75. Maidstone Trial Transcript, pp. 235–236.

76. Ibid. p. 235.

77. This explanation accords with the contents of O'Connor's letter to Lord Edward, which states: "I send you a letter for M'N. and leave it open that you may see it. You can Seal it, and send it to him, and send the Money to Hugh Bell for me." Maidstone Trial Transcript, p. 236.

78. Wilson, *United Irishmen, United States*, p. 10.

79. Statement of John Patten, in Madden, *United Irishmen* (1916), VI, p. 24.

80. Statement of Matthew Dowling, in Madden, *United Irishmen* (1916), VI, p. 25.

81. Statement of John Chambers, in Madden, *United Irishmen* (1916), VI, pp. 26–27.

82. Ibid. p. 27.

83. Ibid. pp. 27–28.

84. Ibid. p. 28.

85. Ibid. p. 28.

86. Thomas Addis Emmet [1828–1919], *Memoir of Thomas Addis and Robert Emmet* (New York, 1915), I, p. 336.

87. See O'Reilly's footnote, Madden, *United Irishmen* (1916), VI, p. 32.

88. Madden, *United Irishmen* (1916), IV, p. 171.

89. Emmet, *Memoir of Thomas Addis and Robert Emmet*, I, pp. 335–336. Also see: T. A. Emmet [1828–1919], *Ireland Under English Rule* (New York, 1903), II, p. 260.

90. Emmet, *Memoir of Thomas Addis and Robert Emmet*, I, p. 336 (emphasis in original).

91. Pelham to General Eyre Coote, 25 July 1797, quoted in Fitzpatrick, *Secret Service Under Pitt*, p. 350.

92. See Fitzpatrick, *Secret Service Under Pitt*, p. 101, and Vane, *Memoirs and Correspondence of Castlereagh*, I, p. 277.

93. Emmet, *Memoir of Thomas Addis and Robert Emmet*, I, p. 337. This false claim has been picked up and repeated elsewhere; for example, in the *Dictionary of National Biography* entry on O'Connor.

94. Madden, *United Irishmen* (1916), IV, p. 16; TCD 873/744.

95. O'Connor, "Memoirs," f. 5, p. 273.

NOTES TO CHAPTER EIGHT

1. NLI Ms. 35,005 (11), 12 June 1802.

2. Fitzgerald, *Emily, Duchess of Leinster*, p. 271.

3. See Lucy Fitzgerald's 1831 letter to Fanny Coutts, Lady Bute, in Campbell, *Edward and Pamela Fitzgerald*, pp. 13–16.

4. NLI Ms. 35,004. Marginal notes attributed to Pamela, Lady Campbell (emphasis in original).

5. Emmet, O'Connor, and MacNeven, *Memoire*.

6. Melesina (Chenevix) St. George Trench. *The remains of the late Mrs. Richard Trench, being selections from her journals, letters, & other papers* (London, 1862), p. 135.

7. NAF, F/7/6330, doss. No. 6988 (15 Pluviose an XI).

8. John Bernard Trotter, *Memoirs of the Latter Years of the Right Honourable Charles James Fox* (Philadelphia, 1812), pp. 47-48.

9. Ibid. p. 48.

10. Georges Lefebvre, *The Thermidorians and the Directory* (New York, 1964), p. 53.

11. Mabell, Countess of Airlie, *In Whig Society, 1775-1818* (London and New York, 1921), p. 46.

12. Ibid. p. 43.

13. NAF, F/7/6330, doss. No. 6988 (15 Pluviose an XI).

14. NAF, F/7/6330, doss. No. 6988 (25 Pluviose an XI).

15. Elliott, *Partners in Revolution*, p. 326.

16. Arthur O'Connor, *L'Etat actuel de la Grande Bretagne* (Paris, an XII). Also, Arthur O'Connor, *The Present State of Great Britain* (Paris, 1804).

17. O'Connor, *Monopoly*, III, p. 531.

18. Drennan to Martha McTier, November 1804, *Drennan-McTier Letters*, III, p. 290.

19. Emmet's Paris Diary, in Emmet, *Memoir of Thomas Addis and Robert Emmet*, I, pp. 351, 356.

20. Madden, *United Irishmen* (1916), V, p. 16; TCD 873/744.

21. Madden, *United Irishmen* (1916), V, p. 17.

22. *Memoirs of Miles Byrne*, I, pp. 307–308.

23. Emmet, *Memoir of Thomas Addis and Robert Emmet*, I, p. 359 (emphasis in original).

24. Ibid. p. 361.

25. PRO F.O. 27/70, 440, "Secret Communication . . . received July 10 1804."

26. Emmet, *Memoir of Thomas Addis and Robert Emmet*, I, p. 365.

27. Ibid. p. 369.

28. Ibid. p. 370.

29. Ibid. pp. 370–371.

30. Quoted in Elliott, *Partners in Revolution*, p. 329.

31. Emmet, *Memoir of Thomas Addis and Robert Emmet*, I, pp. 375–376.

32. Ibid. pp. 378–379 (emphasis in original).

33. *Memoirs of Miles Byrne*, II, pp. 3–4. For O'Connor's appointment see SHAT, O'Connor dossier, arrêté du 4 ventose an XII.

34. Emmet, *Memoir of Thomas Addis and Robert Emmet*, I, p. 379.

35. Ibid. p. 380.

36. PRO F.O. 27/70.

37. Emmet, *Memoir of Thomas Addis and Robert Emmet*, I, p. 360.

38. John Swiney's name was also sometimes rendered as "Swinny" or "Sweeney." A sketch of his activities as a United Irishman can be found in

Sean O'Coindealbhain, "The United Irishmen in Cork County" (Part II), *Journal of the Cork Historical & Archaeological Society*, Vol. LIV, no. 180 (July–December 1949), pp. 74–80.

39. SHAT, C1 no. 13, O'Connor to Augereau, 5 Messidor an XII (translated by the author). See also SHAT, C1 no. 14, O'Connor to Augereau, 25 Messidor an XII.

40. *Memoirs of Miles Byrne*, II, p. 6.

41. SHAT, C1 no. 14, O'Connor to Augereau, 25 Messidor an XII (translated by the author).

42. SHAT, C1 no. 19, Berthier to Augereau, 1er jour complémentaire an XII.

43. *Memoirs of Miles Byrne*, II, pp. 318–319.

44. Ibid. p. 319.

45. *Correspondance de Napoléon Ier* (Paris, 1861), IX (7996), p. 638, Bonaparte to Ganteaume, 19 Fructidor an XII (translated by the author).

46. NAF, AF/IV/1195 doss. 2, Ganteaume a le ministre de la marine, 26 Fructidor an XII (translated by the author).

47. *Correspondance de Napoléon Ier*, IX (8048), pp. 682–683, Bonaparte to Berthier, 5 Vendémiaire an XIII (translated by the author).

48. SHAT, O'Connor dossier, Durosnil to Berthier, 24 Vendémiaire an XIV.

49. SHAT, O'Connor dossier, O'Connor to Berthier, 28 Fructidor an XIII; Berthier to Bonaparte, 12 Janvier 1806.

50. *Memoirs of Miles Byrne*, II, p. 14.

51. SHAT, O'Connor dossier (translated by the author).

52. Andrew O'Reilly, *The Irish Abroad and at Home* (New York: 1856), pp. 85–86.

53. Letters to O'Connor from Pierre Jean Georges Cabanis and Constantin François Volney survive in BIF 2475. The correspondence with Volney began in 1805 and continued through the year of his death, 1820.

54. Benjamin Constant, *Journaux intimes* (Paris: Gallimard, 1952), p. 189 (translated by the author). The other dining companion was Jean-Antoine Gallois (1761–1828).

55. NLI, Ms. 10,961, Bonaparte to the duc de Feltre, 4 Juillet 1811.

56. NLI, Ms. 10,961, O'Connor to Bonaparte, 1 Septembre 1811 (translated by the author).

57. NLI, Ms. 10,961, Bonaparte to the duc de Feltre, 9 Septembre 1811 (translated by the author).

58. PRO H.O. 100/135, pp. 61–78.

59. Ibid. p. 71.

60. Ibid. pp. 65–70.

61. O'Connor Papers, CBF, O'Connor to Burdett, 24 July 1819.

62. PRO H.O. 100/135/61–62.

63. SHAT, O'Connor dossier, O'Connor to Dupont, 7 April 1814.

64. SHAT, O'Connor dossier, report of 26 May 1814.

65. SHAT, O'Connor dossier, O'Connor to Bonaparte, 30 March, 13 April, and 18 May 1815.

66. SHAT, O'Connor dossier, O'Connor to Bonaparte, 13 April 1815 (translated by the author).

67. SHAT, O'Connor dossier, Rapport au Roi, 6 March 1816 (translated by the author).

68. SHAT, O'Connor dossier, undated and unsigned order (translated by the author).

69. SHAT, O'Connor dossier, duc de Feltre to O'Connor, 30 April 1816 (translated by the author).

70. *Memoirs of Miles Byrne*, II, pp. 173–174.

71. Bulletin des Lois No. 210 (Paris, l'Imprimerie Royale, 14 Mai 1818), no. 4097.

72. Frayssinous's full title was *ministre des affaires ecclésiastiques et de l'instruction publique.*

73. In 1842, in response to a question from Madden, O'Connor wrote that he had "totally discarded" Lewins "from his acquaintance" because Lewins had "swindled" him out of "£350 British he lent him" (TCD 873/744).

74. *Memoirs of Miles Byrne*, II, pp. 184–185.

75. Ibid. pp. 184–185.

76. Ibid. p. 185.

77. SHAT, O'Connor dossier, 9 March 1828, 8 September 1830, 24 November 1831.

78. SHAT, O'Connor dossier, report on O'Connor's request, 10 November 1830.

NOTES TO CHAPTER NINE

1. C. F. Volney, *Les Ruines ou Méditation sur les révolutions des empires*, 1791. Jean Gaulmier, a Volney biographer, says that Volney "particularly esteemed" O'Connor (Gaulmier, *Volney* [Paris, 1959], p. 311). Gaulmier reproduces three letters Volney wrote to O'Connor a few months before Volney's death in 1820 (pp. 309, 319, 320). See also Volney's letters to O'Connor in BIF 2475, items 6–21. The two men held similar political and anticlerical views, and shared a strong interest in scientific agronomy.

2. *Memoirs of Miles Byrne*, II, p. 14.

3. His birthday was 4 July 1763 and hers was 8 April 1764.

4. The Marquis de Condorcet, "Avis d'un proscrit à sa fille," BIF 848, item 26 (p. 152). Also see *Oeuvres de Condorcet*, I, pp. xi–xii and 611–623 ("Conseils de Condorcet a sa fille").

5. BIF 2475, item 39, Mme. O'Connor to her son Daniel, 1844 (translated by the author).

6. After her marriage, Eliza usually signed her letters "Mme. Condorcet O'Connor."

7. *Oeuvres de Condorcet*, publiées par A. Condorcet O'Connor et M. F. Arago (Paris, 1847–1849).

8. See BIF 848-885 (especially 848, item 8, letter from Condorcet's former secretary, Cardot, to Mme. Condorcet O'Connor, 22 July 1824).

9. A letter from John Binns in Philadelphia to O'Connor, 25 August 1828, reported: "A few days ago our common friend, General Devereux, called on me and said: 'I saw our friend Arthur O'Connor, at Paris, and he desired to be affectionately remembered to our friend Hudson, and to you.' I expressed my gratification at the interesting account he gave me of your family and domestic felicity" (John Binns, *Recollections*, p. 138).

10. O'Connor Papers, CBF, correspondence folder.

11. A family friend who met Daniel in 1834 described him as "a mild gentlemanly young man, but certainly not the inheritor of his parents' talents" (*Notes and Queries*, First series, V, p. 580 [June 19, 1852]).

12. O'Connor Papers, CBF, correspondence folder. Arthur O'Connor (the younger) to his grandmother, 12 September 1819 (translated by the author).

13. O'Connor Papers, CBF, correspondence folder. Arthur O'Connor (the younger) to his father, undated.

14. O'Connor Papers, CBF, correspondence folder. Unfortunately, neither of these birthday letters was dated. Another letter in Latin from young Arthur to his father, however, was dated 1 January 1820, which would have been when he was eleven years old.

15. O'Connor Papers, CBF, correspondence folder. Arthur O'Connor (the younger) to his father, 13 November 1820. The postscript to this letter reveals imperfections in its author's English syntax: "P.S. Will you be so good as to buy me a handkerchief like that which you bought me for Maman Condorcet; for I intend to give such a one at Mamma for Christmas."

16. BIF 2475, item 39. Eliza's resentment was not long-lived; see items 40-41.

17. TCD 873/768, O'Connor to Daniel Conner, 7 February 1807.

18. O'Connor, *Monopoly*, I, p. 300.

19. TCD 873/760, O'Connor to McCabe, February 1807 (emphasis in original).

20. TCD 873/768, O'Connor to Daniel Conner, 7 February 1807.

21. BIF 848, item 2, "Acte de marriage du général O' Connor," 4 July 1807.

22. The portrait was probably painted in late 1797 (see Drennan to Martha McTier, 20 November 1797, *Drennan-McTier Letters*, II, p. 348). It may have been transported from Ireland to Le Bignon by Eliza Condorcet O'Connor in 1815.

23. TCD 873/760, O'Connor to McCabe, February 1807.

24. O'Connor, *Monopoly*, I, p. 294.

25. Ibid. p. 295.

26. Ibid. pp. 295–296.

27. Ibid. p. 296.

28. *L'Eclaireur du Gatinais*, 12 December 1993 (translated by the author).

29. O'Connor, *Monopoly*, I, p. 299.

30. O'Connor Papers, CBF, O'Connor to Burdett, 24 July 1819, p. 26.

31. NAI 620/35/139, Arthur O'Connor to Roger O'Connor, 13 February 1798.

32. O'Connor Papers, CBF, O'Connor to Burdett, 24 July 1819, pp. 4–5.

33. Ibid. pp. 5, 7.

34. Ibid. pp. 8, 12. One of Roger's "expedients" was a countersuit; see BIF 2475, item 48, 30 May 1810, "The several answers of Arthur O'Connor, Esq, one of the Defendants to the Bill of Complaint of Roger O'Connor Esq., complainant."

35. O'Connor Papers, CBF, O'Connor to Burdett, 24 July 1819, pp. 10, 12, 25.

36. Ibid. pp. 1–2, 6 (emphasis in original).

37. Ibid. p. 24.

38. TCD 873/767, Daniel Conner to McCabe, 5 July 1808.

39. TCD 873/767, Daniel Conner to McCabe, 31 October 1808.

40. TCD 873/760, O'Connor to McCabe, 7 April 1807.

41. This was Madden's opinion as well. After a thorough examination of McCabe's papers, Madden concluded: "I feel bound to declare, that those papers lead to the conviction, that there was no disposition, evinced by O'Connor, to wrong M'Cabe" (Madden, *United Irishmen* [1846], I, p. 339).

42. TCD 873/768, O'Connor to Daniel Conner, 17 March 1807.

43. TCD 873/760, O'Connor to McCabe, 7 April 1807.

44. TCD 873/770, memos of French lawsuits, 1819–1827.

45. O'Connor Papers, CBF, O'Connor to Burdett, 24 July 1819, p. 25.

46. Madden, *United Irishmen, Third Series* (1846), I, p. 343.

47. O'Reilly, *The Irish Abroad and at Home*, p. 107.

48. Ibid. pp. 107–108.

49. Arthur O'Connor, *Lettre au Général Lafayette sur les causes qui ont privée la France des avantages de la révolution de 1830* (Paris, 1831). Also, Arthur O'Connor, *A Letter from Gen. Arthur Condorcet O'Connor to General Lafayette, on the Causes which have Deprived France of the Advantages of the Revolution of 1830* (London, 1831). The quotation is from the London edition, p. 31.

50. SHAT, O'Connor dossier.

51. SHAT, O'Connor dossier, 6 July 1816. In 1842 O'Connor gave 1763 as his birthyear to Madden (TCD 873/744).

52. Lamarque's stature among his contemporaries is indicated by Miles Byrne's identification of him as "the great General Lamarque who took Capri in 1808 and pacified La Vendée in the Hundred Days of 1815." *Memoirs of Miles Byrne*, II, p. 4.

53. SHAT, O'Connor dossier, October 1830.

54. SHAT, O'Connor dossier, 14 [November?] 1831 (translated by the author).

55. *Cork Mercantile Chronicle*, 9 May 1834.

56. Lord Edward's daughter, Pamela, speculated that Lord Morpeth's invitation was motivated by curiosity "to see a Man of '98, a live rebel." Campbell, *Edward and Pamela Fitzgerald*, p. 250. Or perhaps it had something to do with O'Connor's former connections with Devonshire House; Morpeth was a grandson of Georgiana, Duchess of Devonshire.

57. MacDermot, "Arthur O'Connor," p. 67.

58. Read and Glasgow, *Feargus O'Connor*, p. 20.

59. O'Connor Papers, CBF, correspondence file, O'Connor to Sturge, 28 March 1842.

60. Read and Glasgow, *Feargus O'Connor*, pp. 25, 56, 131.

61. *Cork Mercantile Chronicle*, 3 December 1834.

62. Ibid. (emphasis in original).

63. O'Connor Papers, CBF, correspondence file, O'Connor to Sturge, 28 March 1842.

64. Ibid.

65. Ibid.

66. O'Connor Papers, CBF, correspondence file, Sturge to O'Connor, 23 June 1846.

67. O'Connor Papers, CBF, correspondence file, Cooper to O'Connor, 17 July 1846.

68. Madden, *United Irishmen* (1916), IV, p. 21. See also TCD 873/742.

69. May 1841. Quoted in Elliott, *Partners in Revolution*, p. 367.

70. Madden, *United Irishmen* (1916), IV, p. 22.

71. Ibid. p. 21.

72. O'Connor's three-volume work was first published in English as *Monopoly, the Cause of All Evil* (Paris & London, 1848) and later in French as *Le monopole, cause de tous les maux* (Paris, 1849). Both versions were published by Firmin Didot.

73. O'Connor, *Monopoly*, III, pp. 558, 567.

74. Ibid. p. 23.

75. Ibid. p. 155.

76. Stanley H. Palmer, "Arthur O'Connor," *Biographical Dictionary of Modern British Radicals*, I, p. 349.

77. MacDermot, "Arthur O'Connor," p. 67.

78. Madden, *United Irishmen* (1916), IV, p. 163.

79. The journal's ten issues were reissued in book form as *État Religieux de la France et de l'Europe . . . avec les controverses sur la séparation de l'église et de l'état, par MM P.-C. comte de Lasteyrie, Arth. Condorcet-O'Connor, Isambert, et autres publicistes* (2 volumes, Paris and Leipzig, 1844).

80. Ibid., II, p. 4 (translated by the author).

81. Ibid., I, "Avertissement" (translated by the author).

82. Ibid., II, second title page (translated by the author).

83. Madden, *United Irishmen* (1916), IV, pp. 155–156.

84. O'Connor Papers, CBF, correspondence file, O'Connor to the Prefet du Loiret, 18 May 1849 (emphasis in original; translated by the author).

85. Ibid.

86. *Notes and Queries*, First series, V, p. 579 (June 19, 1852). The friend was "J. R. (of Cork)"; see note 33 to chapter 1 above. Madame O'Connor addressed her request to him when she and her husband were in Cork in 1834.

87. TCD 873/747, Madame Condorcet O'Connor to Madden, 13 June 1852.

88. TCD 873/750, Isambert to Madden, 31 October 1852 (translated by Madden).

89. See chapter 4 above.

90. *Burke's Irish Family Records* (London, 1976), p. 265.

91. Some of them are: *The True Political Economy of Ireland, or, Rack-rent, the One Great Cause of All Her Evils* (Dublin, 1835); *The Axe Laid to the Root of Irish Oppression* (Dublin, 1840); *A Letter to the People of Ireland on the Present Disturbed State of the Country Addressed to Christians of All Denominations* (Clonmel, 1822).

92. BIF 2475, item 23 (translated by the author).

93. O'Connor Papers, CBF, Testament de Madame Veuve O'Connor, 26 April 1859 (translated by the author).

NOTES TO CHAPTER TEN

1. G.D.H. Cole, *Chartist Portraits* (London, 1989), p. 354.

2. The legend of Lord Edward's romantic naïveté was given wide circulation early on by Thomas Moore's *The Life and Death of Lord Edward Fitzgerald*.

3. Unsigned report dated 11 June 1793, AAE, Corr. Pol. Angl, v. 587, f. 101 (translated by the author).

4. Lionel D. Woodward, "Les Projets de descente en Irlande et les réfugiés irlandais et anglais en France sous la Convention: d'après des documents inédits," *Annales Historiques de la Révolution Française*, VIII (1931), p 4.

5. Fitzgerald biographer Stella Tillyard examined this charge and found that "cumulative evidence from spies and later researches" has served to "dispel once and for all the idea of Lord Edward as a romantic who was used or led by men more ruthless than himself" (Tillyard, *Citizen Lord*, p. 310).

6. Campbell, *Edward and Pamela Fitzgerald*, p. 250. Emphasis in original.

7. See chapter 7 above.

8. This, for example, was the charge that O'Connor sought to refute in *To the Free Electors of Antrim* (see chapter 5 above).

9. Bernadette Devlin McAliskey, "Foreword" to Conner, *Colonel Despard*, p. 12.

10. MacDermot, "Arthur O'Connor," pp. 68–69.

11. "A new consensus has established itself with surprising speed: recent scholars agree," observes I. R. McBride; "The blame for the inter-communal violence of the 1790s is laid squarely at the door of the Dublin Castle administration, the Orange gentry and the British state itself" ("'When Ulster Joined Ireland': Anti-Popery, Presbyterian Radicalism and Irish Republicanism in the 1790s," *Past and Present*, November 1997, p. 65).

12. O'Connor Papers, CBF, correspondence file, O'Connor to Sturge, 28 March 1842.

Appendix One

The Kilmainham "Memoire"

The initial statement that Emmet, O'Connor, and MacNeven gave to Cornwallis's agents on 4 August 1798 in fulfillment of the terms of their agreement under the Kilmainham pact is reproduced in full below. Cornwallis did not challenge its accuracy but found it politically unacceptable and refused to publish it. The three United Irish leaders themselves had it published after their release from prison; the title page read:

MEMOIRE:
OR, DETAILED STATEMENT OF THE
ORIGIN AND PROGRESS
OF THE
IRISH UNION:
DELIVERED TO THE IRISH GOVERNMENT,
By Messrs. Emmet, O'Connor, and M'Nevin;
TOGETHER WITH THE
EXAMINATIONS
OF THESE GENTLEMEN
BEFORE THE SECRET COMMITTEES OF THE
HOUSES OF LORDS AND COMMONS,
IN THE SUMMER OF 1798.

There are numerous small discrepancies between this version and one reproduced in Castlereagh's Memoirs and Correspondence *(volume I, pp. 353–372). The differences are, for the most part, inconsequential and appear to have been accidental, perhaps caused by separate attempts at deciphering a poorly handwritten original. The discrepancies have been reconciled in the text presented below.*

As to authorship of the document, Emmet's grandson and namesake claimed that "according to family tradition" it was "from the pen of T. A. Emmet," and that "Mr. O'Connor wrote no portion of it" (Memoir of Thomas Addis and Robert Emmet, p. 443). *Be that as it may, it was clearly a work of collaboration signed by O'Connor and MacNeven as well as Emmet. All three shared equal responsibility for producing it and defending its political content.*

The disunion that had long existed between the Catholics and Protestants of Ireland, particularly those of the Presbyterian religion, was found by experience to be so great an obstacle to the obtaining a Reform in Parliament, on any thing of just and popular principles, that some Persons, equally friendly to that measure, and to Religious Toleration, conceived the idea of uniting both Sects, in pursuit of the same object—a Repeal of the Penal Laws, and a Reform, including in itself an extension of the Right of Suffrage to the Catholic.

From this originated the Societies of United Irishmen, in the end of the year 1791; even then it was clearly perceived that the chief support of the Borough Interest in Ireland was the weight of English Influence; but as yet that obvious remark had not led the minds of the Reformers towards a Separation from England. Some individuals, perhaps, had convinced themselves that benefit would result to this country from such a measure; but during the whole existence of the Society of United Irishmen of Dublin, we may safely aver, to the best of our knowledge and recollections, that no such object was ever agitated by its Members, either in public debate, or private conversation, nor until the Society had lasted a considerable time, were any traces of Republicanism to be met with there: its views were purely and in good faith what the Test of the Society avows. Those, however, were sufficient to excite the most lively uneasiness in the friends of Protestant Ascendancy and Unequal Representation; insomuch that the difficulty of their attainments, notwithstanding the beginning union of sects, became manifest. But with the difficulty, the necessity of the measure was still more obvious; and the disposition of the People, to run greater risques, for what they conceived both difficult and necessary to be had, was encreased. This will sufficiently account for the violent expressions and extraordinary proposals that are attributed to that society.—One of the latter was, that of endeavoring at some future, but undetermined time, to procure the meeting of a Convention, which should take into consideration the best mode of effecting a Reform in Parliament, as had been done in the year 1784. It was thought the weight and power of such a body, backed as it was hoped it would, with the support of Catholic and Protestant, and the encreased spirit towards Liberty which arose from the French Revolution, would procure a more favourable issue to the efforts of that Convention than had attended those of the former; but the object as yet went no farther than a Reform in Parliament, only on more broad and liberal principles.

The discussion, however, of political questions, both foreign and domestic, and the enacting of several unpopular laws, had advanced the minds of many people, even before they were aware of it, towards Republicanism and Revolution: they began to reason on the subject, and to think a Republican Form of Government was preferable to our own; but they still considered it as impossible to be obtained, in consequence of the English power and connexion. This, together with its being constantly perceived that the weight of English influence, was thrown into the scale of Borough Interest, gradually rendered the connexion itself an object of discussion; and its advantages somewhat problematical. While the minds of men were taking this turn, the Society of United Irishmen of Dublin, was in the year 1794 forcibly dissolved, but the principles by which it was actuated were as strong as ever; as hypocrisy was not one of the vices of that Society, it brought its destruction on itself by the openness of its discussion, and publicity of its proceedings. Its fate was a warning to that of Belfast, and suggested the idea of forming Societies, with the same object, but whose secrecy should be their protection. The first of these Societies was, as we best recollect, instituted in the year 1795. In order to secure co-operation and uniformity of action, they organized a system of Committees, Baronial, County, and Provincial, and even National; but it was long before the skeleton of this organization was filled up. While the formation of these Societies was in agitation, the Friends of Liberty were gradually, but with a timid step, advancing towards Republicanism; they began to be convinced, that it would be as easy to obtain a Revolution as a Reform, so obstinately was the latter resisted; and as the conviction impressed itself on their minds, they were inclined not to give up the struggle, but to extend their views; it was for this reason that in their Test the words are "an equal representation of all the people of Ireland," without inserting the word Parliament. This Test embraced both the Republican and the Reformer, and left to future circumstances to decide to which point the common strength should be directed; but still the whole body, we are convinced, would rejoice to stop short at Reform. Another consideration, however, led the minds of reflecting United Irishmen to look towards a Republic and Separation from England; this was the war with France: they clearly perceived that their strength was not likely to become speedily equal to wresting from the English and the Borough Interest in Ireland even a Reform; foreign assistance would, therefore, perhaps become necessary; but foreign assistance could only be hoped for in proportion as the object to which it would be applied was important to the party giving it. A Reform in the Irish Parliament was no object to the French—a Separation of Ireland from England was a mighty one indeed.—Thus they reasoned: shall we, between two objects, confine ourselves to the least valuable, even though it is equally difficult to be obtained, if we consider our own internal resources, and much more difficult to be obtained, if we consider the relation of Ireland with the rest of Europe?

Whatever progress the United System had made among the Presbyterians of the North, it had, as we apprehend, made but little way among the Catholics throughout the Kingdom, until after the recall of Lord Fitzwilliam, notwithstanding many resolutions which had appeared from them, manifesting a growing spirit, they were considered as entertaining not only an habitual spirit for Monarchy, but also as being less attached than the Presbyterians to Political Liberty. There were, however, certain men among them of a different description who rejoiced at the rejection of their claims, because it gave them an opportunity of pointing out that the adversaries of Reform were also their adversaries; and that those two objects could never be separated with any chance of success to either. They used the recall of that Nobleman, and the rejection of his measures, to cement together in political union the Catholic and Presbyterian masses.

The modern Societies, for their protection against informers and prosecution, had introduced into their Test a clause of secrecy. They did more—they changed the engagement of their predecessors into an Oath; and mutual confidence encreased, when religion was called in aid of mutual security.

While they were almost entirely confined to the North, but encreasing rapidly there, the Insurrection Bill was passed in the beginning of the year 1796, augmenting the penalties upon administering unlawful oaths, or solemn obligations, even to death: but death had ceased to alarm men who began to think it was to be encountered in their country's cause. The statute remained an absolute dead letter, and the numbers of the body augmented beyond belief.

To the Armagh Persecution is the Union of Irishmen most exceedingly indebted. The persons and properties of the wretched Catholics of that county were exposed to the merciless attacks of an Orange Faction, which was certainly in many instances uncontrouled by the Justices of Peace, and claimed to be in all supported by Government. When these men found that illegal acts of Magistrates were indemnified by occasional statutes, and the Courts of Justice shut against them, by Parliamentary barriers, they began to think they had no refuge but in joining the Union. Their dispositions so to do, were much encreased by finding the Presbyterians of Belfast especially step forward to espouse their cause, and succour their distress. We will here remark, once for all, what we most solemnly aver, that wherever the Orange System was introduced, particularly in Catholic counties, it was uniformly observed, that the numbers of United Irishmen encreased most astonishingly. The alarm which an Orange Lodge excited among the Catholics made them look for refuge by joining together in the United System; and as their number was always greater than that of bigoted Protestants, our harvest was ten-fold.

At the same time that we mention this circumstance we must confess, and must deeply regret, that it excited a mutual acrimony and vindictive spirit, which was peculiarly opposite to the interest, and abhorrent to the feelings of the United Irishmen, and has lately manifested itself, we hear, into outrages of so much horror.

Defenderism has been supposed to be the origin of the modern Societies of United Irishmen: this is undoubtedly either a mistake or a misrepresentation; we solemnly declare, that there was no connexion between them and the United Irish, as far as we know, except what follows:

After the Defenders had spread into different counties, they manifested a rooted but unenlightened aversion, among other things, to the same grievances, that were complained of by the Union. They were composed almost entirely of Catholics, and those of the lowest order, who, through a false confidence, were risking themselves, and the attainment of redress by premature and unsystematic insurrection. In the North they were also engaged in an acrimonious and bloody struggle with an opposite faction, called Peep-of-day-boys. The advantage of reconciling these two misguided parties, of joining them in the Union, and so turning them from any views they might have exclusively religious, and of restraining them from employing a mutually destructive exertion of force, most powerfully struck the minds of several United Irishmen. For that purpose, many of them in the Northern counties went among both, but particularly the Defenders, joined with them, shewed them the superiority of the Union System, and gradually, while Government was endeavouring to quell them by force, melted them down into the United Irish body. This rendered their conduct infinitely more orderly, and less suspicious to Government.

It has been alledged against the United Irishmen, that they established a system of assassination. Nothing has ever been imputed to them, that we feel more pleasure in being able to disavow. In such immense numbers and very various dispositions as were to be found in that body, altho' uniformity of system may have given a wonderful uniformity of action, yet it is unfair and unjust to charge the whole body with the vices of a few of its members: individual grievances produced individual resentments, and the meeting of many sufferers in the same way, frequently caused them to concur in the same resolutions. It appears, indeed, by some trials, that a Baronial Committee once took that subject into consideration, but it was manifest, it was taken up by them as individuals, whose principles, as it afterwards appeared, were not repugnant to the act. A Committee of Assassination has been much talked of—we have heard persons mentioned as members of it, whom we know, from the most private and confidential conversations, to be utterly abhorrent from that crime. We solemnly declare, we believe that such a Committee never existed.—We most positively aver, it never was with the cognizance of a part of the Union. We also declare, that in no communication from those who were placed at the head of the United Irishmen, to the rest of that body, and in no official paper, was assassination ever inculcated, but frequently and fervently reprobated. It was considered by them with horror, on account of its criminality, and with personal dread, because it would render ferocious the minds of men, in whose hands their lives were placed, most peculiarly placed; inasmuch as between them and the rest of that body were they out of the protection of the law. In proof of this assertion, we would beg leave to refer to a sketch of a publication, which we believe was seized among the papers of one of us, at the time of his arrest, and which it was intended should appear, if the paper to which it alluded had not been discontinued.—One other consideration, which we entreat may not offend, will, we hope, be decisive. If such Committee had existed, and if the men at the head of the United Irishmen had thought assassination a justifiable mode of attaining their ends, and had been capable of encouraging such atrocity, possessed as they were of wide-spread means of acting, and powerful controul over men, who, it is now manifest, held the loss of their lives in utter contempt, the poignard would have been directed, not against such petty objects as an obnoxious county Magistrate, or an informer.

We were none of us members of the United System until September or October, in the year 1796; at that time it must be confessed, the reasons already alledged, and the irritations of the preceding summer in the North, had disposed us to a Separation and Republic, principally because we were hopeless that a Reform would ever be yielded to any peaceable exertion of the people. We cannot be accurate as to the progress either of the numbers or organization of the United Irishmen; because, it having been an invariable rule, to burn all the returns, or other papers, after they ceased to be useful; we have no documents with which to refresh our memories, but we apprehend the Report of the Secret Committee to be, in that case, sufficiently accurate, except that the numbers were always much greater than appeared by those reports; the documents on which they rely, only noticed those who went regularly into societies; but great numbers, perhaps at a rough guess, half as many, were sworn to the test, who were prevented by private motives and local circumstances, from committing themselves in that way; we are, however, convinced, that the numbers of the whole body could not latterly be less than 500,000.

The returns from the different societies, and committees upwards, specified among other things, arms and ammunition; they were not originally included in them, nor were they introduced until after the passing of the Insurrection and Indemnity Acts, when the people began to be more than ever carried towards resistance, and were extremely irritated by the indemnified violations of law in the North. The returns also stated, sums of money having been collected; those sums were always very small, and applied towards the spreading of the system in other places, towards the support of persons imprisoned on charges connected with the Union, and in conducting of their defences; any other expences were defrayed by occasional private subscriptions.

The printed Constitution mentions a National Committee; none such, strictly speaking, was ever formed, at first, because to its appointment, two Provincials at least were necessary; and before the organization in any other part of the kingdom could reach to a provincial, the immense numbers in Ulster required the superintendence of a supreme head. Some persons were then chosen by the Northern Provincial, with powers to associate to themselves such others as they should think fit. They were commonly called the Executive. When the organization began in Leinster, and shortly after the French left Bantry Bay, some persons resident in this province were associated to that body; things continued thus until many began to think, that elections should take place pursuant to the Constitution. The fidelity of the people had by that time been so abundantly proved, that men did not hesitate to submit themselves to a guarded election by the Leinster Provincial. National Delegates were therefore chosen by it, who acted for their own province, and occasionally consulted with the Executive of the North on subjects of general importance. The election of National Delegates first took place, as we best recollect, about the latter end of November or December, 1797.

The military organization had no existence until towards the latter end of 1796, and was as near as could be engrafted on the civil: in order to avoid giving alarm, it continued to conceal itself as much as possible under the usual denominations. The Secretary of a society of twelve, was commonly the petty officer; the delegate of five societies to a Lower Baronial, when the population required such an intermediate step, was usually the Captain, and the Delegates from the Lower to the Upper Baronial, was usually the Colonel. All officers to Colonels up, were indispensably elected by those they were to command, but at that point the interference of the Societies ceased, and every higher commission was in the power of the Executive; only as soon as sufficient numbers of regiments were organized in any county, the Colonels were directed to transmit to the Executive the names of three persons, fit, in their opinion, to act as Adjutants General for that county; of those, the Executive chose one; and through this organ all military communications were made to the several counties; in consequence of such arrangements not more than one of the Executive need ever be committed with any county, and that only to a person of his own choice from among the three. It so happened, that the same member was entitled to hold communications with several Adjutants General, which still further diminished the risk to the Executive: we refer to the amended printed Constitution, where the Military Constitution, without being named, is more correctly set forth, than we can now give from memory. As to the manner in which these men were to be provided with arms and ammunition, every man who could afford it was directed to provide himself with a musket, bayonet, and as much ammunition as he could; every other man with a pike, and if he was able a case of pistols; but this, we apprehend, was not strictly adhered to. We have heard it said, that Treasurers were appointed for raising money to purchase arms, but no such appointment was ever made, at least by the Executive. Perhaps some private Societies might have adopted such a measure.

In many instances the lower orders went about to private houses to search for arms; this the Executive constantly endeavoured to prevent; because they were unwilling to raise alarm in their adversaries, or let the members of their body acquire habits of plunder, and be confounded with robbers. They endeavoured to dissuade them from these acts, by representing to the people, that the arms would always be kept in better condition by the gentlemen than by them, and could be easily seized whenever necessary. In other respects our stores were in the arsenal in the Castle, and the military depots throughout the country; our supplies were in the Treasury.

A Military Committee was appointed by the Executive in February, 1798, for the principal purpose of preparing plans of operations, either in case of a premature insurrection, if we should be unfortunately and unwillingly forced into one, or of the invasion from France. As a Committee it did nothing, but some of its members took up the consideration of the latter subject, and framed instructions how to act in case of a landing of a foreign force; these were sent by the Executive to such Adjutants General as had received their appointments; they generally went to use every effort in favour of the French.

Attempts were made with as much zeal as the necessary caution would permit, to introduce the system among the military, the militia especially; but the reports of the agents were mostly confused and unsatisfactory, so that the success of the measure could never be ascertained with any tolerable accuracy.

We have read in some evidence lately given, that a person was appointed Colonel by a Commission from a General in the rebel army; we must beg leave to doubt, if not deny, the truth of that assertion: no General was ever chosen for Leinster, and Colonels were always appointed by their Captains; they derived their authority from this appointment, not from any Commission of a General.

If Irish officers in foreign service had joined in our cause, they would have been gladly received, and rapidly promoted. Indeed an attempt to procure that was actually set on foot; we counted on their attachment to their native soil, and hatred to England, as a substitute for Republicanism, and when they should be convinced, that such a form of Government was the best security for the permanent separation of the two countries, we were sure of their fidelity. It has so happened, however, from the delay of peace on the Continent, or because our agent was over cautious in conducting the negociation, lest it should become known to the respective Potentates, and communicated to the British Court, that nothing in consequence of it has hitherto been effected.

We can aver, that no general plan of insurrection existed before the 12th of March, 1798; but some individuals had perhaps formed local ones, adapted to the taking Dublin, and a few other places. When the North was on the point of rising, after the celebrated Proclamation of General Lake, a plan of operations had been suggested for that occasion, which was destroyed as soon as the people were dissuaded from the enterprise, of which we cannot now speak with any degree of precision.

Several recommendations were occasionally handed down from the Executive through the Committees, the dates or contents of which we cannot undertake to detail, unless they should be called to our recollection. The most remarkable as they now occur to us, was a recommendation to abstain from spiritous and exciseable articles, not so much to destroy the resources of Government, as for the purpose of preserving sobriety, which was so necessary to secrecy, and morality, which was so necessary to good order. It may be right to remark, that the recommendation was, however painful to the people, and contrary to their former habits, most astonishingly complied with. The Executive also directed to discourage the circulation of bank notes, and published a hand bill, cautioning against the purchasing of quit rents, pursuant to a scheme then in agitation, declaring, that as such a sale was an anticipation of the future resources of the country, it should not be allowed to stand good in the event of a revolution. The reasons for these publications are obvious; we must here remark, that many things were entrusted by the Executive to some one of its members. It having been an invariable rule, that no more than one of them should, on any occasion, be committed with persons not of its body; for this reason many things here stated are set forth on the credit of one individual, but believed by the remainder.

About the middle of 1796, a meeting of the Executive took place, more important in its discussions and its consequences, than any that had preceded it; as such we have thought ourselves bound to give an account of it with the most perfect frankness, and more than ordinary precision. This meeting took place in consequence of a letter from one of the Society, who had emigrated on account of political opinions: it mentioned, that the state of the country had been represented to the Government of France, in so favourable a point of view, as to induce them to resolve upon invading Ireland, for the purpose of enabling it to separate itself from Great Britain. On this solemn and important occasion, a serious review was taken of the state of the Irish nation at that period: it was observed, that a desperate ferment existed in the public mind; a resolution in favour of a Parliamentary Reform had indeed been passed early in 1793 by the House of Commons, but after it had been frustrated by several successive adjournments, all hope of its attainment was vanished, and its friends every where proscribed; the volunteers were put down; all power of meeting by delegation for any political purpose, the mode in which it was most usual and expedient to co-operate on any subject of importance, was taken away at the same time. The provocations of the year 1794, the recall of Lord Fitzwilliam, and the reassumption of coercive measures, that followed it, were strongly dwelt on: the county of Armagh had been long desolated by fomented feuds, the two contending factions, agreeing only in one thing, an opinion, that most of the active Magistrates in that county treated one party with the most fostering kindness, and the other with the most rigorous persecution. It was stated, that so marked a partiality exasperated the sufferers, and those who sympathized in their misfortunes. It was urged with indignation, that notwithstanding the greatness of the military establishment in Ireland, and its having been able to suppress the Defenders in various counties, it was not able, or was not employed to suppress these outrages in that county, which drove 4000 persons from their native dwellings. The Magistrates, too, who took no steps against the Orangemen, were said to have overleaped the boundaries of law to pursue and punish the Defenders. The Government and Legislature seemed to take upon themselves those injuries by the Indemnity Act, which screened from punishment, and even honoured the violators; and by the Insurrection Act, which enabled the same Magistrates, if they chose, under colour of law, to act anew the same abominations. Nothing, it was contended, could more justly excite the spirit of resistance, and determine men to appeal to arms, than the Insurrection Act; it punished with death the administering of oaths, which in their opinion were calculated for the most virtuous and honourable purposes. The power of proclaiming counties, and quieting them by breaking open the cabins of the peasants between sunset and sunrise, by seizing the inmates, and sending them on board tenders, without the ordinary interposition of a Trial by Jury, had, it was alledged, irritated beyond endurance the minds of the reflecting, and the feelings of the unthinking inhabitants of that province. It was contended, that even according to the Constitution and example of

1688, when the protection of the Constituted Authorities was withdrawn from the subject, Allegiance, the reciprocal duty, ceased to bind; when the people were not redressed, they had a right to resist, and were free to seek for allies wherever they were to be found. The English revolutionists of 1688 called in the aid of a foreign Republic to overthrow their oppressors. There had sprung up in our own time a much more mighty Republic, which, by its offers of assistance to break the chains of slavery, had drawn on itself a war with the enemies of our freedom, and now particularly tendered us its aid. These arguments prevailed, and it was resolved to employ the proferred assistance for the purpose of separation. We were aware it was suspected that negociations between the United Irishmen and the French, were carried on at an earlier period than that now alluded to, but we solemnly declare such suspicion was ill founded. In consequence of this determination of the Executive, an Agent was dispatched to the French Directory, who acquainted them with it, stated the dispositions of the people, and the measures which caused them, he received fresh assurances that the succours should be sent, as soon as the armament could be got ready.

About October, 1796, a Messenger from the Republic arrived, who, after authenticating himself, said he came to be informed of the state of the country, and to tell the Leaders of the United Irishmen of the intention of the French to invade it speedily with 15,000 men, and a great quantity of arms and ammunition; but he neither mentioned the precise time, nor the place, doubting, we suppose, our caution, or our secrecy. Shortly after his departure, a letter arrived from a quarter, which there was reason to look on as confidential, stating, that they would invade England in the Spring, and positively Ireland. The reason of this contradiction has never been explained; but the consequences of it, and the Messenger not having specified the place of landing, was, that when the armament arrived in December, 1796, at Bantry Bay, they came at a time, and in a port we had not foreknown.

After the intended descent had failed, it occurred to some Members of the Opposition, and their friends in the city, and to some of the most considerate of the United Irishmen, that one more attempt should be made in favour of Parliamentary Reform. They hoped that the terrible warning which had been given by the facility of reaching our coasts, and if the armament had landed, the possibility at least of it succeeding, would have shewn the Borough Proprietors of the necessity of conceding to the popular wish. The storm had dispersed—a cloud big with danger—but it might again collect, and the thunder of republic and revolution again roll, and perhaps burst over their heads. This was then judged the best moment to persuade them, in the midst of their fears, to a measure strictly counter-revolutionary.

We think it but right to state, that no greater connexion than that of private acquaintance and friendship ever subsisted between any of the Members of the Opposition and the United Irishmen, except in this instance, and for the accomplishment of this purpose. In consequence of these joint efforts, a meeting was held at the Exchange; which declared in favour of Reform, and a proposal of that nature was submitted to Parliament. If in the course of that effort for Reform it had not become evident, that success was hopeless, it was the wish of many among us, and we believe the Executive would have gladly embraced the occasion of declining to hold any further intercourse with France, except sending a Messenger there to tell them that the difference between the Government and the People had been adjusted, and that they would have no business a second time to attempt a landing. In fact, no attempt or advance was made to renew the negociation till April, 1797, when an Agent was sent. In the May following, the well-known proclamation of General Lake appeared. This very much encreased the ferment of the public mind, and the disposition of the people to wish for the return of the French, that they might get rid of the severities of martial law. It did more, it goaded many people of the North to press the Executive to an insurrection, independent of foreign aid.

About this time a letter arrived, which assured us the French would come again, and requested that a person should be sent over to make previous arrangements. The eagerness of those in the North who were urgent for insurrection, was checked by making known this communication to them, and entreating for delay; it was resisted likewise by some of the most sober and reflecting among themselves, who were of opinion they were not yet sufficiently prepared for the attempt; those considerations prevailed, particularly as in order to enforce them, an advantage was taken of the wish expressed in Parliament, that the people might rise.

The impatience, however, which was manifested on this occasion, and the knowledge that it was only controuled by the expectation of speedy and foreign assistance, determined the Executive to send a second Agent speedily to France, in answer to the letter. This person departed in the latter end of June 1797. By both these Agents, rather a small number of men, with a great quantity of arms, ammunition, artillery, and officers were required; a small force only was asked for, because the Executive, faithful to the principle of Irish Independence, wished for what they deemed just sufficient to liberate their country, but incompetent to subdue it.—Their most determined resolution, and that of the whole body, being collected as far as its opinion could be taken, always has been in no event to let Ireland come under the dominion of France, but it was offered to pay the expences of the expedition. The number required was 10,000 men at the most, and at the least 5000.

The Executive inclined to the larger number; but even with the smaller, the general opinion among them was, there could be no doubt of success. As to the quantity of arms, by the first Messenger 40,000 stand were specified, but by the second, as much more as could be sent; the difference arose from the disarming that had gone on in the mean time in the North, and from the increasing numbers who were ready to use them. The Executive also instructed its Agents to negociate for a loan of money, if it could be had in France; if not, to negociate with Spain—the sum was half a million. Our second agent, on his arrival at Hamburgh, wrote a memorial, containing those and other details, a copy of which, some way or other, we perceive the Government has obtained, and therefore refer to it. He then proceeded to Paris, to treat further on the business, where he presented a second memorial; the object of this was to urge motives arising out of the new state of affairs, which would induce the Directory not to postpone the invasion. We cannot precisely state the whole of its contents, as, according to the constant practice already mentioned, no copy of it has been preserved; but it went to demonstrate that so favourable a disposition as then existed in the Irish mind, was in no future contingency to be expected. In any subsequent rupture between Great Britain and the French Republic, His Majesty's Ministers must see that Ireland would infallibly become the seat of war, if they did not previously remove their grievances, the existence of which would naturally invite, and prove a powerful auxiliary to the enemy. Such a rupture, it was observed, must be in the contemplation of the British Cabinet, as several of its most leading members declared that they considered the existence of the British Monarchy incompatible with that of the Republic. Conciliation, then, according to every rule of policy and common sense, should be ultimately adopted; and though it should fall short of the wishes of the people, it was asserted, if once possessed of a reasonable share of liberty, they would not be brought to run the chance of a revolution in order to obtain a more perfect system of freedom.

Our second Agent, while at Paris, and pending the negociation at Lisle, was told by some of the persons in power in France, that if certain terms, not specified to him, were offered by the English, peace would certainly be made.—However, after the negociation was broken off, he received positive assurances that the Irish never should be abandoned, until a separation was effected, and that they should be left entirely at their own option to choose their own form of government.

About this time a person came over, informing us that a considerable army was ready, and embarked at the Texel, destined for Ireland, and only waiting for a wind. The troops afterwards disembarked, but we are ignorant of the reason why they never sailed, except perhaps that the wind continued so long adverse, that the provisions were exhausted—and that in the mean time disturbances broke out in the French Government. It may be proper to remark, that in none of the communications or negociations with France, did the Government of that country ever intimate the place they would land, or, except in the first, the force they would bring.

Sometime in the beginning of this year a letter was received from France, stating, the succours might be expected in April. Why the promise was not fulfilled, we have never learned. We know nothing of further communications from any foreign state, nor of the future plan of operations of the French; but we are convinced they will not abandon the plan of separating this country from England, so long as the discontents of the people would induce them to support an invasion.

Let us, then, while Ireland is yet our country, be indulged in a few remarks, which we deem extremely important to its future prosperity; now that we have given these full and faithful details of the past, we cannot be suspected of any but pure disinterested motives in what we are about to say, ere we leave it for ever. The parts we have acted have enabled us to gain the most intimate knowledge of the dispositions and hearts of our countrymen. From that knowledge we speak, when we declare our deepest conviction that the Penal Laws, which have followed in such doleful and rapid succession—the House Burnings—Arbitrary Imprisonments—and Free Quarters—and above all, the Tortures to extort confessions—neither have had, or can have, any other effect but exciting the most deadly rancour in the hearts of almost all the people of Ireland, against those of their countrymen who have had recourse to such measures for maintaining their power, and against the connexion with Great Britain, whose men, and whose aid have been poured in to assist them.

The matchless fidelity which has marked the Union—the unexampled firmness and contempt of death, displayed by so many thousands at the halbert, in the field, in the gaol, and at the gibbet, exempt us from claiming any belief on our personal credit. If the hearts of the people be not attached by some future measures, this nation will be again, and more violently disturbed, on the next coming of a foreign force. If a Reform be adopted, founded upon the abolition of Corporations and Buroughs, as constituent bodies, and the equal division of the representatives among those who may be entitled to the elective suffrage, the best possible step will be taken for preserving the Monarchical Constitution, and British Connexion. For the success of this measure we would not now answer—but of this we are sure, you must either extirpate or reform.

The heavy and still agitated minds with which we write, will, we hope, not only apologize for any inaccuracy of style, but likewise serve the much more important purpose, of excusing any expressions that may not be deemed sufficiently circumspect. Much as we wish to stop the effusion of blood, and the present scenes of useless horrors, we have not affected a change of principles, which would only bring on us the imputation of hypocrisy, when it is our most anxious wish to evince perfect sincerity and good faith. We however entreat Government to be assured, that, while it is so much our interest to conciliate, it is far from our intention to offend.

ARTHUR O'CONNOR.
THOMAS ADDIS EMMETT.
WM. JAMES M'NEVIN.

Appendix Two

O'Connor's Testimony to the
Parliamentary Secret Committees

After their "Memoire" had been rejected (see Appendix One), O'Connor and other United Irish leaders were required to testify before special committees of the upper and lower houses of the Irish parliament, and the government published edited transcripts of their testimonies. O'Connor, Emmet, and MacNeven subsequently published their own versions of what they had told the committees.

The official government version of O'Connor's House of Commons examination appeared in Appendix XXXI of "Report from the Committee of Secrecy of the House of Commons in Ireland, as reported by the Right Honourable Lord Viscount Castlereagh, August 21, 1798." The parallel report from the House of Lords simply reproduced the same page and a half of O'Connor's testimony, an indication that these were summaries or excerpts rather than complete verbatim transcripts. O'Connor maintained that after his examination by the two committees he immediately, upon being returned to his prison cell, reconstructed the sessions from memory and put them in writing. These, too, obviously cannot be considered verbatim transcriptions of the questions asked him and his answers. A comparison of the two versions, however, gives a reliable indication of the essence of what transpired; the full texts of both are reproduced below. Taken together, they constitute indispensable documents concerning O'Connor's place in the history of the United Irishmen and his perception of his role.

While the government's staccato rendition contains only direct answers to sharply posed questions, O'Connor's extended account makes it appear as if he was in full control of the interrogations. In the latter, his response to almost every question was a lengthy political justification of the United Irishmen that often included harsh portrayals of the government his questioners represented. It may seem unlikely that the committee members would have tolerated O'Connor's eloquent harangues at such length, but perhaps they allowed him free rein in the hope that he would inadvertently disclose information that otherwise might have remained concealed.

The Government's Version

Thursday, 9th August, 1798

Arthur O'Connor, Esq., sworn

Q. When did you become an United Irishman?

A. About November 1796.

Q. When did the military organization begin?

A. About the middle of 1796.

Q. Were you a member of the National Executive?

A. I was, and continued so from November 1796 to January 1798.

Q. When did the communications with France commence?

A. Before I was an United Irishman, I believe in the middle of 1796, at the same time that the military organization was formed.

Q. When was it agreed to accept the offer of alliance from France?

A. I understood it was accepted at a meeting of the Executive in summer 1796.—I was apprized of the offer and acceptance by my brother members of the Executive after I became a member of it, and before the arrival of the French in Bantry Bay.

Q. Was it the determination of the United Irishmen in the north to rise if the French had landed?

A. The Directory thought they would rise.

Q. When was the first communication from France after the expedition to Bantry Bay?

A. The first which of my own knowledge I can speak of was in August 1797,—It stated, that a fleet lay in the Texel with 15,000 men on board, and that the armament was destined for Ireland. I was arrested, and in confinement for some months before that time.

Q. Was it mentioned to the Irish Executive where the descent was intended?

A. It was not in the dispatch which I saw.

Q. Was there any intelligence brought of the intended invasion at Bantry?

A. There was, by a messenger who arrived here about November 1796.

Q. Was there a resident agent appointed to go to Paris in spring 1797?

A. There was, whilst I was in prison; and a second person was sent in June following; I saw this person on his return to Ireland from France about November 1797. He reported that no armament was then ready, but that one would shortly be ready. I understood that when a French fleet was ready the expedition would take place.

Q. Have you heard that there were some conversations on this subject between persons of this country and General Valence, prior to October 1796?

A. I have heard there were; they did not however lead to any thing decisive.

Q. Was there any connexion with the English or Scotch societies?

A. Any connexion with them was between individuals: the Irish Executive wished to keep clear of them.

Q. Do you know of any loan being negotiated with France or Spain?

A. Instructions were given to the agent to negotiate a loan of half a million in France or Spain, on the security of the new Irish government. Says, his situation in the Executive was filled up when he left Ireland in January last.

O'Connor's Version

The Examination of Arthur O'Connor, before the Secret Committee of the House of Lords, August the 9th, 1798.

Committee. Were you of the Executive of the Irish Union?

O'Connor. I was a Member of the Executive from the time I became a Member of the Union.

Com. When did the communication between the Union and France begin?

O'Connor. You, I suppose, have the Report I signed and delivered to the Irish Government, in conjunction with Mr. Emmett and Mr. M'Nevin?

[The Chancellor nodded assent; but none of the other Members of the Committee].

O'Connor. In that Report you will find the whole of that important transaction detailed. You will there find that the first alliance that was formed between the Union and France was in the middle of 1796. You will see that before the Executive entered into any alliance with France, or that it resolved on resistance to the tyranny of the Irish Government, a solemn meeting was held, when, after considering the uniform system of coercion and opposition, which had been pursued from 1793 by the Irish Government against the Irish People; and finding that 1796 had opened with the sanguinary laws, called the Insurrection and Indemnity Acts, whereby the most sacred rights of the Constitution were destroyed, the most gross violations of the laws by the Magistrates were indemnified—that the expulsion of 4000 unoffending inhabitants of the county of Armagh, from their homes and properties, left no doubt that all protection was at an end, the Executive were decidedly of opinion, that by the principles of the Constitution, as established by the Revolution of 1688, they were justified in calling in foreign aid, and in resisting a Government which had forfeited all claims to obedience.

Com. You are under a mistake: the Insurrection and Indemnity Acts were not passed until the end of 1796.

O'Connor. I am confident I cannot be mistaken; for I know that these acts were what filled up the measure of that oppression which decided the Executive to seek foreign aid; and, I am confident, it did not come to that determination until May, 1796; and I also recollect that I left this country in February, 1796; and before I left it, the Attorney General had moved these two bills; but if you can have any doubts, your Journals will clear them up.

Com. When did the Military Organization begin?

O'Connor. Shortly after the Executive had resolved on resistance to the Irish Government, and on an alliance with France, in May, 1796.

Com. Were there no communications with France before the middle of 1796?

O'Connor. None. I can confidently affirm, that until the conduct of the Irish Government forced the Executive to resist, which was, as I have stated, in the middle of 1796, no alliance whatsoever was formed between the Union and France.

Com. Did the Executive imagine the North would rise if the French landed?

O'Connor. We had no doubt but the North was sensible of the tyranny of the Government, and that they would take the first opportunity to free their country.

Com. When was the first communication with France after the Bantry Bay expedition?

O'Connor. I was a close prisoner in the Tower, from February, 1797, to August following it; in August I heard of the first communication after the Bantry Bay expedition.

Com. What did the dispatch contain?

O'Connor. It stated that a considerable force of 15,000 or 20,000 men were embarked at the Texel, and that they would sail in a week.

Com. What prevented their sailing?

O'Connor. The wind continued directly contrary for several weeks after, and the changes which took place on the 4th of September probably had some effect on the expedition.

Com. Was it mentioned in the dispatch where the landing should take place?

O'Connor. It was not; the Directory do not communicate such important intelligence, except to those to whom it may be absolutely necessary.

Com. Had you any intelligence of the invasion at Bantry Bay?

O'Connor. There was a messenger who arrived in November, 1796; he said the French would arrive shortly, but did not say where.

Com. Had you any other intelligence?

O'Connor. We received a letter about the time of this messenger's arrival, (a French agent,) which stated that the expedition was postponed; this has never been accounted for.

Com. Was there a person sent in spring, 1797, to France?

O'Connor. During the time these messengers were sent off I was a close prisoner.

Com. Did you see Dr. M'Nevin on his return from France?

O'Connor. I shall not answer any thing about Dr. M'Nevin, nor any other person.

Com. Oh! he has been here.

O'Connor. If so, there is the less occasion for you to ask me about him; I shall not answer any questions of any one.

Com. Did you see any person who returned from France towards the end of 1797?

O'Connor. I did.

Com. What intelligence did he bring?

O'Connor. When he left France, he was assured that assistance would be sent, though no time was mentioned; but so considerable a change had taken place in France on the 4th September, 1797, and our messenger having left Paris before that period, and not arriving here till after, we did not know what measures the new arrangement might give rise to.

Com. Have you heard that some conversation on Irish affairs had passed between General Vallence, and some persons of this country?

O'Connor. I cannot conceive that General Vallence could have any thing to do with the business; he was an emigrant.

Com. Was there any connexion between the Union and the British and Scotch societies?

O'Connor. The Executive carefully avoided any.

Com. Was there not some connexion between individuals?

O'Connor. I cannot say what individuals may have done; the Executive was careful to confine itself to the affairs of Ireland. As one of the Executive, I can say, I never had the most distant with any British Society; nor did I ever interfere with the politics of England.

Com. Do you know any thing of a Loan being negotiated for with France or Spain?

O'Connor. Some of our agents were ordered to negotiate for half a million with either of these Powers.

Com. Was your place in the Executive filled up when you left this in January, 1798?

O'Connor. My place in the Executive of Leinster was filled up.

Com. Were you not proprietor of The Press?

O'Connor. I was, until it was destroyed by the Irish Government.

Com. Was it not for the purpose of promoting the Union that you set it up?

O'Connor. The inculcating Union amongst my countrymen, was a principal object; I had also in view to expose the outrages and tyranny of the Irish Government; but it was not set up by the Union; it was my own individual undertaking; it was under my sole controul; and it was set up by me on the broadest basis, for the support of the liberties of my country.

ARTHUR O'CONNOR

The Examination of Arthur O'Connor before the Secret Committee of the House of Commons, 16th of August, 1798.

Committee. Explain the first formation of the alliance between the Irish Union and the French.

O'Connor. If you have seen the report I signed and delivered in conjunction with Emmett and M'Nevin, it will not be necessary I should go very fully into that important transaction; but if you have not seen it, I will explain it more fully.

Com. We have not seen the report you allude to.

O'Connor. Sometime in 1795, or the beginning of 1796, a letter was received by the Executive of the Union from France, from some individuals of the Union, who had fled from persecution; in which they mentioned, that they had made such a representation of the state of Ireland, that they believed the French would be induced to treat with the Union, to free us from the tyranny under which we groaned. This letter was not acted upon by the Executive at the time it was received, from their unwillingness to have recourse to foreign aid, except in the last resort, and in the hope, that the effects of the popular mind from the tyrannical measures which Government had pursued, would induce them to abandon their measures of coercion, and to adopt measures congenial to the wishes of the people. But when the Executive saw the year 1796 open with the Insurrection Bill—that 4000 unoffending inhabitants of the county Armagh had been driven from their homes, on account of their religious opinions, by a lawless banditti, who were not only not restrained by Government, but aided and instigated by its Magistracy, and that an act was passed to indemnify the most gross violation of the most sacred laws by the Agents and Magistrates of Government. Roused by these fresh instances of tyranny, the Executive of the Union held a most important meeting to consider the state of the country—to determine on what measures these sanguinary, tyrannical proceedings of Government made it necessary for us to adopt. The views and conduct of those who exercised the powers of Government were coolly and dispassionately discussed. The Executive were convinced, and the same conviction was in every mind, that a system of monopoly and usurpation had absorbed every part of the Constitution which belonged to the people; that those who exercised the assumed right of representing the people of Ireland, were self-constituted; that they acted with the sole view of advancing their individual interests; and that what was called the Emancipation of the Irish Legislature in 1782, was nothing more than freeing a set of self-constituted individuals, from the absolute controul of the British Legislature, that they might be at liberty to sell themselves to the corrupt controul of the British Ministry. The Executive considered, which had the Constitution on their side, they who contended that the House of Commons should be filled with the real Representatives of the People of Ireland, or those individuals who contended, that it should be filled with themselves. This was the great point at issue, by which the past, the present, and the future conduct of the Irish Government was to be judged, without even appealing to the imprescriptible right of a People to put down oppression. Standing on the ground of the Constitution, the Executive looked back upon the sanguinary, tyrannical measures, which had been invariably pursued by the Irish Government and Legislature, under the controul of the British Ministry from 1793, they were convinced, that if the most faint connexion existed between those who filled the places of the People's Representatives, and the People, no Government or Legislature durst commit such unexampled outrages as those which had been perpetrated, and indemnified in Ireland; that no lawful or just Government could by any possibility be driven to burn houses, or to torture the persons of the people to extort obedience. The Executive looked back to the melancholy history of Ireland, they saw how dreadfully it had been torn and wasted by religious dissentions. The first object of the Executive was to destroy religious discord, and promote brotherly love and affection among all the people of Ireland, be their religious belief what it may. The next object of the Union was to promote a Reform of the Government, and to regain those rights which were the people's birthright by the Constitution; yet the oath which bound the people to these first duties of Christianity, Morality, and the Constitution, was punished with death by the Insurrection Act, which by some other of its clauses broke down every barrier of Liberty: that not only every effort was made to oppose us in these our exertions to destroy religious discord, but that no means were left untried to organize a sect, founded upon the diabolical oath of extermination, whose institution was avowedly for the purpose of perpetuating religious discord and rancour. This was not all—the expulsion of 4000 Irish citizens, with every aggravation of cruelty and horror, which was followed by the Indemnity Act, left no doubt on the mind of the Executive, that all the excesses and outrages were either openly or secretly the acts of the Government and Legislature of Ireland. Struck with the enormity of these acts and outrages, the Executive looked back to the history of James II, and after comparing his conduct with the conduct of the Irish Government, they were decidedly of opinion, that the conduct of the Irish Government had been beyond comparison, more tyrannical and cruel. They were of opinion; that if the people were justified in calling in foreign aid, to rescue their liberties and constitution from James's government, it was infinitely more justifiable in us to call in foreign aid. The Executive were of opinion, that the Irish Government had not only forfeited all title to obedience from the people, but that we were called on to resist its most unparalleled usurpation and tyranny. That as the people of Ireland had been disarmed, contrary to the right of every free people; and as the tyranny under which the Government was upheld, was supported by the men and the money of one foreign nation, we stood peculiarly necessitated to seek the aid of some other foreign power. Actuated by this reasoning, the Executive sent to seek an alliance with France, in May, 1796, which was actually formed in the August following, the first which was formed between the Irish Union and France.

Com. Did you not go to Hamburgh, and afterwards to Switzerland, in the summer of 1796, in company with another person?

O'Connor. This question points at Lord Edward Fitzgerald; and as it is notorious he did accompany me to Switzerland in 1796, and although my friend is no more, I will not answer any thing, which could in the most distant manner lead to the disclosure of any act of his; besides, I am not bound by the stipulation I have entered into, for saving the lives of those you have in your power, to disclose any act of my life prior to my becoming a Member of the Union; but so little am I inclined to withhold the account of any part of our conduct, and so fully am I convinced of the rectitude of what we have done, that if you will be satisfied with the substance of the transactions of the Union, without leading to names or persons, I will give it.

Com. Well, we will be content with the substance, without any allusion to names or persons.

O'Connor. In May, 1796, after the important meeting of the Executive I have just mentioned was held, they sent to France, to adjust the terms of the alliance, to plan the manner the succours should be seconded, so as to ensure success. The most important part of the terms was, that France was to assist Ireland in freeing herself from the tyranny of those who exercised the Government of Ireland, and that Ireland should be free to frame whatever constitution she might think fit to adopt. The same expedition which was afterwards equipped, and sent to Ireland under Hoche, was agreed on, and every thing was settled, which could ensure success on its landing. At the same time it was proposed to the person who formed this first alliance between France and the Union, that a body should be sent against England to cause a diversion, to retaliate for the Quiberon expedition. To dissuade the French from the invasion of England, this Irish negociator used every argument in his power. He said, from his knowledge of England, the best men of that country would be most hostile to any interference of the French in the government of their country, on the same just principles that they condemned the interference of England in the Government of France.—That the situation of Ireland and England were very different, that in Ireland the people were most solicitous for the aid of France, to rescue them from foreign and domestic tyranny; but that the majority of the people of England would be averse to their interference—that many of the people of England were beginning to see and feel the ruin the Ministers had brought on the nation, by engaging in the war; but that if they invaded their country, it would bury all consideration of the injustice of the war, under the immediate consideration of self defence; that it would prove the greatest support to an unpopular Ministry, by giving them an unlimited power over the remaining wealth of England, in any way they might wish to take it, while a guinea could be extorted. These, together with other arguments, were thought conclusive by those to whom they were addressed, and the invasion of England in 1796 was abandoned.

Com. Was not M. Barthelemy privy to these transactions?

O'Connor. I will not answer any question where the name of any person is mentioned.

Com. But he is a foreigner.

O'Connor. I care not; the name of a foreigner or a countryman shall be equally inviolable with me.

Com. Was it not at Paris this first alliance was formed?

O'Connor. It was not; if it was, you would have no need to ask me the question.

Com. Was it at Lisle?

O'Connor. It was not.

Com. Were you of the Executive?

O'Connor. I was of the Executive from the time I became a Member of the Union in 1796, until I was obliged to fly my country abruptly in January, 1798, to avoid being taken off by a foul plot which was laid by some of the under agents of the Irish Government, but which my respect for the safety of those who gave me the intimation of it, obliges me to keep secret.

Com. Inform us of the progress and extent of the organization.

O'Connor. When I was imprisoned in February, 1797, the organization had made considerable progress in Ulster, and things were in train to extend it to the other three provinces. On my liberation in the August following, I found the means we employed before my imprisonment had been successful in extending the organization, particularly in Leinster; but that it had been thrown into confusion by the burnings, hangings, and torturings, which had been extended from Ulster to the other parts of the country.—But to such a degree had the minds of the people been exasperated by the cruelties of the Government, the disposition towards the Union was so strong in the three provinces, that in four months after my liberation I was enabled as one of the Northern Executive (there being no Executive for Leinster during this period) to organize 70,000 men in Leinster only, while the number of those who took the test of the Union was nearly equal to the population of the three provinces; to such a degree did the Irish Government raise the resentment of the people against it, by the cruelties it practiced to support its powers, and to keep down the national spirit for liberty.

Com. Was not your object in forming the organization to effect a revolution?

O'Connor. If our mere object had been to effect a revolution, the British Ministry, and the Irish Government were effecting one more violently and rapidly than we wished for; we clearly perceived, that the measures, they adopted to prevent revolution, were the most effectual that could be devised to ensure it. When we viewed the state of the British empire, we were convinced we need not take much pains merely to make revolution. If that was our sole object, we knew that the Irish Government, of itself, could not exist one month; we saw that it was the men and the money of England, which upheld the Irish Government; we therefore looked to the state of Great Britain, and considered the state of its actual Government, and we were of opinion, that the measures which the present Ministry had pursued, were the most rapidly ruinous which could be adopted. We examined her state before the war, we saw, that as before the enormous expenditure, which the war occasioned, the Minister could not extort more than sixteen millions annual revenue, it would be impossible, after hundreds of millions of the national capital had been squandered, that thirty millions annual revenue, could by any physical possibility, be extorted, which was the least her peace establishment could amount to. But that even supposing thirty millions annual revenue could be raised on Great Britain, experience convinced us, that liberty must be destroyed by such additional means of corruption being thrown into the hands of the Executive; and we were convinced, that a nation which had lost her liberty could not long support such monstrous burthens, on the principle, that capital, like fluid, would find its level; we were of opinion, that as the profits of capital would be higher in France than in England, the vast exhaustion of capital which had taken place in France, would be replenished on a peace, by the flowing in of a considerable portion of British capital, and that this disposition on the part of the British capitalist, to transport his wealth, would be farther encreased by a desire to avoid the enormous taxes, to which his industry and his profits would be exposed. These considerations, amongst many others, left no doubt on our minds, that the powers of England, by which alone the tyranny and usurpation of the Irish Government and Legislature were supported, must be very shortly destroyed.

Com. If you did not organize for the purpose of effecting a revolution, what other object had you in view?

O'Connor. We saw with sorrow the cruelties practiced by the Irish Government had raised a dreadful spirit of revenge in the hearts of the people; we saw with horror that to answer their immediate views, the Irish Government had renewed the old religious feuds; we were most anxious to have such authorities as the organization ready constituted to prevent the dreadful transports of popular fury. We hoped that by having Committees for each barony, County Committees, and Provincial Committees; by holding out the benefits of the revolution to those who supported it, and by withholding its benefits from those who should disgrace it by popular excesses, we should have been able to restrain the people. But those who had monopolized the whole political power of the Constitution, finding, that they stood in need of some part of the population, and that from their monopoly being so directly opposite to the interest of all classes of the Irish nation, they could not hope for the support of any (be their religion what it may) on the score of politics, except those in the pay of Government. Finding how necessary it was to have some part of the population on their side, they had recourse to the old religious feuds, and set on foot an organization of Protestants, whose Fanaticism would not permit them to see, they were enlisted under the banners of religion, to fight for political usurpation they abhorred. No doubt, by these means you have gained a temporary aid, but by destroying the organization of the Union, and exasperating the great body of the people, you will one day pay dearly for the aid you have derived from this temporary shift.

Com. Government had nothing to do with the Orange System, nor their oath of extermination.

O'Connor. You, my Lord, [Castlereagh] from the station you fill, must be sensible that the Executive of any country has it in its power to collect a vast mass of information, and you must know from the secret nature, and the zeal of the Union, that its Executive must have the most minute information of every act of the Irish Government. As one of the Executive, it came to my knowledge, that considerable sums of money were expended throughout the nation, in endeavouring to extend the Orange System, and that the Orange oath of extermination was administered; when these facts are coupled, not only with general impunity, which has been uniformly extended towards all the acts of this infernal association, but the marked encouragement its members have received from Government, I find it impossible to exculpate the Government from being the parent and protector of these sworn extirpators.

Com. Were not some of the Union very Monarchical?

O'Connor. My first political acquaintance with the body of my Catholic countrymen, to whom I suppose you allude, was in 1791, whilst I was High Sheriff of the county of Cork, when I defended the Catholics from an attack which was made upon them by the monopolists of our representation in that part of Ireland. At that time the Catholics of Ireland were just beginning to feel the influence of the French Revolution, and to be sensible of the degrading state to which centuries of oppression had reduced them; they were, however, strongly addicted to Monarchy, and made their first advances in pursuit of freedom in a very humble manner; but the contempt and insult with which their first petition was scouted from the House of Commons, roused them to a sense of their rights as men.—In 1792, they again petitioned, but in terms of boldness proportioned to the insult with which their former petition had been treated. They were joined by the Presbyterians, and the contemptuous manner with which both petitions were refused, created an union of sentiment, whereby the Catholics were led to examine what title to power those had who thus insultingly denied the joint desires of the great mass of the Irish nation. They passed from any explanation with the Irish Parliament, and negociated with the British Ministry, whom they found controuled every act of the Government and Legislature of Ireland. While the Catholics were succeeding with the British Ministry in England, the Borough Mongers of Ireland were most active amongst the Grand Juries in the summer of 1792, in pledging lives and fortunes, never to grant the claims of their Catholic countrymen. When the Parliament met in 1793, the mandate came from the British Ministry to accede to a partial emancipation of the Catholics. This was not all: in the session the House of Commons resolved that the National Representation stood in need of Reform: they raised the hopes of the Irish but to blast them afterwards. This most impolitic conduct brought the Irish Government into the utmost disrepute, and was followed by a declaration on the part of the Catholics in 1793, to stand or fall with their countrymen on the great question of obtaining a National Representation. From this time the Irish Government seemed to abandon all idea of conciliating the Catholics, and to think only of punishing them for what they thought ingratitude. In pursuance of this plan, all idea of Catholic Emancipation and Parliamentary Reform was scouted; British troops were poured into Ireland, and prosecutions commenced against some of the Catholic and Presbyterian leaders in 1794, on such evidence as clearly demonstrated they were undertaken from vindictive motives of resentment. These measures were calculated to eradicate the inveterate predilection for Monarchy from the hearts of the Irish Catholics. In 1795, the British Ministry appeared sensible of the consequences which had resulted from the measures which had been pursued hitherto in Ireland; and an attempt was entered on to regain the Catholics, by sending Lord Fitzwilliam, with powers to choose his own Councils. The hopes of the national mind were raised, particularly of the Catholics; but the recall of Lord Fitzwilliam, the abandonment of the projected political changes, the renewal of the reign of terror and coercion, totally alienated the minds of the Catholics from their confirmed propensity to Monarchy. No doubt the French Revolution had a great and powerful effect in exciting the Catholics of Ireland to attain their long lost Liberty; but it was the measures of the British Ministry, and the Irish Government, which hurried them into their present violent detestation of Monarchy, and their present ardent love, Representative Democracy, which was confirmed in the minds of the very lowest orders, by being familiarized with the organization of the Union, and by observing its good effects.

Com. Why, what opinion have the lower classes of the people of political subjects?

O'Connor. The lowest societies of the Union conversed freely of the corruption, the usurpation, and the venality of Parliament. While I was a member of the House of Commons, you know the frequent conversation amongst the Members was—how much has such an one given for his seat? From whom did he purchase? Has not such an one sold his borough? Has not such a Lord bought? Has not such a Peer so many Members in this House? Was not such a Member with the Lord Lieutenant's Secretary, to insist on some greater place or pension? Did not the Secretary refuse it? Has he not gone into the Opposition? These, and such like facts, are as well known to the lowest classes of the Union as to yourselves.

A Member of the Com. Mr. O'Connor is perfectly right; I have heard the lowest classes of the people talk in that style.

O'Connor. The people are conscious you are self constituted, and not their delegates; men who have no other object in view but to advance their own individual interests.

A Member of the Com. That we are a parcel of placemen and pensioners?

O'Connor. Exactly so.

Com. What is the object the people have in view at present?

O'Connor. I believe they have laid by for the instant all idea of speculative politics, and think only how they shall annihilate the insupportable usurpation and cruelty of the British and Irish Government, and how they shall best avenge the blood which has been shed, and the tortures which have been inflicted, to support a Government they detest.

Com. Was there not a disunion in the Executive?

O'Connor. From the time I was elected one of the Executive, I never experienced any disagreement.

Com. Were there not men who could influence the people to disobey the orders of the Executive?

O'Connor. On the contrary, they were always obeyed with the most zealous alacrity. No doubt the secret manner in which we were obliged to conduct the business of the Union, gave great scope to intrigue; yet I found that wherever religious prejudices were placed in the way of political liberty, the people invariably disregarded the former, and adhered to the latter.

Com. Did not the Executive form a plan of a Constitution for Ireland's future Government?

O'Connor. The Executive never thought itself invested with power to meddle with the future Constitution of Ireland, that could have been the work only of those, whom the people of Ireland might elect for that express purpose. We were elected solely for to devise means of wresting power out of the hands of men, who had violated every part of the Constitution, and liberties of Ireland, and outraged every feeling and right of man, by the means they employed to retain their usurpation.

Com. What do you think would tranquilize the people of Ireland, and induce them to give up their arms?

O'Connor. That is a question which would require the best head to answer, and the best heart to execute; I am not so ignorant of human nature as to suppose, that those men who have so long engrossed the enormous emoluments of ill, and unjustly acquired power, will ever restore them to the people, however manifest it must appear to an unprejudiced mind, that the most dreadful ruin awaits the present fruitless effort which is made to retain them.

Com. But what, in your opinion, would tranquilize Ireland, and induce the people to give up their arms?

O'Connor. Under the present system of usurpation and corruption, every source by which the Irish nation could acquire wealth, is betrayed to Great Britain, and even the wretched pittance her industry gathers is thrown a prey to monopolists of her political power, who have sold her dearest rights. By this double plunder, the people of Ireland are destitute, not only of every convenience and comfort of life, but of the bare necessities to support their existence. If you would tranquilize a people, you must cease to oppress them—you must cease to betray them; make them happy, and you will make them tranquil. The great and main source, from which the wants of a people are supplied, is agriculture; yet near two millions worth of the rude produce of the agriculture of Ireland is annually exported to pay non-resident landlords; for this there is no return; it is all loss to the Irish nation, and is, of itself, a sufficient drain to impoverish a greater nation for extent than Ireland. The commerce of Ireland has to cope with the most commercial nation on earth in its very vicinage, under the disadvantage of a general admission of every species of manufactured and foreign produce on one side, and of as unlimited rejection on the other, with scarcely one exception. When the agricultural produce of a people—when their home and foreign markets are sold, the consequence must be, that they must experience a great dearth of national capital; hence the best machinery, and the most extensive division of labour, by both which, labour is so wonderfully abridged, the low profits which result from abundant capital, and the being able to give long credits, are all lost to a nation bereft of every means to acquire wealth. By this cruel injustice, England can supply the people of Ireland with their manufactures cheaper than the Irish can manufacture their own materials, whereby our manufactures (the other great source for acquiring national capital) shares the same fate with our agriculture; and the abused laws by which the fisheries of Ireland have been destroyed, compleat the catastrophe of the ruin of Irish industry, in the several ways of acquiring wealth with which God and Nature have endowed her. But this is not all; the small portion of wealth which the Irish nation acquires under these mutilated means is subject to a thousand of the most gross extortions. A most monstrous establishment (and that for one-tenth of the nation only), under the name of supporting the Ministers of Religion, but really for the purpose of the most flagrant corruption—a vast military establishment, which those who exercise the powers of Government are obliged to keep up, as the sole means by which they can maintain the actual usurpation of all popular and constitutional rights—sinecure places—pensions—and the various ways which are hourly devised for draining the people. These, if you would tranquilize the people, you must abolish—you must restore to them those means for acquiring wealth which God and Nature gave them—you must not subject the wealth they do acquire to any exaction which is not absolutely necessary, for the support of a Government capable of affording them protection. The result of the pillage which the Irish nation at present undergoes is, that it diminishes national capital—that wages are low, and employment so doubtful, the greatest causes of national misery. The next great evil which results from this great dearth of national capital is, that land has become the only material the people have to work on, which cannot be exported; every one is forced to hire it, as his only means of employment; and the competition has made the rents of land much higher than they otherwise would be, whilst the tythes (the most impolitic of imposts) are an endless source of vexation and litigation between the people and the Ministers of Religion. If you would correct all these evils, restore to the Irish nation its just rights; then wealth must flow in from every quarter; thousands of means of exercising industry will present themselves; wages will be liberal; rents will be moderate; and it will be as impossible to disturb the public mind, when the reign of justice shall be established, as it will be to tranquilize it as long as the actual system of usurpation, plunder, and tyranny shall be continued. It is oppression which has armed the people of Ireland—by justice only you can disarm them. A just Government, which emanates from the people, and which exists but for the people's protection and happiness, need never dread their arms, or desire to see them disarmed. As long as you are anxious to disarm the people, so long you have no reason to expect they should be tranquil.

Com. You have made politics and political economy your study: what political changes do you think would tranquilize Ireland?

O'Connor. Restore the vital principle of the constitution, which you have destroyed, by restoring to the people the choice of Representatives, who shall controul the Executive, by frugal grants of the public money, and by exacting a rigid account of its expenditure. Let the people have Representatives they can call friends—men in whom they can place confidence—men they have really chosen—men chosen for such time, that if they should attempt to betray them, they may speedily have an opportunity of discarding. Give us such a House of Commons, and I will answer for the tranquility of my country. Place but the public purse in the hands of such Representatives, and I will answer for it, the people of Ireland will not have to complain of the profligacy, the tyranny, or usurpation of Government or Legislators.—How such a House of Commons could be chosen (if it was not the interest of those who monopolize the national representation to oppose it) would not be a difficult task to devise.

Com. Was not the Union to destroy the constitution?

O'Connor. We could not have an intention of destroying a constitution, of which we did not believe there was one particle in existence. A House of Commons so far chosen by the people, and so far independent of the Crown, as to controul it, by its sole exercise of power over the public purse, was the vital principle of the Constitution, it was by taking the demands from time to time, to this power over the public purse, that those rights, one after another, have been gained, which rights constitute the constitution. The instant such an House of Commons ceased to exist, and that it was supplanted by a House of Commons which represents itself; from that instant the vital principle which created the Constitution, and which alone could preserve it from bankruptcy and ruin, was at an end. It was not to destroy this vital principle of the Constitution, it was to put down a Parliament of self constituted men, who first destroyed every vestige of the Constitution, and then committed every outrage and cruelty to support their usurpation.

Com. Why, did you not intend to set up a Republic?

O'Connor. I have already told you we did not conceive that any power was vested in us to set up any Constitution. We were chosen solely for the purpose of putting down your usurpation of the Constitution and Liberty of the Irish nation. I know not whether those who would have been chosen by the people of Ireland for the purpose of forming a Constitution, would have adopted the Constitution you have destroyed. I know not whether it is possible to build up such a Constitution, now it has been destroyed. I know not whether they would have formed a Constitution purely representative, from a conviction that an elective government, in which the people, whether by their delegates, or in their proper persons, exercise a controul over the government, I hold to be a Republic. As such, the Constitution (as long as a House of Commons made any part of it) was a Republic; but whether the future government of Ireland may be less, equally, or more democratical than the Constitution, those who shall be chosen to frame it can alone determine.

Com. Was there any thing implied in the Oath of the Union, than what was set forth in the Test?

O'Connor. Certainly not; for all we wanted was to create a House of Commons which should represent the whole people of Ireland; and for that purpose we strove to dispel all religious distinctions from our political Union, and after we had destroyed your usurpation of our national representation, and that we had set up a real representation of the whole people of Ireland, we were convinced there was no evil which such a House of Commons could not reach; we were satisfied, that to set up such a House of Commons was our right, and that whether the other parts of the Constitution could stand or not, after the House of Commons was restored to the Constitution, yet we were assured that our liberties would exist, but that without a constitutional House of Commons, the Government must of its own nature speedily end in bankruptcy and ruin, from the vast expence of the corruption and force which it required to uphold it.

Com. How was the late rising occasioned?

O'Connor. I have already told you how; from the beginning of the French Revolution the measures pursued by the British Ministry and the

Irish Government have worked up the minds of the people of Ireland to their present highly irritated state—at one time raising their hopes—at another time blasting those hopes; at one time promising Emancipation and Reform—and at another time resisting both with fire and sword—burning houses—hanging—lashing—and torturing—means unjustifiable to support any system, and which a just Government could not for one instant stand in need of. These no human patience could endure, and yet (from a conviction that they were practised to goad the people to a premature attempt to put down their oppressors) as long as I could remain, I used every means in my power to endure a little longer; but when, to avoid being dispatched, I was forced to fly, those into whose hands the executive power of the Union was vested, yielded to the pressing solicitations of the people of the most oppressed parts, who were desirous to risk their lives, in order to rid themselves of the cruelties they hourly experienced.

Com. Are there not Committees forming at the present moment?

O'Connor. I know not what Committees are forming; but I am well assured the people of Ireland will never abandon the Union, and that its principles will never be eradicated from their hearts until we obtain our object.

Com. How can deputations be sent to France?

O'Connor. By as many ways as there are human devices.

Com. Could you get one to go to France now?

O'Connor. Thousands, if necessary.

Com. How is that possible?

O'Connor. Unless you destroy every vestige of commerce, we can find no difficulty in sending to France. Not a ship that sails, that contains an United Irishman, that does not contain a faithful messenger.

Com. Do you know any thing of the future plans of the French?

O'Connor. I do not; but I firmly believe they will never abandon their engagements with us.

Com. Were there many men of property in the Union?

O'Connor. Men of property usually consult their own personal interests, which is a great check to any generous or disinterested exertion of patriotism; such men seldom run great hazards in the public cause. If we had been content with a hollow support, we might have had abundance of them; however, there were many of considerable property, who upon principle were of the Union.

Com. Would you not have destroyed the Protestant Religion, and the Protestant Establishment?

O'Connor. The destruction of Religion is one thing, the destruction of Establishments another; the great and just principle upon which the Union is formed is the most perfect freedom for all religions alike. We are of opinion that the present monstrous Protestant Establishment in Ireland is a grievous burden on Presbyterians, Catholics, Quakers, Protestants, in short, on all the people of Ireland—highly unjust to those who are not of the Protestant religion, and highly injurious to the Protestant religion itself; for we are convinced it would work a very desirable change in the Protestant Clergy of Ireland, if they were made to owe their maintenance to a faithful discharge of their functions, instead of obtaining it by a base and disgraceful cringing to corrupt patrons; and that if there was no other objection to tythes than their being an endless source of discord between a Christian Ministry and the People, they ought to be abolished.

Com. How did you mean to pay the half million you wished to borrow from France or Spain?

O'Connor. When the present Government can borrow millions on millions, we could have had no difficulty in paying half a million. If millions can be had out of Irish industry, by a Government which has sacrificed every means of acquiring wealth, we have no doubt a Government that restores those rights could easily find means to discharge any debts we should contract in the contest.

Com. Do you imagine Ireland could exist as an independent nation?

O'Connor. I have not a doubt of it. We have five millions of a brave hardy people, and if we had the government in our hands but for a short time, to organize and to arm them, we could defy the whole world. Once possessed of a country, they would fight for it; and it is one of the strongest countries in Europe by nature. It must have a tactic peculiar to itself, and the people of Ireland must execute that tactic.

Com. Could not Great Britain destroy your trade with her navy?

O'Connor. I doubt if the rest of the world would allow her to shut them out from so good a market. If we were once free, I doubt she could effect it. I doubt she could have power, after the separation of Ireland, to act so injurious a part; but as Ireland has no foreign dominion, and I trust never will, if her whole foreign trade was carried on by foreign ships, it is of little matter. The old notion that a carrying trade is the most beneficial, is nonsense; the home trade should be the great national object, and that would be most flourishing. There is no convenience nor a comfort of life that we could not find in our island; and the temporary inconvenience and loss we should feel by being obliged for a long time to supply ourselves, would be compensated in a great measure, by the number of hidden resources we should discover.

ARTHUR O'CONNOR

Appendix Three

This book review originally appeared in Saothar, Journal of the Irish Labour History Society, *XXVII, 2002.*

Jane Hayter Hames, *Arthur O'Connor, United Irishman* (The Collins Press, Cork, 2001), ix + 338pp, E25.40.

The bicentenary of the 1798 rebellion continues to stimulate renewed interest in that period and is probably responsible for this first book-length biography of Arthur O'Connor, who was indisputably one of the most important leaders of the United Irishmen. Scholars wishing to learn about O'Connor's life were long reliant on source materials collected in the 19th century by R. R. Madden and on Frank MacDermot's 1966 article in *Irish Historical Studies*. Although the recent upsurge in scholarly work on 1798 did fill some gaps in our knowledge of this enigmatic figure, a proper biography has been badly needed.

An attempt to remedy that glaring deficiency in the historical literature is certainly to be welcomed but, unfortunately, Hames, who refers to O'Connor as her 'kinsman' (p. ix), has chosen to honour her ancestor with an uncritical report of his own view of his life. Her narrative tells his story well and in an engaging way, but is not sufficiently reliable as an historical account. A salient example is her treatment of the highly improbable family tradition regarding a supposed royal lineage. 'There are several reasons why the story of Arthur O'Connor's descent from O'Connor Kerry rings true,' writes Hames (p. 20), but gives none while devoting several pages to retailing the undocumented legend and chastising historians for their scepticism.

Biography is a narrative art but this book draws too heavily on fiction-writing techniques and exhibits a tendency to spin tales out of insufficient evidence. There is, for example, a great deal of speculation about a woman identified as O'Connor's 'lover' and his 'mistress' with whom he was 'deeply involved' (pp. 81, 231), but there is no solid indication that this unnamed woman existed. Likewise, while Hames does not go as far as to invent dialogue, she does frequently imply knowledge of her subject's mental state: 'A strange recklessness invaded his astute mind' (p. 170) or 'Here his ideas buzzed like angry bees' (p. 73).

Her main source is O'Connor's unpublished memoirs, and that is both the greatest strength and the fatal weakness of this biography. Previously, MacDermot was the only researcher to seriously examine these memoirs and report on their contents but his mistaken assertion that they only covered the period up to 1793 indicates that he did not have access to the important sections that continue through 1798. Hames is to be commended for extracting a great deal of useful material out of the complete version, which is no easy task because deciphering O'Connor's handwriting requires patience and skill. On the other hand, her over-reliance on this material, and her uncritical approach to it, undermines the usefulness of her research. Hames's narrative does not go irredeemably astray because the unpublished memoirs, in my opinion, are essentially truthful; but they do contain errors of fact and in many particulars are characterised by subjectivity and unconscious biases not untypical of the genre. Moreover, O'Connor wrote them late in life when his social attitudes had become more inflexible, especially with regard to Catholics and Catholicism. In short, they require a critical exposition that Hames does not provide.

Hames commonly simply states O'Connor's opinions without evaluating them, thereby leaving the impression that they are statements of fact. In many instances this is innocuous but her uncritical presentation of his harsh views on factional opponents is certainly problematic. To quote without comment O'Connor's assessment of Thomas Addis Emmet is to implicitly endorse it (p. 123). Also, her subject's negative pronouncements on Catholic colleagues deserve particular caution because of the historiographical importance of the relationship between Protestant and Catholic leaders of the United Irishmen. But Hames blandly echoes O'Connor's assertion that Catholic members were a source of 'endless intrigues' as if this were an uncomplicated fact. Especially troubling is her tacit acceptance of O'Connor's claim that Lord Edward Fitzgerald fully shared his opinions of these 'vile men' and their 'dastardly conduct' (p. 158). That claim needs more than O'Connor's biased testimony to sustain it and Hames does not provide corroborating evidence.

There are numerous other instances where O'Connor's assertions go unchallenged. With regard to the pact that O'Connor, Emmet, and other United Irish leaders made with the government, saving their lives in exchange for political concessions, Hames declares that O'Connor 'had no interest in his own salvation' (p. 190). That was O'Connor's contention but should it be taken at face value? She also accepts too easily O'Connor's dubious depictions of his relationships with his influential uncle, Lord Longueville (p. 59), and with Walter 'Watty' Cox, the publisher of the *Union Star* (pp. 155, 159).

French archival sources are of crucial importance for a biography of O'Connor, who spent the last fifty years of his life as an exile in France. Furthermore, they are essential for understanding O'Connor's role in the 1796 United Irish negotiations with the French government. Hames's inattention to the French sources makes her dependent on O'Connor's memoirs and on secondary material that invariably exaggerates the role of Theobald Wolfe Tone and understates that of O'Connor. Her two references to the diplomatic archives suggest that she did not visit them but reproduced the citations from a secondary source. One of these reads, 'Archives Nacionale *[sic]*, Paris, Corr. Pol. Ang. 590 fos 217-23'. However, the 'Corr. Pol. Ang.' is not at the Archives Nationales but at the Archives des Affaires Etrangères. The secondary source is almost certainly Marianne Elliott's *Partners in Revolution* (1982), which contains an identical erroneous citation. The inattention to these important French archives very much weakens Hames's book.

The book is also plagued by an indefensible number of small errors. Proper names were apparently transcribed from O'Connor's handwritten pages without checking them against printed sources: 'Cribleur' for Crublier, 'Hedoville' for Hédouville, 'Thurgot' for Turgot, 'Ducket' for Duckett. The publisher's copy-editors should be taken to task for not noticing names that are rendered in various versions: Truguet/Trugnet, MacSheehy/McSheehy, Barthélemy/Bartholomey. A 'John Swiney' is mentioned in one place and a 'Sweeney' in another without recognition that they are the same man (pp. 123, 216). Elsewhere, Lord Edward Fitzgerald's brother Henry is mistaken for Lord Edward himself (p. 58). One of Thomas Addis Emmet's descendants is misidentified as his son (p. 244), while MacDermot's article is cited in support of an assertion that O'Connor visited Ireland in 1839 (p. 264) but no such visit is mentioned in that article or anywhere else that I am aware of. Edmund Burke was sixty-three not seventy-three when he met O'Connor (p. 82). With regard to a 1796 meeting between O'Connor, French diplomat Charles Reinhard, and an unnamed third person, Hames claims that O'Connor suspected this third individual of being 'sold to the British' (p. 111) but, in fact, it was Reinhard himself whom O'Connor (mistakenly) distrusted.

Compounding these problems is a very poor index, and the book's notes and references are also inadequate. More than 250 references simply say 'Bignon papers,' which is meant as a pointer to O'Connor's memoirs and correspondence. There are no page numbers or further location clues, making these references virtually useless to future researchers.

Although I have dwelt on the shortcomings of this biography from a historian's point of view, I would not wish to leave the impression that it is utterly without value. It is an attractive, well-illustrated book that may serve to stimulate interest in a previously neglected figure, and that is certainly a good thing. Perhaps, however, it is better to think of it not as a biography but as an autobiography mediated through the pen of Jane Hayter Hames.

Clifford D. Conner

Suggestions for Further Reading

The sources upon which this biography is based can be found in the footnotes and in the bibliography. The books listed below are ones that should be readily available to readers who wish to inquire further into the life and times of Arthur O'Connor.

Fortunately, one of O'Connor's most important written works has been reissued in a recent edition: *The State of Ireland*, edited by James Livesey (Dublin, 1998). Other important contemporary writings that should not be difficult to find include Wolfe Tone's memoirs: *Life of Theobald Wolfe Tone*, edited by Thomas Bartlett (Dublin, 1998), and the correspondence between William Drennan and Martha McTier: *The Drennan-McTier Letters, 1794–1801*, edited by Jean Agnew and Maria Luddy (Dublin, 1999).

For general background on the United Irishmen, the 1798 rebellion, and the French connection, Marianne Elliott, *Partners in Revolution: The United Irishmen and France* (New Haven and London, 1982) is indispensable. Nancy J. Curtin, *The United Irishmen: Popular Politics in Ulster and Dublin 1791–1798* (Oxford, 1998) provides a concise introduction to the subject. Also worth consulting are Paul Weber, *On the Road to Rebellion: The United Irishmen and Hamburg, 1796–1803* (Dublin, 1997); Thomas Pakenham, *The Year of Liberty* (London, 1972); *The Great Irish Rebellion of 1798*, edited by Cathal Póirtéir (Cork and Dublin, 1998); and *The French Are in the Bay*, edited by John A. Murphy (Cork and Dublin, 1997).

Among the best biographies of O'Connor's friends and colleagues are Stella Tillyard, *Citizen Lord: The Life of Edward Fitzgerald, Irish Revolutionary* (New York, 1999); Fintan O'Toole, *A Traitor's Kiss: The Life of Richard Brinsley Sheridan* (New York, 1998); and Marianne Elliott, *Wolfe Tone: Prophet of Irish Independence* (New Haven, 1989). For O'Connor's unfortunate codefendant at Maidstone, see *A Patriot Priest: The Life of Father James Coigly, 1761–1798* (Cork, 1998), edited by Dáire Keogh. Although the actual contact between O'Connor and Edward Marcus Despard was at most minimal, their activities were significantly intertwined; see Clifford D. Conner, *Colonel Despard: The Life and Times of an Anglo-Irish Rebel* (Conshohocken, Pennsylvania, 2000). And finally, O'Connor's nephew is the subject of an important new biography: Paul Pickering, *Feargus O'Connor: A Political Life* (London, 2008).

For more information about those of O'Connor's associates who emigrated to America—especially John Binns, Thomas Addis Emmet, and William James MacNeven—two worthwhile studies are recommended: David A. Wilson, *United Irishmen, United States* (Ithaca, New York and London, 1998), and Michael Durey, *Transatlantic Radicals and the Early American Republic* (Lawrence, Kansas, 1997).

Bibliography

Agnew, Jean and Maria Luddy, eds. *The Drennan-McTier Letters, 1794–1801* (Dublin: The Women's History Project in association with Irish Manuscripts Commission, 1999).

Airlie, Mabell, Countess of. *In Whig Society, 1775–1818, compiled from the hitherto unpublished correspondence of Elizabeth, Viscountess Melbourne, and Emily Lamb, Countess Cowper, afterwards Viscountess Palmerston, by Mabell, Countess of Airlie* (London, New York: Hodder and Stoughton Ltd., 1921).

Barras, Paul. *Mémoires de Barras, Membre du Directoire*, ed., George Duruy (Paris: Hachette, 1895).

Barthélemy, François. *Mémoires de Barthélemy, 1768–1819*, ed., Jacques de Dampierre (Paris: Plon, 1914).

Bartlett, Thomas, Kevin Dawson, and Dáire Keogh. *Rebellion: A Television History of 1798* (Dublin: Gill and Macmillan, 1998).

Baylen, Joseph O. and Norbert J. Gossman. *Biographical Dictionary of Modern British Radicals*, Vol. I: 1770–1830 (Sussex: Harvester Press, 1979).

Beames, M. R. "Peasant Movements: Ireland, 1785–95," *Journal of Peasant Studies*, II, no. 4 (July 1975).

The Beauties of the Press (London, 1800).

Binns, John. *The Recollections of the Life of John Binns* (Philadelphia, 1854).

Bonaparte, Napoléon. *Correspondance de Napoléon Ier* (Paris: Imprimerie Impériale, 1861).

Burke, Bernard. *A Second Series of Vicissitudes of Families* (London: Longman, Green, Longman, and Roberts, 1860).

——————. *Burke's Irish Family Records* (London: Burke's Peerage, 1976).

Burke, Edmund. *The Correspondence of Edmund Burke*, ed., R. B. McDowell (Cambridge, 1969).

Byrne, Miles. *Memoirs of Miles Byrne*, edited by his widow (Dublin: Maunsel & Co., 1907).

Campbell, Gerald. *Edward and Pamela Fitzgerald* (London: Edward Arnold, 1904).

Castlereagh, Robert Stewart. *Memoirs and Correspondence of Viscount Castlereagh, Second Marquess of Londonderry*, ed., Charles Vane, Marquess of Londonderry. Vol. I: The Irish Rebellion (London: Henry Colburn, 1848).

Cole, G. D. H. *Chartist Portraits* (London: Cassell, 1989).

Condorcet, Marquis de. *Oeuvres de Condorcet,* publiées par A. Condorcet O'Connor et M. F. Arago (Paris, 1847–1849).

Conner, Clifford D. *Colonel Despard: The Life and Times of an Anglo-Irish Rebel* (Conshohocken, Pennsylvania: Combined Books, 2000).

Constant, Benjamin. *Journaux intimes* (Paris: Gallimard, 1952).

Curtin, Nancy J. "The Transformation of the United Irishmen into a Mass-based Revolutionary Organisation, 1794–6," *Irish Historical Studies,* XXIV, no. 96 (November 1985), pp. 463–492.

——————. *The United Irishmen: Popular Politics in Ulster and Dublin, 1791–1798* (Oxford, 1998).

d'Alton, Ian. *Protestant Society and Politics in Cork, 1812–44* (Cork: Cork University, 1980).

Daunt, W. J. O'Neill. *A Life Spent for Ireland* (London, 1896).

Debidour, A., ed. *Recueil des Actes du Directoire Exécutif* (Paris, 1913).

Desbrière, Édouard. *Projets et Tentatives de Débarquement aux Iles Britanniques: 1793–1805* (Paris: Librairie Militaire R. Chapelot et Ce., 1900).

Dickson, David, Dáire Keogh, and Kevin Whelan, eds. *The United Irishmen: Republicanism, Radicalism and Rebellion* (Dublin, 1993).

Dickson, William Steel. *A Narrative of the Confinement and Exile of William Steel Dickson, D.D.* (Dublin, 1812).

Durey, Michael. *Transatlantic Radicals and the Early American Republic* (Univ. Press of Kansas, 1997).

Elliott, Marianne. *Partners in Revolution: The United Irishmen and France* (New Haven and London: Yale, 1982).

——————. *Wolfe Tone: Prophet of Irish Independence* (New Haven: Yale, 1989).

Emmet, T. A., Arthur O'Connor, and W. J. MacNeven. *Memoire; or, Detailed Statement of the Origin and Progress of the Irish Union: Delivered to the Irish Government by Messrs. Emmett, O'Connor, and McNevin; together with the Examinations of these Gentlemen before the Secret Committees of the Houses of Lords and Commons, in the Summer of 1798* ([London], [1802]).

Emmet, Thomas Addis [1828–1919]. *Ireland Under English Rule* (New York, 1903).

——————. *Memoir of Thomas Addis and Robert Emmet* (New York: Emmet Press, 1915).

Escande, Georges. *Hoche en Irlande 1795–1798* (Paris: Félix Alcan, 1888).

Evidence to Character, or, The Innocent Imposture: Being a Portrait of a Traitor by his Friends and by Himself (London, [1798]).

Fenwick, John. *Observations on the Trial of James Coigly, for High Treason* (London, 1798).

Ffolliott, Rosemary. *The Pooles of Mayfield and Other Irish Families* (Dublin: Hodges Figgis, 1958).

Fitzgerald, Brian. *Emily, Duchess of Leinster, 1731–1814: A Study of Her Life and Times* (London: Staples Press, 1949).

Fitzpatrick, W. J. *Ireland Before the Union* (London and Dublin, 1867).

——————. *Secret Service Under Pitt* (London, New York: Longmans, Green, 1892).

——————. *The Sham Squire, and the Informers of 1798* (Dublin: W. B. Kelly, 1869).

——————, ed. *The Life, Times, and Cotemporaries* [sic] *of Lord Cloncurry* (Dublin, 1855).

Foreman, Amanda. *Georgiana, Duchess of Devonshire* (New York: Random House, 1998).

Fox, Charles James. *Memorials and Correspondence of Charles James Fox*, ed., Lord John Russell (London: Richard Bentley, 1853–1857).

Gaulmier, Jean. *Un Grand Témoin de la Révolution et de l'Empire, Volney* (Paris: Hachette, 1959).

Gilbert, John Thomas, ed. *Documents Relating to Ireland, 1795–1804* (Dublin, 1893).

Granville, G. L.-G. *The Private Correspondence of Granville Leveson Gower, 1781–1821*, edited by his daughter-in-law, Castalia, Countess Granville (New York: E. P. Dutton, 1916).

Guillon, Edouard Louis Maxime. *La France et l'Irlande pendant la Révolution* (Paris: Armand Colin, 1888).

Hames, Jane Hayter. *Arthur O'Connor, United Irishman* (Cork: Collins, 2001).

Hayes, Richard. *Biographical Dictionary of Irishmen in France* (Dublin: M.H. Gill and Son, 1949).

Holland, Lady Elizabeth. *The Journal of Elizabeth Lady Holland*, ed., the Earl of Ilchester (London: Longmans, Green, 1908).

Inglis, Brian. *The Freedom of the Press in Ireland, 1784-1841* (London, 1954).

Jones, E. H. Stuart. *An Invasion that Failed: The French Expedition to Ireland, 1796* (Oxford: Basil Blackwell, 1950).

Kavanaugh, Ann C. *John FitzGibbon, Earl of Clare: Protestant Reaction and English Authority in Late Eighteenth-Century Ireland* (Dublin, 1997).

Kennedy, William Benjamin. "French Projects for the Invasion of Ireland, 1796–1798" (Unpublished dissertation, University of Georgia, 1966).

Keogh, Dáire, ed. *A Patriot Priest: The Life of Father James Coigly, 1761–1798* (Cork, 1998).

King, Charles R., ed. *The Life and Correspondence of Rufus King* (New York, 1971).

Lasteyrie, P.-C., comte de, Arthur Condorcet O'Connor, and M. Isambert. *État Religieux de la France et de l'Europe . . . avec les controverses sur la séparation de l'église et de l'état* (Paris and Leipzig, 1844).

Lecky, William Edward Hartpole. *A History of Ireland in the Eighteenth Century*, New Edition (London: Longmans, Green, 1892).

Lefebvre, Georges. *The Thermidorians and the Directory* (New York: Random House, 1964).

MacDermot, Frank. "Arthur O'Connor," *Irish Historical Studies*, XV (1966), pp. 48–69.

MacNeven, William James. *Pieces of Irish History* (New York, 1807).

Madden, R. R. *Lives and Times of the United Irishmen, Second Series* (London, J. Madden & Co., 1843).

_____. *Lives and Times of the United Irishmen, Third Series* (Dublin: James Duffy, 1846).

_____. *Lives and Times of the United Irishmen*, edited by Vincent Fleming O'Reilly (New York: Catholic Publication Society of America, 1916).

I. R. McBride. " 'When Ulster Joined Ireland': Anti-Popery, Presbyterian Radicalism and Irish Republicanism in the 1790s," *Past and Present*, no. 157 (November 1997), pp. 63–93.

Moore, Thomas. *The Life and Death of Lord Edward Fitzgerald* (London, 1831).

Murphy, John A., ed. *The French Are in the Bay: The Expedition to Bantry Bay 1796* (Cork and Dublin: Mercier Press, 1997).

O'Coindealbhain, Sean. "The United Irishmen in Cork County," *Journal of the Cork Historical & Archeological Society*. Part I: vol. LIII, no. 178 (July–December 1948); Part II: vol. LIV, no. 180 (July–December 1949).

O'Connor, Arthur. *Address from Mr. O'Connor to the Free Electors of the County of Antrim* (Dublin, 1797).

_____. *Arthur O'Connor's Letter to Lord Castlereagh* (pamphlet dated 4 January 1799; no further publication data provided).

_____. *A Letter from Gen. Arthur Condorcet O'Connor to General Lafayette, on the Causes which have Deprived France of the Advantages of the Revolution of 1830* (London: Edward Rainford, 1831). [French edition: *Lettre au Général Lafayette sur les causes qui ont privée la France des avantages de la révolution de 1830* (Paris, 1831).]

_____ [Pseud.: "A Stoic"]. *The Measures of Ministry to Prevent a Revolution Are the Certain Means of Bringing It On* (London: Eaton, 1794).

_____. *Monopoly, the Cause of All Evil* (Paris & London: Firmin Didot, 1848). [French edition: *Le monopole, cause de tous les maux* (Paris: Firmin Didot, 1849).]

_____. *The Present State of Great Britain* (Paris, 1804). [French edition: *L'Etat actuel de la Grande Bretagne* (Paris, an XII).]

_____. *Speech of Arthur O'Connor, Esquire, delivered in the House of Commons of Ireland on Monday, May 4, 1795, upon the important question of Catholic Emancipation* (London, 1795).

_____. *The State of Ireland*, ed., James Livesey (Dublin: Lilliput Press, 1998). [The original publication date was 1 February 1798.]

O'Connor, Roger. *The Chronicles of Eri* (London, 1822).

O'Conor, the Rev. Charles. *Memoirs of the Life and Writings of the Late Charles O'Conor of Belanagare, Esq. M.R.I.A.* (Dublin, undated).

O'Reilly, Andrew. *The Irish Abroad and at Home; at the Court and in the Camp. With Souvenirs of "The Brigade." Reminiscences of an Emigrant Milesian* (New York: D. Appleton and Company, 1856).

O'Toole, Fintan. *A Traitor's Kiss: The Life of Richard Brinsley Sheridan* (New York: Farrar, Straus and Giroux, 1998).

Pakenham, Thomas. *The Year of Liberty: The Great Irish Rebellion of 1798* (London: Granada, 1972).

The Parliamentary Register: or, History of the Proceedings and Debates of the House of Commons of Ireland, XI–XII (Dublin, 1791–1793).

Patterson, M. W. *Sir Francis Burdett and His Times (1770–1844)* (London: Macmillan, 1931).

Pickering, Paul. *Feargus O'Connor: A Political Life* (London: Merlin Press, 2008).

Póirtéir, Cathal, ed. *The Great Irish Rebellion of 1798* (Dublin: Mercier, 1998).

Powell, Martyn J. "Charles James Fox and Ireland," *Irish Historical Studies*, XXXIII (November 2002), pp. 169–190.

Read, Donald and Eric Glasgow. *Feargus O'Connor: Irishman and Chartist* (London: Edward Arnold, 1961).

Report from the Committee of Secrecy of the House of Commons in Ireland, as reported by the Right Honourable Lord Viscount Castlereagh, August 21, 1798.

Rose, J. Holland. "Papers Relating to the Irish Rebellion," *English Historical Review*, XXV (October 1910), pp. 748–752.

Shapin, Steven. *A Social History of Truth* (Chicago: University of Chicago Press, 1994).

Sheridan, Richard Brinsley. *The Letters of Richard Brinsley Sheridan*, ed., Cecil Price (Oxford: Clarendon Press, 1966).

_____. *The Speeches of the Late Right Honourable Richard Brinsley Sheridan* (London, 1816).

Smyth, Jim, ed. *Revolution, Counter-Revolution and Union: Ireland in the 1790s* (Cambridge: Cambridge University Press, 2001).

Sorel, Albert. "Les vues de Hoche: La Vendée, l'Irlande et le Rhin," *Revue de Paris*, July/August 1895, pp. 225–253.

Stuart, Dorothy Margaret. *Dearest Bess: The Life and Times of Lady Elizabeth Foster, Afterwards Duchess of Devonshire, from her Unpublished Journals and Correspondence* (London: Methuen, 1955).

Tillyard, Stella. *Citizen Lord: The Life of Edward Fitzgerald, Irish Revolutionary* (New York: Farrar, Straus and Giroux, 1999).

Tone, Theobald Wolfe. *Life of Theobald Wolfe Tone*, compiled and arranged by William Theobald Wolfe Tone, edited by Thomas Bartlett (Dublin: The Lilliput Press, 1998).

Trench, Melesina (Chenevix) St. George. *The remains of the late Mrs. Richard Trench, being selections from her journals, letters, & other papers*, edited by her son, the Dean of Westminster (London: Parker and Bourn, 1862).

The Trial of James O'Coigly, . . . Arthur O'Connor, esq., John Binns, John Allen, and Jeremiah Leary . . . at Maidstone in Kent (London: M. Gurney, 1798).

Trotter, John Bernard. *Memoirs of the Latter Years of the Right Honourable Charles James Fox* (Philadelphia: Samuel R. Fisher, 1812).

Volney, C. F. *The Ruins, Or, Meditation of the Revolutions of Empires: and The Law of Nature* [1791], (reprint edition: Baltimore: Black Classic Press, 1991).

Weber, Paul. *On the Road to Rebellion: The United Irishmen and Hamburg, 1796–1803* (Dublin: Four Courts Press, 1997).

Wells, Roger. *Insurrection: The British Experience, 1795–1803* (Gloucester: Alan Sutton, 1983).

The Whole Proceedings . . . against the Right Hon. Sackville Earl of Thanet, Robert Fergusson, Esq., and Others, for a Riot and Other Misdemeanours: Tried at the Bar of the Court of King's Bench, April 25, 1799 (London: R. Ogle, 1799).

Wilson, David A. *United Irishmen, United States: Immigrant Radicals in the Early Republic* (Ithaca, New York: Cornell University Press, 1998).

Woods, C. J. "The Secret Mission to Ireland of Captain Bernard MacSheehy, an Irishman in French Service, 1796," *Journal of the Cork Historical and Archaeological Society*, vol. LXXVIII, no. 228 (July–December 1973), pp. 93–108.

Woodward, L. D. "Les Projets de descente en Irlande et les réfugiés irlandais et anglais en France sous la Convention: d'après des documents inédits," *Annales Historiques de la Révolution Française*, VIII (1931), pp. 1–30.

INDEX

at Maidstone jail, 117, 130-133; in various Dublin jails; 133-135; at Kilmainham jail, 139-146; at Fort George, 79, 148-161;

Kilmainham pact negotiations, 9-10, 139-148, 161-162, 203, 263-277, 279-297, 300;

marriage and family, 10, 40, 181-185, 199;

negotiations with France, xii, 7-8, 10, 57-76, 85, 110, 112, 146-147, 164, 172, 202, 208n26, 301;

on trial at Maidstone, 118-131;

physical appearance, 5-7, 12, 161-163, 182;

place in history, 3-4, 7-9, 58, 71-75, 201-202, 205-206;

relations with and attitude toward Catholics, 7, 9-12, 15, 28-30, 47-49, 53-57, 65, 67-68, 82-83, 96, 102, 126, 134, 153-154, 178, 194-197, 199, 204, 264, 266-267, 290-291, 297, 300;

relations with his uncle, 14-15, 25-28, 30-34, 39, 47, 90, 204, 300;

writings of, 25, 94, 105, 184-185, 187, 193-195, 197-198, 206; Kilmainham pact "Memoire," 263-277; *Letter to Lord Castlereigh*, 146-148, 157; *Lettre au Général Lafayette . . .* , 191-192; *Measures of Ministry to Prevent a Revolution . . .* , 41-42; *Monopoly, the Root of All Evil*, 160, 185-186, 196-197, 259n72; *State of Ireland*, 105-108, 147, 202, 303; *To the Free Electors of the County of Antrim*, 89-90, 105, 147, 262n8; testimony to parliamentary committees, 144-149, 279-297; unpublished memoirs, xi, 7-8, 11-12, 15, 18-21, 24-46, 53, 56, 58-61, 65, 67-71, 75-77, 80-87, 89-90, 93, 95-96, 98, 100-101, 103, 109-113, 116-118, 123-126, 128, 130, 132, 134-135, 140, 144, 158, 160, 165, 196, 198, 207n1, 209n34, 300-301

O'Connor, Feargus, 11, 17, 193-195, 197

O'Connor, Roderick, 17

O'Connor, Roger (brother of Arthur O'Connor), 13-18, 22-23, 77, 124, 131, 141, 148-150, 152, 159-160, 184, 187-190, 193, 257n34

O'Connor, Rory, 13

O'Connor Kerry, 17, 299

O'Connor (or O'Conor) of Belanagare, 81-82

O'Conor, Charles, 82

O'Flanagan, Thomas, 97-99

O'Grady (Austrian general), 37

O'Grady, Standish (Lord Guillamore), 20-21, 193

Orangemen, Orange Order, 13, 97, 99, 102, 261n11, 266, 272, 289-290

orators, oratory, 4, 7, 9, 44, 47-49, 60, 85, 194, 202

O'Reilly, Andrew, 173, 191

O'Reilly, Richard, 175-176, 187-188; the "O'Reilly affair," 175-176

O'Reilly, Vincent Fleming, 158

Orléans, Duke of, 62, 191. *See also* Louis Philippe (1773-1850)

O'Shee, Richard, 75

Osterly, Middlesex, 111

Ovid, 183

Oxford, Earl of, 38, 123, 162; Lady Oxford, 162-163

Paine, Thomas, 203

Palais Royal, 167, 191

Paris, ix, xi, 20, 35-36, 41, 46, 48, 56, 61-62, 74, 102, 110, 125, 161-167, 172-173, 175, 177, 181, 183-184, 197, 203, 275, 280, 283, 287

parliament, British, 38-39, 41, 44, 46, 94, 118, 142, 193-195, 285

parliament, Irish, 7-8, 15, 29-32, 36, 38, 40-41, 47-49, 60, 64, 76, 83, 90, 106, 135, 144-145-146, 148, 162, 201, 204, 215n27-28, 215n33, 263-266, 272-274, 279, 281, 285-286, 289-291, 294-295

Parsons, Sir Laurence, 31, 215n27, 215n33

Patton, John, 157-158

Pays Bas (the Netherlands), 75. *See also* Holland

Peep-of-Day Boys, 267

Pelham, Lord Thomas, 151, 234n66

Pemberton, William, 97-98